COMPETITIVE BUSINESS MANAGEMENT

The growth of global corporations has led to the development of new business strategies whose complexity and configuration rest on corporate networks; corporate cross-culture and intangible corporate and product assets. In global markets, corporations compete in a competitive marketspace dimension, in other words, competitive boundaries in which space is not a stable element of the decision-making process, but a competitive factor whose complexity depends on markets increasingly characterized by time-based competition and over-supply. In view of today's fierce competition from US and Southeast Asian corporations, this book highlights global business development policies based on innovation, sustainability and intangible assets.

The book assesses competitive business management from a global perspective, examining business development policies linked to the profitability of global firms. It forces readers to actively think through the most fundamental policies developed by global firms in the current competitive landscape and provides answers to questions such as: What are the new drivers of global capitalism?; How do global businesses deal with new local nationalism?; Which governance systems and behavioural norms qualify global businesses?; What are the main business policies that characterize competitive business management in a global competition perspective?

Competitive Business Management neatly explains the global business management domain and helps readers to gain an understanding of global development business policies.

Silvio M. Brondoni is Full Professor of Management at the University of Milano-Bicocca, Department of Economics, Management and Statistics, Milan, Italy.

Edited by

Silvio M. Brondoni

Competitive Business Management.
A Global Perspective

Routledge
Taylor & Francis Group
LONDON AND NEW YORK

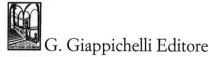

G. Giappichelli Editore

First published 2018 by Routledge

2 Park Square, Milton Park, Abingdon, Oxfordshire OX14 4RN
52 Vanderbilt Avenue, New York, NY 10017

Routledge is an imprint of the Taylor & Francis Group, an informa business

First issued in paperback 2020

British Library Cataloguing-in-Publication Data
A catalogue record for this book is available from the British Library

ISBN: 978-88-921-1609-2 (hbk-G. Giappichelli Editore)
ISBN 13: 978-1-138-34222-4 (hbk)
ISBN 13: 978-0-367-58951-6 (pbk)

Typeset in Simoncini Garamond
by G. Giappichelli Editore, Turin, Italy

CONTENTS

ACKNOWLEDGEMENTS

The Editor wishes to gratefully acknowledge the precious contribution of Professor Mirian Palmeira, Federal University of Parana, Professor Andrè Richelieu, École des Sciences de la Gestion de l'Université du Québec à Montréal, and Professor Christina Marta Suciu, Academia of Economic Studies of Bucharest, who provided constructive comments to the manuscript.

Preface
GLOBAL BUSINESS MANAGEMENT

Silvio M. Brondoni

SUMMARY: I. From marketing to zero defects product and market-driven management. – II. The global competitive business management. – III. Global competition, outside-in management and hybrid innovation. – IV. Market-driven management and web revolution: global management of price, brand and marketing channels. – V. Competitiveness, corporate governance, ownership and global markets.

The growth of global corporations has led to the development of new business strategies whose complexity and configuration rest on:

– Corporate networks. Global markets promote the development of corporate networks where performance (related primarily to global economies of scale and to the increasing importance of corporate finance and private equity) is linked to 'downsizing' policies, rendering the organization leaner and more responsible through targeted personnel selection, outplacement, outsourcing, and transforming 'country managers' into 'key business managers'.

– Corporate cross-culture. Global markets and corporate networks favour an increasingly heterogeneous organization and cross-cultural interrelations among employees, co-makers, and customers. Nevertheless, numerous cases of failure exist linked to the management's incapacity to identify cross-cultural issues and to appropriately and effectively deal with these. As the current global scenario is becoming increasingly complex, global managers will have to become more perceptive and responsive to the multicultural challenges and risks. Corporate strategies therefore aim to manage cultural differences and turn these into a competitive advantage, exploiting corporate culture as an intangible asset whose fundamental quantitative performance indicators tend to synthesize the levels of network efficiency.

– Intangible corporate and product assets. Global markets emphasise the priority of intangible product assets (pre-sale services, post-sale assistance, design, and logistics) and above all the competitive predominance of intangible corporate assets, i.e., corporate culture, information system, and brand equity.

In global markets, corporations compete in a competitive marketspace dimension, in other words, competitive boundaries in which space is not a stable element of the decision-making process, but a competitive factor whose complexity depends on markets increasingly characterized by:

– Time-based competition. Globalization accentuates the competitive dynamics and pushes corporate strategies towards growth policies based on time compression and time value, defining time as an important competitive factor. Particularly, time compression entails immediate effects on business reorganization, assigning specific economic value to time consumption efficiency.

– Over-supply. For many products, global markets compete on production capacity, above and beyond potential demand. Over-supply thus becomes a structural factor for the firm, whose profitable growth requires hypothesizing the progressive overabundance of more sophisticated and low cost products sold at reduced prices to motivate increasingly disloyal intermediate and final demand.

The resurgence of economic nationalism is creating a new political scenario for corporate strategies of global businesses. Some elements of contemporary economic nationalism, e.g., trade barriers, are expected to entail a of old-fashioned protectionism inescapably inconsistent with established global value chains. However, both governments and multinational corporations are mandated to 're-invent' a positive relation between corporations and the collective interests.

In view of today's fierce competition from US and Southeast Asian corporations, global business development policies are based on innovation, zero defects products, sustainability, and intangible assets.

I. From marketing to zero defects product and market-driven management

The valuable scientific contributions of prestigious colleagues over the course of a long-term research project carried out by a much larger group of authoritative business economists who dedicated knowledge, time, and commitment to fostering the development of economic-management disciplines. This complex research project is based on the market-driven management manifesto titled "New Trends in Business and Business Management" developed on University of Milano-Bicocca.

"The recent developments in the world economy, characterized by competitive contexts dominated by the globalization of markets and structural over-supply, push companies to configure a new market-oriented philosophy", in other words, market-driven management (J.-J. Lambin, S.M. Brondoni, Symphonya, Emerging Issues in Management (www.unimib.it/symphonya), n. 2, 2000-2001).

In a business-market approach, the concept of customer value management is central, i.e., a continuous approach aimed at offering selected and higher value asset/service aggregates than competitors. Such market orientation is therefore intended to ensure efficiently meeting demand (intermediate and final) and supply, developing products (new or improved, able to better satisfy 'demand bubbles' than competitors), and organizing physical exchange and communications flows (push/pull communication).

A market-based business approach is an innovative reality where market orientation is manifested when all business functions (production, sales, programming and control, marketing, finance) are: responsive to the needs of demand; conscious of the conduct of competitors; determined to achieve solutions that overcome the functional barriers and physical space of competition.

Market orientation therefore does not result in a simple proclamation, but presupposes a 'market-driven' philosophy, which requires: reorganizing the firm based on markets rather than products or plants; a motivated business culture based on results and attentive to the variability of demand and the instability of the competitive domain; the predisposition of new metrics for intangible and tangible factors to estimate business performance in external and changing contexts.

In summary, the management of a "market-driven business and economy" is characterized by: 1) a cultural dimension developed through corporate governance that proposes the affirmation and dissemination of corporate responsibility and behavioural norms according to a business vision consistent with the complexity of global markets and competitive contexts; 2) an analysis dimension based on continuously monitoring the competition system, developing a business management approach based on instability, constrained by pull/push communication flows; 3) an action dimension in which time is a key factor of marketing programs and the associated economic-business monitoring (time-based competition) in a business management approach focused on mutable demand and competition.

The novelty of this approach is in defining a business model based on: global rather than international/local development policies; management that is primarily focused on competition rather than on demand; and competition policies geared to controlling global supply rather than satisfying demand segments.

II. The global competitive business management

The competitive business management in a global perspective deepens business development policies linked to the profitability of global firms.

The firm will be forced to actively think through the most fundamental policies developed by global firms in the current competitive landscape:

– What are the new drivers of global capitalism?

– How do global businesses deal with new local nationalism?

– Which governance systems and behavioural norms qualify global businesses?

– What are the main business policies that characterize competitive business management in a global competition perspective?

Global markets redefine market-space competition and affirm a global business economy with distinctive traits including: resource management without physical and administrative boundaries; increasingly sophisticated products that rapidly become obsolete through easy imitation at a reduced cost; competitive interrelationships between transnational networks that go beyond multinational (or multidimensional) organizations – typically European – and linked to smaller market spaces; and finally, transforming national markets into complex socio-economic systems, where communication and distribution are global, nation-states are confronted with supranational organizations, and enterprises exercise multidimensional values of both responsibility and corporate social responsibility.

The strategic objective of achieving and maintaining global competitiveness will remain central, but three developments are expected: 1) reassessing the balance between national autonomy and economic globalization where the "without limits" globalization business model must transform into a "within limits" model. Unmanaged globalization undermines democracy and encourages populism; 2) the climate change debate will gain intensity over voluntary versus public regulation. Voluntary regulation of corporate behaviour has resulted in substantial improvements, but cannot be regarded as a substitute for the more effective exercise of state authority; 3) the collaborative economy will create a new form of competition that facilitates peer-to-peer transactions between customers and service providers by integrating local players into a global organization and offering new low-cost opportunities for entrepreneurs.

III. Global competition, outside-in management and hybrid innovation

The globalization of markets has characterized the business landscape with an unprecedented, accelerating, and complex mix of risks and opportunities. Particularly in natural resource procurement markets, large global companies are called on to confront sustainable global goals and local problems, which require high investments in local areas and the involvement of local public regulators and civil society as a whole.

A single large company, even if global, cannot easily achieve effective and efficient solutions with sustainable levels of risk. A collaborative approach among competitors (business coalitions) can generate long-term solutions that share value creation for all actors involved.

The growing complexity of the external environment and the globalization of markets force companies across many industries to expand their activities through developing network relations to anticipate and satisfy customers while seizing new business opportunities. By adopting an outside-in management approach, companies are able to develop a global scale learning platform by strengthening their ability to gain insights from the outside.

The network structure promotes market knowledge and learning from every periphery in the competitive scenario and allows companies to participate in partnerships and collaborations with stakeholders to more efficiently manage their innovation processes.

An important opportunity for manufacturing firms to strengthen their competitiveness in the global market is modernizing their business model to enable developing hybrid innovation processes. In particular, companies must develop new business models in which both value creation and value capture occur in a value network that can include suppliers, partners, distribution channels, and coalitions. Thus, value networks strive for product innovation, but also for production system innovation to achieve greater flexibility in global business management.

IV. Market-driven management and web revolution: global management of price, brand and marketing channels

The emerging web revolution entails managing multichannel strategies by experimenting with new organizational solutions in search of a new reference model. Logistics have also begun to change dramatically, disrupting the classic configurations where logistics actors played a functional role in bringing efficiency to a process where a large number of producers offered goods to a myriad of consumers.

The growing complexity of today's business systems has led to the substantial modification of retailer policies. In particular, in recent years, large-scale retailers have found ways to become more competitive by devising new policies aimed at creating competitive customer value. The creation of such value translates into the entire marketing channel's ability to compete according to the principles of timeliness, effectiveness, efficiency, and optimization.

Indeed, in over-supply markets, competition develops between the marketing channels where the processes are managed to quickly respond to market changes and satisfy unstable and changing demand.

In price management has become very popular at the global level the advance selling or advance pricing, i.e. the phenomenon of suppliers offering favourable conditions to customers who purchase in advance. This practice is known as advance price and defines a scenario where customers purchase a service before they actually intend to use it. In exchange for the commitment of buying in advance, the buyer is offered a number of benefits, such as price discounts or the ability to choose before other customers.

Finally, a firm that pursues a market-driven management approach will tend to better understand and form relationships with the market.. In particular, a market-driven brand management perspective becomes a key factor in affirming corporate supply in highly competitive global markets.

V. Competitiveness, corporate governance, ownership and global markets

The elimination of space and time barriers to the circulation of information and capital, the growing complexity and importance of business/stakeholder relationships, and the establishment of corporate social responsibility principles have changed the corporate governance approach of listed companies.

Indeed, the prerequisites have been created to attenuate behavioural differences, which for a long time have characterized companies with wide ownership dispersion (outsider systems) and those with concentrated ownership or control (insider systems).

A pervasive improvement of the corporate governance approach in a global perspective is strictly linked to international principles and recommendations focused on a social responsibility and sustainability approach, that facilitate the convergence between insider and outsider corporate governance systems. In particular, the shared medium- to long-term value orientation of top executives and investors is affirming regardless of the ownership structure of companies and the characteristics of risk capital markets.

In global firms, corporate responsibility is aimed at pursuing partial and overall business results characterized by high levels of profitability and efficiency with a focus on sustainable development. For this reason, CSR represents an action that a firm chooses to take and potentially affecting the social welfare of stakeholders. Promoting the effectiveness of a CSR-oriented strategy requires enterprises to govern their costs and benefits, and develop dynamic relationships with stakeholders.

Milan, March 2018

Silvio M. Brondoni
Full Professor of Market-Driven Management
University of Milano-Bicocca
Editor in Chief of "Symphonya. Emerging Issues in Management"
(http://symphonya.unimib.it/)
silvio.brondoni@unimib.it

Part 1
CONCEPTUAL FRAMEWORK

Chapter 1

COMPETITIVE BUSINESS MANAGEMENT AND GLOBAL COMPETITION. AN INTRODUCTION

Silvio M. Brondoni

ABSTRACT: *Global markets redefine market-space competition and affirm a global business economy with distinctive traits including: resource management without physical and administrative boundaries; increasingly sophisticated products that rapidly become obsolete through easy imitation at a reduced cost; competitive interrelationships between transnational networks that go beyond multinational (or multidimensional) organizations – typically European – and linked to smaller market spaces; and finally, transforming national markets into complex socio-economic systems, where communication and distribution are global, nation-states are confronted with supranational organizations, and enterprises exercise multidimensional values of both responsibility and corporate social responsibility.*

SUMMARY: 1.1. Globalisation and competition. Emerging issues in global business management. – 1.2. Market-space competition: competitive landscapes in global firms. – 1.2.1. Networking and competitive global business management. – 1.3. Global markets, competitive landscapes and market-driven management. – 1.3.1. Competitive business management, over-supply and bubble demand. – 1.3.2. Market-driven management and global economies of scale. – 1.3.3. From marketing management to market-driven management. Competitive customer value. – 1.4. Competitive global business, market-driven management, product and corporate intangible assets.

1.1. Globalisation and competition. Emerging issues in global business management

Globalisation has led to new competition boundaries between enterprises, changing the traditional temporal and spatial competition relationships (Lambin and Brondoni, 2001).

Global markets transcend the traditional view of the localism and staticity of competition spaces that characterized corporate competition policies until the early 80s (Levitt, 1983; Brondoni and Lambin, 2001). With globalisation, individual local contexts aim to develop and achieve specific and partly contingent competitive advantages (from time to time, and ascribable to aspects of production, marketing, R&D, etc.) coordinated in a wider economic and business management system (market-space management) (Brondoni, 2015b).

In global markets, firms therefore compete according to the market-space competition logic, namely, with competition boundaries where the space is not a known and stable decision-making element, but a competitive factor that is determined by – and changes as a result of – the actions/reactions of the firms, competitors, and authorities of the many areas in which businesses operate. Business policies based on an open competition space (market-space management) endeavour to overcome the usual limitations of direct control and proximity characterizing the physicality of activities (invariance of goods produced, amount realized with direct controls, reduced number of customers and suppliers, static localization of production facilities, etc.) and instead affirm operating contexts characterized by: the dominance of intangible resources; competitive adaptability; management flexibility (Best, 2004; Webster, 2002: Lambin, 2000; Day, 1999; Rayport and Sviokla, 1994; Day, 1990). Globalisation profoundly changes the traditional industrial production principles (i.e., the direct and controllable coordination of workers, technologies and materials, standardizing the temporal sequence of processes), which in extreme synthesis is always characterized by: efficient production processes and the greatest possible number of standardized goods; organisational structures based on a rigid and planned division of tasks; the presence of workers at production sites (Brondoni, 2008).

In global markets, the strategic leverage of organizations moves from product characterization (supply differentiation) to the qualification of overall knowledge held and managed by a corporation. Information systems (internal and among companies) thus become critical to business development; collaboration between companies is achieved through specific information channels and flows; and finally, processes organized according to a sequential logic are transformed into relations developed in project-oriented networks, up to arriving at virtual firms.

Therefore, new flexible forms of organization postulate the division of structures in terms of space, time, and functions performed.

In terms of space, production is not implemented through a single process nor necessarily located permanently in a given location. Production processes are usually divided among different units and do not assume a stable spatial location, since the information flows that generate production enable the physical transfer of outputs (also partial) anywhere in the world, directly from individual units and without any time constraints.

Moreover, with regard to time, market-space management affects the temporal efficiency of production and the supply chain of defined goods. Networks variously articulated and localized replace sequential productions and processes, so that the production/delivery time determines the overall realization and logistic needs of the operational units comprising the network. The globalisation of ICT digital technologies determines pressing rhythms on competition (time-based competition), producing new business policies in terms of: launching innovations; imitation of products and services; competitive pricing.

Finally, with respect to the functions performed, market-space management tends to suggest a fundamental change in relationships and collaborations with customers, partners and co-makers, overcoming the typical limitations of interface cooperation and instead aimed at achieving more narrow and selective interactions between inter-company teams. In this sense, the economic and financial crisis of 2007-2008 (which in practice concluded the first globalisation phase) has further contributed to changing the competitive relationships between companies by developing new market-driven management policies, focusing on the critical success factors of global companies, amongst which their network alliances, the ever-larger size of companies and a multi-dimensional competitive landscape (Brondoni, 2014; Cappellin and Wink, 2009).

Thus, with the globalisation of markets, new trends have affirmed in economic and business management. The intangible elements of the business economy now outweigh the tangible elements, time becomes a critical management function, and mobility (of people, goods, knowledge and ideas) affirms new relation systems in the context of a global business economy (Salvioni, 2010).

1.2. Market-space competition: competitive landscapes in global firms

Global markets redefine the competitive space (market-space competition) and affirm a global business economy whose distinctive characteristics are: resource management without physical and administrative boundaries; increasingly sophisticated products that quickly become obsolete through ease of imitability at a reduced cost; competitive interrelationships developed between transnational networks, far beyond multinational (or multi-domestic) organizations, typically European, and linked to reduced market spaces; and finally, the transformation of national markets into complex socio-economic systems in which communication and distribution are global, nation-states are confronted with supranational organizations, and enterprises exercise both multidimensional responsibility and corporate social responsibility values (Salvioni, 2003).

In global markets, unstable customer groups (demand bubbles), constant benchmarking with competitors, waning competitive boundaries, and the high substitutability of products overall stimulate companies to adopt a strong orientation to competition management policies to deal with: consumption characterized by uneven growth rates; unstable demand; and above all, changing consumption potentialities, because these are not predictable with traditional purchasing trends, since consumption does not develop in a simple and linear form in time or in space.

Indeed, in global markets, companies tend to constitute a complex life system (Golinelli and Gatti, 2001) that is competition-oriented and with a competitive landscape that dominates the traditional space and time dimensions (i.e., with performance and competitive positions related to closed markets and to an elementary enterprise-products-market combination). The competitive market-space conditions often determine overlapping and changing boundaries where space and time contribute to forming and altering the competitive context of reference, making it, amongst other things, very difficult to evaluate via the usual performance and position indicators the conditions of potential market domination. The competitive space generated by market-space management behaviours is in fact difficult to define in the sphere of basic activities, and is more ascribable to the intangible resource systems that pro tempore contribute to characterizing the competitive profile of defined business realities (Brondoni, 2012c).

1.2.1. Networking and competitive global business management

Business development based on the open competition space (market-space management), precisely due to progressive market-space competition growth, generates mega-organizations, formed by global networks operating in expanded market spaces, valorising intangible assets on the basis of very extensive and sophisticated market information (Lambin, 2014). In fact, the sharing of intangible resources pursued by market-space management policies usually relate to different structures of the same network, and very often relate also to a complex system of organizations united in market competition due to alliances and joint ventures.

In any case, the global business economy seeks to extend the areas of activity in the intangible dimension, thus configuring complex inter-firm systemic relations, which from extremely blurred and unstable boundaries jointly determine the competitive purchasing, processing, distribution, and sales positions of goods and companies, since these refer to a complex and generally variable matrix (Brondoni, 2008; Dunning and Lundan, 2008).

Modern global bread production processes, i.e., a very traditional prod-

uct and seemingly far from the market-space competition logic, is a sympto-
matic example of competitive interdependence at the level of enterprise and
business management systems dominated by intangible resources. Indeed,
fresh bread today is no longer an elementary good characterized by artisanal,
milled, and local production processes. For consumers, fresh bread is normally associated with fragrant bread that is still warm and purchased locally.
In reality, bread is a complex product that is not always easily classifiable. In
many nations, fresh bread is industrial bread that is frozen, prebaked, or
even fully baked (and therefore with raw materials and processing stages that
are part of the production process without any time and space constraints),
subject to the free movement of goods, transported from production sites to
points of sale, proposed to consumers with a short baking completion time,
allowing having freshly baked bread 24 hours a day; therefore, vastly expanding the competitive boundaries in terms of production, sales, and competencies.

Companies today face high-intensity competitive conditions, global markets and highly fragmented research, production, and sales processes in a
multiplicity of coordinated phases. Unlike in the past, no business can therefore rely solely on its own resources, knowledge, and competencies.

The global business economy therefore interfaces with a competitive
space in which, on the one hand, markets are open and information permea-
bility is high, and on the other, the dimensional growth of companies is fostered with networking models to address the high instability of demand (volatility of consumption choices; purchasing non-loyalty; lack of repurchasing
loyalty) and supply (creation of demand bubbles and acceleration of obsolescence in US-focused companies or zero-defects product development in Jap-
anese/South-Korean corporations) (Kim, 1997; Brondoni, 2012).

Globalisation thus changes the business structure and particularly the
role of strategic alliances, imposing collaborative network strategies among
groups of companies, with competitive relationships that tend to form closed
cooperation relations in the pursuit of a global vision coherent with
companies of vast dimensions.

Business development thus abandons the predominance of production in
the large capitalist factories of the 50s and 60s where they guaranteed equal
treatment to efficient and inefficient workers, according to the average yield
of the professional categories; a simple and consistent mechanism with a
production model based on 30/40 years working in the same company.

Moreover, since the 80s, the global economy has profoundly changed companies, production, products, and workers (in an increasing locational, commercial, and production dynamism) with various forms of collaboration and
no guarantees of stability (short-term contracts; training contracts, temporary

staffing, ongoing independent collaborations; etc.) (Paliwoda et al., 2013).

The global business economy imposes structured, widespread, and highly interconnected organizations (networks). These complex structures privilege management skills and outsourcing relations with co-makers and external partners (competitive alliances).

The corporate culture in particular affirms cross-cultural management oriented to overcoming the physical competition sphere and the primacy of business localism.

In global markets, the network business culture makes it possible to homologate organizations with the constructive, stimulated, and controlled uniformity of communication network systems (internet, intranet, extranet), presupposing multi-level performance evaluations that entail estimating the strategic harmony (consistency of business results and processes, complementarity relations, chairman leadership) and operational harmony (interdependence of structures, shared responsibilities, management leadership).

Open markets emphasize the centrality of the competitive approach to the market (market-driven management) and cross-cultural management, namely, business management that is highly profit-focused on a local and global basis, and does not fall back on the organization (as closed and low competition markets postulate), but in contrast is valorised by the opportunities that open markets offer, namely, the variability of demand and the instability created by competition.

1.3. Global markets, competitive landscapes and market-driven management

Globalisation and new competition boundaries impose a new competitive market-oriented management philosophy (market-driven management) where competitive customer value management predominates, i.e., sales to unstable customer groups (demand bubble) with direct and continuous competition (Mair, 1994; Brondoni, 2009).

In fact, firms operating with market-driven management in a global economy approach are characterized by:

– Sales targeted on markets (i.e., directly referring to competitors first, and then to demand), rather than focusing on satisfying demand segments (with a subordinate role to the competitive dimension).

– Market policies based on continuous innovation to meet changing and unstable demand.

– Finally, new metrics to evaluate the key competition factors (especially intangible) that determine business performance.

Market-driven management assumes critical importance in the development of businesses that deal in open markets where the competitive approach starts from the bottom to force the encounter between supply and demand, generating transactions and communication flows simultaneously (push/pull communication). Market-driven management by its very nature determines a market policy that counteracts the protectionist measures adopted by nation-states, as in the case of the 'Made in China'. However, protectionist defence measures are in fact weak – such as those adopted in Europe in the 1960s to counter (in vain) the invasion of Japanese motorbikes – as they are based on elementary competition matrices (the simple defence of national productions), without reference to competition differentials and demand-matching ability (Lansbury et al., 2007; Brondoni, 2012c). Market-based organizations are in fact very communication-oriented and permeable to information, also requiring that all business functions (production, sales, planning and control, marketing, and finance): are aware of the conduct of competitors, anticipate demand expectations, and finally, are resolute in proposing solutions beyond the tasks of the individual functions and the physical spaces of natural competition (Webster, 2002).

Market-driven management therefore favours an outside-in view based on: identifying high-value supplies to bring demand, creating the maximum pro tempore value by designing and delivering goods to specific demand bubbles, and finally, acquiring time-based market knowledge (Ireland et al., 2002; Inauen and Schenker-Wicki, 2011; Arrigo, 2012).

Market-driven management is thus defined as: a cultural dimension, with standards of conduct and values (corporate responsibility) consistent with the complexity and transparency of global markets, continuous monitoring-based analyses of the competitive system according to a modern business economy in unstable conditions, and finally, an action dimension where time is the key factor (time-based competition) in a management approach based on the variability of supply and demand relations.

1.3.1. Competitive business management, over-supply and bubble demand

In global markets, over-supply, the instability of purchases, and high competitive tension often become important structural factors of the development of enterprises that plan the progressive overabundance of goods in a competitive approach (amongst others, able to be produced at decreasing costs due to continuous technological development), goods that are also offered with an abundant variety of alternatives to meet increasingly sophisticated consumer needs and stimulate non-loyal demand. Such contexts on the one hand emphasise the role of multi-market and multi-business enterprises, and on the other, reduce the competitive significance of the business sector. Thus, traditional analyses based on the sector's maturity/newness give way to high-intensity competition activities (Keegan and Schlegelmilch, 2001; Brondoni, 2009).

In a context of global hyper-competition, high-revenue organisations foster supply innovation and create consumption bubbles, rapidly meeting (time to market) and duly abandoning (time competition) these, leaving imitator competitors the residual part of the bubble (typically dispersive and not very profitable for the numerous alternatives offered) (Brondoni, 2013; Levitt, 1996).

Hyper-competition strategies break the static rules of oligopolistic one-to-one competition and instead propose a systemic competition model developed according to a market-driven management approach.

The competitive approach to the market is thus evident from the bottom to force the encounter of supply and demand by developing trade and communication flows (push/pull communication). In addition, in global markets, market-driven management in large corporations imposes sophisticated market strategies primarily aimed at overcoming the local protectionism measures of nation-states that still operate in a space fragmentation approach.

In global markets, a market-driven management philosophy implies: a corporate culture motivated by results, market policies mindful of the instability of competition and demand variability, corporate reorganization based on markets instead of products; predisposition to new evaluation metrics of intangible factors to estimate business performance.

1.3.2. Market-driven management and global economies of scale

Large corporations that have long operated in contexts dominated by market globalisation exalt the achievement of viable cost economies (procurement, production, distribution, communications, sales).

Globalisation requires abandoning the competitive reference to a closed domain coinciding with particular physical or administrative contexts (a product category, a country, a region, a geographic area, etc.) (Park and Hong, 2011).

In global markets, traditional competition trends are surmounted, focusing on the simple expansion of sales volumes of given products in defined geographical areas, and development policies favour customer satisfaction that is highly competition-sensitivity, opening product classes and stimulating the search for innovative intersections between supply gaps and unmet demand needs.

The vast economic-financial advantages that can be achieved through the pursuit of ever-growing economies of scale (supply-driven management) do not however exclude behaviours based on meeting demand and primarily focused on competitive benchmarking (market-driven management) (Gnecchi, 2009).

Under global competition conditions, the market-driven approach thus requires developing long-term corporate policies with competitive cost advantages evaluated in relation to demand and especially superior benchmarking with respect to competitors.

In open markets, without the defence of geographic and administrative boundaries, enterprises adopt very flexible management behaviours characterized by the absolute dominance of intangible resources and aimed at taking advantage of global economies of scale. In global economies of scale, the search for the minimum production costs entails: 1) complex outsourcing functions; 2) dynamic localization of plants , and 3) large scale commercialization to meet demand that is little motivated to purchase, volatile in selection preferences, and non-loyal in repurchasing (i.e., the typical conditions of over-supply, today exacerbated by falling prices of basic raw materials) (Douglas and Craig, 1989; Brondoni, 2008).

Competition between global companies on open markets has radically changed the traditional character of industrial production consisting of: long structures with rigid task division, workers present at production sites, massive production of uniform goods; stocks of raw materials, semi-finished and finished products stored in the proximity of production sites and consumption markets.

Market-space competition instead emphasizes global economies of scale, the value of which does not depend on the degree of exploitation of elementary production factors, but on the intensity of sharing defined resources in a networking system, i.e., the sophistication of collaborative relationships between internal and external structures and co-makership. Such new competition fosters the development of network enterprises with high managerial skills, able to dominate the communication, research, and development of new products, marketing, control, and finance.

1.3.3. From marketing management to market-driven management. Competitive customer value

Market-driven management is a business strategy (dominated by customer value management and direct and continuous benchmarking with competitors) that has developed with globalisation since the 80s mainly as a result of the numerous innovations Toyota introduced (lean production; just-in-time; total quality; mass customisation; demand bubble management) (Kotabe, 1996). The Toyota Production System is based on an alternative mass production process to the assembly line, that is, large-scale production introduced by Henry Ford and improved by Alfred P. Sloan's GM with production specialization (based on supply segmentation and demand differentiation). The Toyota Production System was invented in the textile industry in the 1940s and 1950s, and then developed in Toyota, which in the immediate aftermath of the war, after a devastating and lost conflict, recorded serious shortcomings in raw materials, labour, and financial means. The Toyota Production System was designed by Sakichi Toyoda, Kiichiro Toyoda, and engineer Taiichi Ohno based on the principle of 'doing more with less', i.e., using the scarce resources available to dramatically increase plant productivity. The Toyota Production System is based on a seemingly simple concept: eliminating any type of waste in production processes. In particular, the Toyota Production System envisages the following phases: 1) identifying value for customers; 2) developing a value creation process; 3) generating value flow; 4) customer participation in pulling (pull) the value flow; 5) developing continuous supply improvements (kaizen). The remarkable results of the Toyota Production System fostered the global affirmation of this new production philosophy, renamed Lean Production, to emphasize the importance of eliminating unnecessary phases and processes. The Toyota Production System is also specifically designed to contain stocks of raw materials, semi-finished products, and finished products, bringing the customer closer to production and sales points (just-in-time) through an information system capable of managing the input/output logistics flow, producing only when customer demand is immediately downstream in the flow. Pull production is opposed to traditional systems (push production) where production programs are decided previously and are inevitably distant from the time of satisfying actual demand (Ohno, 1978; Shingo, 1981; Shingo, 1988).

In recent years, market-driven management has been adopted by companies competing in open markets, reformulating the traditional marketing management approach introduced in the 50s by Alfred P. Sloan of GM to win supremacy over the product orientation established in the 30s by Henry Ford with the legendary black T model.

The traditional concept of marketing focuses on the customer's needs and defines segments of competition, thus providing a partial view of the market. In fact, segmentation presupposes a fundamental requirement to activate the demand disaggregation process. Defining demand segments requires the stability of purchasing behaviours, which in turn derive from the stability of the competitive market dynamics. Conversely, demand bubbles consist of temporary groupings of buyers formed on the basis of business programs, specific in terms of time and space, and planned to disrupt particular competitive equilibria.

Conversely, in saturated or stagnant global markets, the aggressiveness of competition is vital, and anticipating the actions of one's rivals becomes the primary objective. In these competitive conditions, demand bubbles consist of temporary groupings of buyers formed on the basis of business programs, specific in terms of time and space, and planned to disrupt particular competitive equilibria (Lambin, 2014).

In other words, marketing management requires knowledge of demand (and especially the stability of the purchasing behaviours of the various segments) to enable offering a product that can occupy a given market space. Therefore, with marketing management, the management process starts from demand, thereafter defining the characteristics of a product intended to fill a specific supply gap (market space) that tends to be stable in the longer term.

Instead, with market-driven management, the market orientation is primarily aimed at identifying a temporary competitive space, namely, maintaining the demand gap highly unstable - in terms of sales volumes and customer expectations- due to continuous innovative proposals. Therefore, in global markets with high competitive pressure, marketing dominance is replaced by the primacy of communications and intangible corporate and product resources to manage high instability, with a predominance of competition, and where intermediate demand and global trade play a central role (Percy, 2014).

In other words, the market-driven management process assumes first that the firm focuses on competition (market-space) (Lambin, 2002; Brondoni, 2002; Reinartz, 2002) to identify temporal demand opportunities (demand bubble), then choosing the product characteristics that are most consistent with a global expected demand to offer contingent (but solid) differential and defensible advantages in time and space with specific competitive pricing (before and better than competitors) (Lambin, 2008; Brondoni, 2005).

In summary, as the Kenichi Ohmae theoretical framework indicates, market-driven management becomes a critical corporate policy to compete in saturated markets dominated by an unstable customer base and scarce loyalty (Ohmae, 2001). In global markets characterized by fickle and non-loyal consumers, market-driven management is very attractive, since it favours: 1) activities focused on competitive profitability rather than on simple customer satisfaction (Brondoni, 2012b); 2) market policies based on innovation, imitation, and competitive pricing to stimulate uncertain and unstable customers to purchase; and 3) performance metrics with even a very short-term horizon.

Market-driven management exalts business management aimed at imposing new purchasing behaviours that emphasize competitive customer value, where final demand tends to no longer be positioned at the end of the transaction chain, with a marginal, passive, and conditional position in the selection with limited marketing investments. Conversely, demand arises in a circular relationship with trade and producers, expressing new buying patterns based on non-loyal behaviours alongside known loyalty mechanisms.

In market-based organizations, the corporate culture requires all business functions (production, sales, planning and control, marketing, and finance) to do better than their competitors and be forward looking with outside-in management based on the supply of goods with a higher value than competitors and on the time-based acquisition of market knowledge.

Market-driven management thus entails:

– A culture and values (corporate responsibility) consistent with the complexity and transparency of global markets (Borgonovi, 2007; Zucchella, 2007; Salvioni, 2003).

– Continuous monitoring of the competitive system through pull/push digital and analogue corporate communication flows.

– Finally, an operational dimension, where time is the critical success factor to manage the revenue variability of demand (Brondoni, 2015a).

1.4. Competitive global business, market-driven management, product and corporate intangible assets

The global managerial economics entails multiple competition spaces characterized by different levels of intensity. Market-driven management thus refers to a plurality of environments characterized by specific competitive conditions that can typically be summarized as: 1) economies in scarcity of supply (D > O) dominated by forms of monopolistic markets with a business economy focused on price competition, cartels and agreements, and sales/supplies managed locally with separate markets. The oil industry is a prime example of global markets with economy of scarcity; 2) economies in conditions of controlled competition, with supply and demand in dynamic equilibrium (D $\cong$ O), namely, markets with static oligopoly where global corporations manifest widespread internationalization and the centrality of marketing policies (typically non-price competition, with communication, advertising and sales promotion prominence) as, for example, in the global industrial beer and tobacco product markets; 3) economies in over-supply conditions (D < O), referring to markets with dynamic oligopoly in which managerial economics emphasizes the centrality of digital and analogue communication flows, the criticality of innovation and imitation policies (active and passive) for the continued development of intermediate (trade) and final demand.

The globalisation of markets highlights a profound rethinking of the long-term business development philosophy, which tends to reconcile the volumes offered and the customer satisfaction (supply-driven management) with a priority focus on competition, considering that product features are more and more common to all competitors as a result of widespread and rapid imitation processes (market-driven management) (Brondoni, 2009).

A weak market orientation may today undermine the competitive business strength due to: excessive decision centralization; a progressive insensitivity to the opportunities of local markets; bureaucratic implementation of corporate strategies at the local level; damaging the brand's competitive value; the deterioration of brand equity. In fact, the brand represents the relationship between supply and demand with respect to specific identifying features compared to competing offers (brand image) and affirmed attributes (brand awareness). By consequence, brand equity or the state in a defined moment of the brand's relationship with the asset that originates from the internal and external information flow system and in a competitive perspective linked to business performance.

A purely physical conception of the competitive space is therefore primitive and limiting with respect to competitive plans in which specific geographic contexts are entrusted with expressing particular and partial competitive advantages (i.e., relating to production, marketing, R&D, etc.) to be coordinated in a wider operating and revenue system (market-space management).

Competition in global markets creates a multi-dimensional space resulting in the simultaneous presence of very different competitors in a specific geographic area with competitive behaviours that generally foresee: saturated markets and very volatile demand; time-based competition; and finally, communication processes that determine sales and production. In these contexts, the competition logic becomes 'first community, second business' or rather 'selling first and then producing', with the disruption of traditional competitive behaviours (typical of unsaturated markets with slow imitation processes and where communication follows production and sales) as synthesized in the 'first business, second community' model or 'producing first and then selling'. In other words, a new competitive approach with a reversal in the hierarchy between customer satisfaction, production, and competitive advantage: goods are in fact produced only when the level and intensity of sales opportunities and the degree of satisfaction that buyers demand are known.

The evolution of the structure of the competitive space is further reflected in the drastic reduction of competitive action and reaction times.

The extension of competitive fronts and the need for a coherent information system with reduced decision-making times determine very short-term competitive horizons related to a multiplicity of elements (products, prices, promotions, etc.) that require the simultaneous and real-time decisions of numerous subjects. Business development therefore requires innovative space-time competitive relationships that more specifically concern: very short decision times and time-based competition, with the reduction of non-action times; competition spaces linked to the business attractiveness and thus not affected by local management control constraints.

In short, global markets require businesses to deal with competition boundaries where competitive business behaviours are dominated by complex spatial coordinates (market-space management), intangible product resources (typically consisting of design, brand, pre-sales and after-sales services) and intangible business resources (specifically regarding the enterprise culture, corporate information system, and brand equity) (Perrini and Vurro, 2010).

In particular, product intangible assets are ascribable to:

– Product brand and product brand equity. In a managerial perspective, the brand expresses the awareness and image relationship created by a particular offer with a given market. With reference to the brand as an intangible asset, brand equity synthesizes the state, at a given moment, of the specific relationship established by a defined offer with a given market (Brondoni, 2001). Therefore, brand equity is the brand competitive value and expresses the market value, at a certain date, of the brand knowledge (i.e., the competitive value of awareness and image) that establishes itself with the demand of reference. Brand equity is an intangible and complex asset as it is the result of multiple determinants and for the company represents an intangible resource able to create value. In global markets with high competitive dynamics, significant brand equity reveals the existence of a positive differential achieved against competing offers, able to ensure – pro tempore – the firm's supply stability.

– Product design. The tangible and intangible components of product design are closely related to market and marketing research aimed at identifying specific consumer needs. New product design consists of: product design research (analysis of social, economic, and technological trends; identifying new consumer profiles and emerging needs; identifying competition gaps and generating ideas for new products and services; evaluating consumer expectations and identifying the functional product characteristics); concept design (innovation process management, product engineering, research on materials, finishes, and colours, etc.); brand design (product portfolio and brand portfolio reorganization, competitive brand and corporate identity positioning). Product design presupposes first the improvement of customer satisfaction, which in global markets is subject to intensive competition and constitutes a necessary (i.e., a sort of prerequisite attained by all competitors) but insufficient condition to outpace competitors. In this sense, achieving a differential advantage requires focusing the design of the offer on a superior interpretation of specific and distinctive features, and this requires gathering information on competitors (competitive market survey) (Hestad, 2013; Brondoni, 2015).

– Pre/post sales services. Pre-sales services are directly designed and produced by manufacturers and/or specialized financial companies (although subsidiaries or affiliated with the manufacturers) for end customers or sales intermediaries (retailers, wholesalers, influencers). Pre-sale services are structured in two main types: on the one hand, services related to product marketing and aimed at stimulating the purchasing decision; on the other hand, services related to financial products and designed to generate economic-financial reasons for selection. By contrast, after-sales services (support, product up/downgrading, maintenance, repairs, spare parts, learning and training, trade merchandising) ensure the full after-sales functionality of products and services. After-sales services (characterised by customization and information flows from customers to the firm) generate major costs, particularly in the presence of high customer satisfaction objectives and tight control over when and how the dedicated structures intervene. In global markets, after-sales costs (often incurred before sales) and the benefits of customization (in the medium-long term) conflict with product profitability objectives, pushing towards outsourcing key services and developing different after-sales outsourcing policies characterised as:

– Outsourcing for cost. Minimizing the cost of services (profit first of all), structuring the operating centres in cascades of subcontractors and moving virtual centres – such as call centres – to countries with low labour costs and strong localization incentives. Typical examples include corporations able to govern global economies of scarcity (such as Ge, Vodafone, Shell, Eni) with entirely passive trade and consumers, as well as local monopolies (in Italy, for example, Telecom, Alitalia, Enel, Rai, Fs, Mediaset) where after-sales services effectively keep customers at a distance.

– Outsourcing for branding. Outsourcing after-sales services enhances brand and repurchasing loyalty (satisfaction first of all) as highlighted in large firms and more generally in global economies with controlled, competition, final demand, and active trade.

– Outsourcing for value. Outsourcing after-sales services to maximize the profitability of branding policies and pre-sales services (especially logistics for trade, and consumer credit for customers), which subordinate repurchasing and after-sales loyalty (thus in a 'business value first of all' perspective) as in the case of firms operating in over-supply economies with trade hard competition and non-loyal consumers.

The intangible corporate assets governable by firms are linked instead to:

– Corporate culture. The criticality of the corporate culture is particularly evident in large corporations that deal in global markets, according to a conception of the competition space without physical boundaries (market-space competition). In complex organizations oriented to overcoming the physical competition space (market-space management), the corporate culture becomes central in the governance of internal, external, and co-makership relations, since these relationships are based on narrow and widespread interactions pursued in real-time (Trompenaars *et al.*, 2011). Corporate culture thus expresses the corporate personality, permeating every event in the organisation's life, in dealing with the external environment (customers, intermediaries, competitors), and above all, in the internal structure with respect to various operating units, articulated by type of relationship (employees, co-makers, partners). In external relations, the corporate personality affects the image, i.e., the differential competitive characteristics, while within the organization, the corporate personality is intended to assert high identification to achieve the alignment of objectives, interests, and behaviours. Such alignment expresses the firm's guiding values and behavioural rules, setting the stage to act unitedly to achieve common goals.

– Corporate information system. The information system is a critical intangible resource whose attributes derive from the organisation's dominant culture and the characteristics of which configure the integration and adaptation lines (in relation to a defined corporate identity) allowing an organization to remain in tune with the many contexts in which it operates. The information system thus conforms to the corporate culture and the competitive environment of reference, with the specific articulation of the subsystems that compose it. Moreover, in high competition markets, the information system tends to constitute a cross-company system to enhance the local organizations' ability to relate to the market through network relationships.

– Corporate Identity. Finally, a global corporation with a strong competitive stance (market-driven management) sees a fundamental factor in corporate identity development. The control of the global competitive space can in fact be pursued by the overall corporate identity, that is to say, irrespective of brands referring to particular offers and rather correlated to brand equity referring to a corporate identity. The corporate identity phenomenon has become particularly important with globalisation, as global markets penalize brand fragmentation that determines higher marketing and promotion costs with high volatility rates, and instead tends to concentrate the communication activities on the corporate identity.

However, in today's global markets, sustainable business development does not primarily depend on volumes or the attributes of individual products, with easily imitable tangible characteristics and with intangible supply resources (product intangible asset) distinguished by high volatility, especially in relation to marketing costs (Day and Reibstein, 2004). In this sense, the market-driven orientation, precisely due to the outside-in approach that distinguishes it, highlights the primacy of corporate intangible assets that enable (especially for the purpose of local profitability) finalizing and enhancing the intangible supply resources (i.e., the so-called 'product intangible assets').

More generally, in the hyper-competition dominion of global markets with high competitive tension, the intangible corporate and product economy take on specific importance for corporate success and vitality (Salvioni and Bosetti, 2014). A business is highly profitable only for organizations that have continuous information flows from the markets to shape innovation supply and create consumption bubbles (demand bubbles), rapidly satisfying these (time-to-market), and duly abandoning them (time competition), leaving imitator competitors the residual portion of the bubble (usually dispersed and scarcely profitable due to the numerous alternative offers).

References

Arrigo E., *Alliances, Open Innovation and Outside-in Management*, Symphonya. Emerging Issues in Management (symphonya.unimib.it), (2), 53-65, 2012. http://dx.doi.org/10.4468/2012.2.05arrigo.

Bellini N., Hilpert U. (eds.), *Europe's Changing Regional Geography. The Impact of Inter-Networks*, Routledge, Abingdon, 2013.
Best R.J., *Market-Based Management*, Prentice Hall, Upper Sadle River, 2004.
Borgonovi E., *Sustainable Economic Growth in the Global Society*, Symphonya. Emerging Issues in Management (symphonya.unimib.it), (2), 50-63, 2007. http://dx.doi.org/10.4468/2007.2.06borgonovi.

Brondoni S.M., *Brand Policy and Brand Equity*, Symphonya. Emerging Issues in Management (symphonya.unimib.it), (1), 5-25, 2000-2001. http://dx.doi.org/10.4468/2001.1.02brondoni.

Brondoni S.M., *Global Markets and Market-Space Competition*, Symphonya. Emerging Issues in Management (symphonya.unimib.it), (1), 28-42, 2002. http://dx.doi.org/10.4468/2002.1.03brondoni

Brondoni S.M., *Managerial Economics and Global Competition*, Symphonya. Emerging Issues in Management (symphonya.unimib.it), (1), 14-38, 2005. http://dx.doi.org/10.4468/2005.1.02brondoni.

Brondoni S.M., *Market-Driven Management, Competitive Space and Global Networks*, Symphonya. Emerging Issues in Management (symphonya.unimib.it), (1), 14-27, 2008. http://dx.doi.org/10.4468/2008.1.02brondoni.

Brondoni S.M., *Market-Driven Management, Competitive Customer Value and Global Networks*, Symphonya. Emerging Issues in Management (symphonya.unimib.it), (1), 8-25, 2009. http://dx.doi.org/10.4468/2009.1.02brondoni.

Brondoni S.M., *Innovation and Imitation: Corporate Strategies for Global Competition*, Symphonya. Emerging Issues in Management (symphonya.unimib.it), n. 1, 10-24, 2012. http://dx.doi.org/10.4468/2012.1.02brondoni.

Brondoni S.M., *Managerial Economics and Global Corporations*, Giappichelli, Turin, 2012b.

Brondoni S.M., *Market-Driven Management and Corporate Growth*, Giappichelli, Turin, 2012c.

Brondoni S.M., *Innovation and Imitation for Global Competitive Strategies. The Corporation Development Models of US, Japan, Korea,and Taiwan*, Symphonya. Emerging Issues in Management (symphonya.unimib.it), (1), 12-27, 2013. http://dx.doi.org/10.4468/2013.1.02brondoni.

Brondoni S.M., *Global Capitalism and Sustainable Growth. From Global Products to Network Globalisation*, Symphonya. Emerging Issues in Management (symphonya.unimib.it), (1), 10-31, 2014. http://dx.doi.org/10.4468/2014.1.02brondoni.

Brondoni S.M., *Global Networks, Outside-In Capabilities and Smart Innovation*, Symphonya. Emerging Issues in Management (symphonya.unimib.it), (1), 6-21, 2015a. http://dx.doi.org/10.4468/2015.1.02brondoni.

Brondoni S.M., *Product Design Management and Global Competition*, Symphonya. Emerging Issues in Management (symphonya.unimib.it), (2), 13-24, 2015b. http://dx.doi.org/10.4468/2015.2.02brondoni.

Brondoni S.M., Lambin J.-J, *Ouverture de Brand Equity*, Symphonya. Emerging Issues in Management (symphonya.unimib.it), (1), 1-4, 2000-2001. ttp://dx.doi.org/10.4468/2001.1.01ouverture.

Cappellin R., Wink R., *International Knowledge and Innovation Networks: Knowledge Creation and Innovation in Medium Technology Clusters*, Edward Elgar Publishing, Cheltenham, 2009.

Day G.S., *The Market-Driven Strategy*, The Free Press, New York, 1990.

Day G.S., *The Market-Driven Organization*, The Free Press, New York, 1999.

Day G.S., Reibstein D.J, *Managing Brands in Global Markets*, in H. Gatignon-J.R. Kimberly-R.E. Gunther (eds.), *Alliance on Globalizing*, University Press, Cambridge, 2004.

Douglas S.P., Craig C.S., *Evolution of Global Marketing Strategy: Scale, Scope and Synergy*, Columbia Journal of World Business, Fall, 47-59, 1989.

Dunning J.H., Lundan S.M., *Multinational Enterprises and the Global Economy*, Edward Elgar, Northampton, 2008.

Gnecchi F., *Market-Driven Management, Market Space and Value Proposition*, Symphonya. Emerging Issues in Management (symphonya.unimib.it), (2), 33-45, 2009. http://dx.doi.org/10.4468/2009.2.04gnecchi

Golinelli G.M., Gatti M., *The Firm as a Viable System*, Symphonya. Emerging Issues in Management (symphonya.unimib.it), (2), 38-63, 2000-2001. http://dx.doi.org/10.4468/2001.2.04golinelli.gatti.

Hestad M., *Branding and Product Design. An Integrated Perspective*, Routledge, Abingdon, 2013.

Inauen M. Schenker-Wicki A., *The Impact of Outside-in Open Innovation on Innovation Performance*, European Journal of Innovation Management, 14, (4), 496-520, 2011. http://dx.doi.org/10.1108/14601061111174934.

Ireland R.D., Hitt M.A., Vaidyanath D., *Alliance Management as a Source of Competitive Advantage*, Journal of Management, 28, (3), 413-446, 2002. http://dx.doi.org/10.1177/014920630202800308.

Keegan W.J., Schlegelmilch B.B., *Global Marketing Management: A European Perspective* , Pearson Education, Harlow, 2001.

Kim L., *Imitation to Innovation: The Dynamics of Korea's Technological Learning*, Harvard University School Press, Cambridge, Massachusetts, 1997.

Kim L., *Korea's National Innovation System in Transition*, in Kim L. and Nelson R. (eds.), *Technology, Learning and Innovation: The Experiences of Newly Industrialising Economies*, Cambridge University press, Cambridge, 2000.

Kotabe M., *Global Sourcing Strategy in the Pacific. American and Japanese Multinational Companies*, in G. Boyd, (ed.), *Structural Competitiveness in the Pacific*, Edward Elgar, Cheltenham, 1996.

Lambin J.-J., *Market-Driven Management*, McGraw-Hill, London, 2000.

Lambin J.-J., *Strategic Marketing Revisited after September 11*, Symphonya. Emerging Issues in Management (symphonya.unimib.it), n. 1, 2002, 7-27. http://dx.doi.org/10.4468/2002.1.02lambin.

Lambin J.-J., *Changing Market Relationships in the Internet Age*, UCL, Louvain, 2008.

Lambin J.-J., *Rethinking the Market Economy*, Symphonya. Emerging Issues in Management (symphonya.unimib.it), (2), 4-15, 2014. http://dx.doi.org/10.4468/2014.2.02lambin.

Lambin J.-J., *Rethinking the Market Economy. New Challenges, New Ideas, New Opportunities*, Palgrave Macmillan, London, 2014.

Lambin J.-J., Brondoni S.M., *Ouverture de Market-Driven Management*, Symphonya. Emerging Issues in Management (symphonya.unimib.it), n. 2, 2000-2001, 1-11. http://dx.doi.org/10.4468/2001.2.01ouverture.

Lansbury R.D., Suh C-S., Kwon S-H., *The Global Korean Motor Industry: The Hyundai Motor Company's Global Strategy*, Routledge, Abingdon, 2007.

Levitt T., *The Globalization of Markets*, Harvard Business Review, May-June, 92-102, 1983.

Levitt T., *Innovative Imitation*, Harvard Business Review, September-October, 63-70, 1996.

Mair A., *Honda's Global Local Corporation*, McMillan, New York, 1994.

Ohmae K., *Globalization, Regions and the New Economy*, UCLA, Center for Globalization and Policy Research, Working Paper n. 1, January 2001.

Ohno T., *Toyota Seisan Höshiki*, Diamond Ed., Tokyo, 1978 (First English version: T. Ohno, *Toyota Production System: Beyond Large-Scale Production*, Productivity Press Inc., New York, 1988).

Paliwoda S., Andrews T., Chen J., (eds.), *Marketing Management in Asia*, Routledge, Abingdon, 2013.

Park Y.W., Hong P., *Building Network Capabilities in Turbulent Competitive Environments. Practices of Global Firms from Korea and Japan*, CRC Press, Routledge, Abingdon, 2011

Percy L., *Strategic Integrated Marketing Communications*, 2nd ed., Routledge, Abingdon, 2014.

Perrini F., Vurro C., *Corporate Sustainability, Intangible Assets Accumulation and Competitive Advantage Constraints*, Symphonya. Emerging Issues in Management (symphonya.unimib.it), (2), 25-38, 2010 http://dx.doi.org/10.4468/2010.2.03 perrini.vurro.

Raiport J.F., Sviokla J.J., *Managing in the Marketspace*, Harvard Business Review, November-December, 1994.

Reinartz Werner, *Customizing Prices in Online Markets*, Symphonya. Emerging Issues in Management (symphonya.unimib.it), n. 1, 2002, 55-65. http://dx.doi.org/10.4468/2002.1.05reinartz.

Salvioni Daniela M., *Corporate Governance and Global Responsibility*, Symphonya. Emerging Issues in Management (symphonya.unimib.it), n. 1, 2003, 44-54. http://dx.doi.org/10.4468/2003.1.05salvioni.

Salvioni D.M., *Intangible Assets and Internal Controls in Global Companies*, Symphonya. Emerging Issues in Management (symphonya.unimib.it), (2), 39-51, 2010. http://dx.doi.org/10.4468/2010.2.4salvioni.

Salvioni D.M., Bosetti L., *Sustainable Development and Corporate Communication in Global Markets*, Symphonya. Emerging Issues in Management (symphonya. unimib.it), (1), 1-19, 2014. http://dx.doi.org/10.4468/2014.1.03salvioni.bosetti.

Shingo S., *A Study of the Toyota Production System from an Industrial Engineering Viewpoint (Produce What Is Needed, When It's Needed)*, Productivity Press Inc., New York, 1981.

Shingo S., *Non-Stock Production*, Productivity Press Inc., New York, 1988.

Trompenaars F., Hampden-Turner C., *Riding the Waves of Culture: Understanding Diversity in Global Business*, 3rd ed., Nicholas Brealey Publishing, Boston, 2011.

Webster F.E. Jr., *Market-Driven Management*, John Wiley & Sons, New York, 2002.

Zucchella A., *Network Social Responsibility*, Symphonya. Emerging Issues in Management (symphonya.unimib.it), (2), 64-71, 2007. http://dx.doi.org/ 10.4468/2007.2.

Chapter 2

THE SHARING ECONOMY.
A NEW STRATEGY TO COMPETE
IN THE GLOBAL MARKET

Jean-Jacques Lambin

ABSTRACT: *The name "sharing economy", is an umbrella term with a range of meanings used to describe economic and social activities involving online transactions. Also known as "collaborative economy", "on-demand economy", "peer-to-peer economy" or "gig economy". This multitude of names is suggestive of the confusion that surrounds this concept*[1]. *The two most popular names are "collaborative economy" and "sharing economy" are often used interchangeably and will be adopted in this essay.*

2.1. Defining the sharing or collaborative economy

The main obstacle to a deeper understanding of the collaborative/sharing economy' has been ambiguity about its definition. The name "sharing economy" is widely used in the Anglo-Saxon literature (both professional and academic), while the name "collaborative economy" is used in every

---

[1] Frenken K., Schor J. (2017), *Putting the Sharing Economy into Perspective*, Environmental innovation and Societal Transitions, 23, 3.

EU publication. The word "sharing", evokes familiar exchanges and intimate relationships, which seem to be at odds with economic activity dominated by anonymous and rational transactions, rather than by altruistic behavior. Also, most services proposed are not really sharing. *Airbnb* is not sharing, it's renting short term, but providers and users are supposed to be ready to share. On the other hand, "collaboration" evokes is a purposeful relationship which relies on the will of all parties to cooperate in order to achieve shared objectives. In other words, the collaborative economy matches people who want to share assets and services online. The two names designate the same activity but from a different perspective. The collaborative economy evokes a longer term relationship while sharing economy refers more to short term transactions.

A common academic definition of the two term would refer to a hybrid market model of peer-to-peer exchange (or sharing), coordinated through community-based online services, where *individual consumers grant each other temporary access to their under-utilized physical assets, possibly for mon*ey[2]. The keywords in this definition are: peer-to-peer, temporary access, underutilized assets.

The collaborative economy involves three categories of actors: (a) service providers who offer assets, resources, time and/or skills and who are ready to share with other individuals on an occasional basis; (b) users of these services individuals or households; and (c) intermediaries that connect, via an online collaborative platforms, providers with users and that facilitate transactions between them. Service providers can be either individuals offering service on an occasional basis or professional services providers.

2.2. Spirit of the collaborative economy

Entrepreneurial capitalism traditionally follows a top-down strategy in its relations with the market. The initiative comes from the firm targeting a well defined, but passive group of potential users. The collaboration/ sharing business model deeply modifies the supplier-customer relationship by creating more equalitarian and lateral relationships similar to a form of partnership.

Collaboration is a purposeful relationship in which all parties strategically choose to cooperate in order to achieve shared or overlapping objectives. The collaborative economy relies on the will of the users to share. But

[2] Frenken and Schor (2017), *ibidem.*

in order to make an exchange, users have to be trustworthy and trust each other. The following five principles are central in the collaboration business model [3].

– *Openness*, which includes not only open standards and content but also financial transparency and an open attitude towards external ideas and resources.

– *Peering*, which replaces hierarchical models with a more collaborative forum. Tapscott and Williams cite the development of Linux as the "quintessential example of peering".

– *Sharing,* which is a less proprietary approach to exchange (among other things) products, intellectual property, scientific knowledge.

– *Trust,* assured reliance on the character, ability, strength, or truth of someone or something or the belief that someone or something is reliable, good, honest, effective.

– *Acting globally*, which involves embracing globalisation and ignoring "physical and geographical boundaries" at both the corporate and individual level.

In a way, the collaboration economy model refashions the traditional business model among international companies which is insular, closed, secretive and hierarchized, by substituting new practices such as:

– intellectual property by the idea of sharing of propriety information,
– competitive by open collaboration,
– hierarchized by horizontal peers communities,
– pricing by open source and free access for everyone,
– paid labor by cooperation, voluntary help and hedonism,
– market power by co-creation with users,
– one-way communication by a multilateral communication platform.

The success of the open source movement has paved the way of the freely exchange of other kinds of peer produced contents.

2.3. Influence of the open source movement

The term "open source" refers to something people can modify and share because its design is publicly accessible. The term originated in the context of software development to designate a specific approach to creating com-

---

[3] Tapscott D. and Willyams A.D. (2006), *Wikinomics, How Mass collaboration Changes everything,* Penguin Books, New York.

puter programs. Today, however, "open source" designates a broader set of values – what we call *"the open source way"*[4]. Open source projects, products, or initiatives embrace and celebrate principles of open exchange, collaborative participation, rapid prototyping, transparency, meritocracy, and community-oriented development.

The open source movement has developed a new philosophy about in-tellectual property, maintaining that knowledge should be free. It is important to note the historical links between the collaborative economy and activity such as the collaborative software movement that harnesses the unpaid work of software engineers to write code and solve problems collectively. The success of the open source movement paved the way for other kinds of peer produced content such as Wikipedia and citizen science which is produced by massive numbers of volunteers as well as *shared online* content such as file-sharing, video posting, music sharing. There is a strong historical and global connection between the emergence of peer-to-peer platforms and a widespread feeling that the new technology-enabled practices these platforms allow for empowering people, also for crowd-funding to raise capital, for crowd-sourcing to collect data[5].

2.4. Other online economic platforms

Keeping in mind the notion of under-used or idle assets, one can distinguish the collaborative e conomy from other economic forms:

– *Product-service economy*. When a consumer gains access to a product by renting or leasing a good whilst the service provider retains ownership, we are on a business-to-consumer (B2C) platform or in the product-service economy and not in the collaborative economy. An example is car-rental with *Hertz*.

– *Second-hand economy*. When goods are sold or given away between consumers, as it occurs on online platforms such as *Ebay* or *Facebook*, we are in the second-hand economy and not in the collaborative economy.

– *On-demand economy*. When Internet platforms that bring consumers together to provide each other with services we are not in the collaborative economy but in the on-demand economy. An example of such a platform is *Uber* for short term car ride.

---

[4] On this subject see: Raymond E.S. (1997), *The Cathedral and the Bazaar.* Raymond is an open-source software advocate. Retrieved from Wikipedia, July 2017.

[5] Benkler Y. (2006), *The Wealth of Networks: How Social Production Transforms Markets and Freedom*, Yale University Press, New Haven.

– *Gig economy.* When hiring self-employed individuals to carry out work around the home (concierge or home health services, child care, gardening etc.), we are in the gig (or task-based) economy. An example is the platform *Task Rabbit* or *Listminut* a online platforms that matches freelance workers with local demand, allowing consumers to find immediate help with everyday tasks.

By contrast, in the case of *Blablacar*, the consumer occupies a seat that would otherwise not have been used as the driver had planned to go from A to B anyway. Hitchhiking[6] and carpooling are examples of ride-sharing and part of the collaborative economy. Indeed, in the context of transportation, this distinction between on-demand economy and collaborating economy has become clearer over time as most commentators now call *Uber* and *Lyft* ride-hailing companies instead of ride-sharing.

2.5. Excess capacity of shareable goods

In essence shareable goods are goods that by nature provide owners with excess capacity, providing the consumer with an opportunity to lend out or rent out their goods to other consumers[7]. Excess capacity of a consumer good is present when the owner does not consume the product all the time.

As stated by Rachel Botsman[8]: "Do we need a power drill? *That power drill will be used around 12 to 15 minutes in its entire lifetime.* Instead of purchasing can we share? Because *what we need is the hole, not the drill*".

A majority of consumer goods can be understood as having excess capacity, or being idle physical assets, including houses, cars, boats, clothing, books, toys, appliances, tools, furniture, computers, etc. The few exceptions would include, for example, eyeglasses and mobile phones. Another dimension of excess capacity is the lumpiness of some goods. Many items can only be purchased with excess capacity such as the unused memory capacity of computers.

Under-utilized assets and excess and idle capacity is also key to the current discussion about home collaborative platforms, such as *Airbnb*. When a house owner is away for holidays or a business trip, or has a spare bedroom,

---

[6] Hitchhiking is a precursor of the sharing economy.

[7] Benkler Y. (2004), *Sharing nicely: on shareable goods and the emergence of sharing as a modality of economic production*, Yale Law Journal, 114, 273-358

[8] Botsman Rachel (2010), *What's Mine Is Yours: The Rise of Collaborative Consumption*, Harper Collins.

the asset is not utilized. That is, the unoccupied house can be considered as temporary idle capacity. If, however, a person were to buy a second home and rent it out to tourists permanently, that constitutes running a commercial lodging site, such as a B2B or a hotel. The potential market of under-utilized or of idle assets is substantial, in particular in affluent economies.

2.6. Sharing under-used assets

The notion of sharing of under-used asset is central to the definition of sharing economy, because it distinguishes the practice of sharing of goods from the practice of on-demand personal services. It expands the existing market to the market of unused assets. There is a fundamental difference between ordering a taxi through *Uber* or *Lyft* and taking a ride through *Blablacar* or another hitchhiking or carpooling platform[9], the consumer creates new capacity by ordering a taxi on demand to drive the passenger from A to B. Without the order, the trip would not have been made in the first place. In this case, the term now coming into common use is the on-demand economy.

2.7. Lower transaction costs of sharing

A while ago, companies would have assumed that most people didn't want to spend the night in a stranger's house, that they wouldn't really trust a stranger to drive them around. Historically, sharing was confined to trusted individuals such as family, friends and neighbors. However, as noted by Juliet Schor[10], there is something new about the collaborative economy, which is called "*stranger-sharing*". With the customer review system, there is an implied trust in the brand itself: one presumes *Uber* is doing its due diligence on its drivers, one presumes that *Airbnb* is making sure that the users are not going to feel unsafe in the property. What is new is that users now also lend goods to strangers or to unknown people, because the Internet has enormously decreased transaction costs between unknown other, in particular the costs related to search and arranging a contract with strangers. Sharing economy firms sell reductions in transaction costs in three main ways:

---

[9] Meelen T. and Frenken K. (2015), *Stop Saying Uber is part to the Sharing Economy*, FastCompany, January.

[10] Schor Juliet (2014), *Debating the Sharing economy*, Great Transformation Initiative, October.

– by cutting the cost of searching and sorting through the various options;
– by enabling trust between the parties to the transaction and
– by facilitating payment in a way that is predictable and transparent.

The these reductions on transaction costs make possible a more efficient use of assets, to the benefit of both owners and prospective users of those assets. The digital platforms are able to make stranger-sharing less risky and more appealing because they source information on the profile of users and the profile of providers, via the exchange of ratings systems and reputations[11].

2.8. Coverage of the collaborative economy

The collaborative economy covers a great variety of sectors and is rapidly emerging across Europe[12]. Many people in the EU have already used, or are aware of collaborative economy services, which range from sharing houses and car journeys, to domestic services The four sectors in which collaborative economy platforms have the most significant presence are:

1. *Accommodation*: through platforms, people rent out properties or parts of properties. Examples of such companies are: *Airbnb, HomeAway, HouseTrip, 9Flats*, as of February 2016, *Airbnb* claimed a presence in 34,000 cities covering more than 190 countries, 2 million listings, and more than 60 million guests hosted. *Airbnb* is valued at $31 billion[13]. *Home Away*, with a similar business model covers 190 countries. It is a public company valued at $3.4 billion. *Flats* has a strong European presence with 100,000 listings.

2. *Transportation*: two different broad categories of platform can be distinguished in this sector. The first group of platforms facilitate the hiring of assets such as cars, motorbikes and bicycles. Examples are *ZipCar, EasyCar, car2go, Autolib and Velib*. The second group of platforms help their users to rent assets together with labour and human capital. Examples *include BlablaCar, Sidecar, Uber and Lyft. Car2go* offers transportation on demand using 'by-the-minute' rates.

---

[11] Rating systems.

[12] Petropoulos Geogios (2017), *An economic review of the collaborative economy*, Policy Contribution, Issue 5, Brueghel, 4.

[13] In March 2017, *Airbnb* raised $1 billion in additional funding, bringing their total funding raised to date to more than $3 billion and valuing the company at $31 billion.

3. *Online labor markets such as Amazon Mechanical Tusk, Adtriboo, TaskRabbit, Oltretata, Freelancer, Crowdsource, Listminut and Clickworker:* these platforms specialize in micro-tasking by matching employers and on demand workers.

4. *Finance:* crowd funding platforms such as *Kickstarter* and *IndieGogo* match entrepreneurial projects with funders (venture capital financing). Peer-to-peer lending platforms such as *Lending Club* and *Prosper* connect individuals and SMEs with potential peer-lenders, without the involvement of any financial institution.

2.9. The gig economy and freelance workers

Encompassing many of the listed benefits of the sharing economy is the idea of the task-based economy, also called the "gig economy". Through monetizing unused assets, such as renting out a spare guestroom on *Airbnb*, or providing personal services to others, such as becoming a driver with *Uber*, people are in effect becoming freelance or task-based workers.

Freelance work entails better opportunity for employment, as well as more flexibility for workers, as people have the ability to pick and choose the time and place of their work. As freelance workers, people can plan around their existing schedules and maintain multiple jobs if needed. The social protection of these free lance workers is problematic however, as evidenced by the hot ongoing debate in France (*les intermittents*) regarding the free lance workers in the theatrical sector.

The collaborative economy is one of many forces that is creating a new temporary workforce across a range of countries, shifting labor from full-time to independent work. As of 2016, close to one in three workers in many European countries earn all or part of their income from freelance (or non-employment) work [14].

Controversy and confusion surrounds the thousands of *Uber* drivers worldwide. Despite being the largest taxi company in the world, they employ no drivers. *Uber* refers to its drivers as independent contractors. This term has caused anger amongst some drivers due to the lack of employee benefits and security.

---

[14] Sundararajan Arun (2017), *The Collaborative Economy: Socioeconomic, Regulatory and Policy Issue*, Directorate-General for Internal Policies, Internal Market and Consumer protection, European Parliament.

2.10. Low rate and simple system in Belgium

A tax rate of 10% will be applied to services between individuals. This provides a legal framework for activities currently taking place in the "grey zone", and helps combat fraud. Today, most activities in the sharing economy are subject to tax at a rate of 33%. The new legislation will apply to income up to 5000 euro. This prevents unfair competition with small businesses and professional entrepreneurs.

Rather than requiring the individuals to report their income to the tax authorities, registered platforms will have to withhold taxes at source and send the information to the tax authorities. Administrative charges will be minimal for the individuals who render the services. Those who want to turn a second job in the sharing economy into a profession must switch to self-employed status in a primary or secondary profession. In other words, contributions to Social Security are not owed as long as the income does not exceed 5000 euro. This new legal framework enters into full force on 1 March 2017.

With this new legislation for the sharing economy, Belgium moves to the forefront of peer-to-peer economies in Europe. Up to now, the United Kingdom has been the leader in stimulating the sharing economy. Last month, the British Minister of Finance announced a tax exemption of up to 2 500 euro for incomes earned in the sharing economy. The French government recently rejected a proposal for advantageous treatment of incomes up to 5 000 euro. The Italian government is currently considering a system similar to the Belgian legislation but with more red tape.

2.11. The uberization business model

A noted above, *Uber* is not part of the sharing economy, but part of the on-demand economy. Yet its operational business model has been largely adopted by most digital platforms. *Uberization is a business model in which services are offered on demand through direct contact between a customer and a supplier, usually via mobile technology.* The term "uberization" is derived from the company name *Uber,* very successful all over the world in the taxi industry. The *Uber* company developed a mobile application that allows consumers to submit a city trip request which is then routed to *Uber* drivers who use their own cars. Start-up companies all over the world are trying to apply the same business model to every industry possible. Naturally, not all will be a success. However there are indications that a number of industries will eventually follow in the footsteps of *Uber* and disrupt a whole industry. Due to its popularity, and due to the confusion around the term sharing economy, *Uberization* is becoming the generic name for an economic system based on *sharing underused assets or services.*

It requires the utilization of computing platforms, such as mobile applications, in order to facilitate peer-to-peer transactions between clients and providers of a service, bypassing the role of centrally planned corporations. The model has much lower operating costs compared to a traditional business. Around the world, a new wave of peer-to-peer, access-driven businesses is shaking up established categories. The *uberization* business model has the following characteristics:

– elimination of middlemen, but direct online contacts between suppliers and customers;
– intensive use of the new digital technologies (smart phones, tablets, mobile internet, GPS, ...);
– very limited fixed cost and low transactions costs;
– almost instantaneous connection between the customer and the service provider depending on their geographic proximity through a digital platform;
– the customers are paying the platform and the service providers are paid by the platform after deduction of a commission;
– reciprocal evaluation of the customers and of the providers;
– substantial savings on costs by bypassing regulation and legal constraints imposed to traditional competitors.

By way of an example and referring to the *Uber*'s case in the taxi industry,

Uber's value to customers is : Reducing wait time – increased cab reliability – standardized (and often cheaper) pricing of cab rides – Hassle-free payment for rides using card/wallet – Simplicity and reactivity – Security of the relationship assumed by the platform.

Uber's value proposition to drivers lies in: Increased income – constant stream of ride requests – few waiting time around for a consumer – flexible working hours – choice of their own work timings – availability during off hours – Reducing wait time.

One of the most powerful mechanisms is the peer review mechanism by which the consumers rate their experience afterwards to see how conventions and protocols are being put into practice.

2.12. Uberization: a capitalism without capital

Uberization is a disruptive model displacing competitors and established business. The phenomenon of "Uberization" has been criticized for its role in facilitating the decline of labor-intensive industries, and hence for threatening jobs. *Uber* removes the middleman, – i.e. the taxi dispatcher – from the buyer/seller equation, allowing each driver to be his own boss and work independently of a central company, thanks to the magic box that is the Internet. The current labor climate, in which the job market is shifting away from traditional employment and towards part-time and temporary work, self-employment and alternative working arrangements, actually creates a perfect recipe for the Uberization of labor. It could help both highly skilled workers, who don't want to be employees or are seeking a more flexible work schedule, as well as low-skilled laborers who can find flexible part-time work when it's convenient for them.

Unlike websites that act as online store front, collaborative platforms are not direct service providers. Instead the platform allows "users" (purchasers of services) to connect and transact with "providers. Internet platforms are "light weight" businesses with few assets and risk. Uberization is a new form of capitalism which does not require fresh capital for its development, since the objective is to monetize underused but already established markets or existing assets. *Alibaba* holds not stock; *Airbnb* does not invest monies in building new hotels but simply rent unused apartment or spare rooms in existing houses [15]. Similarly for *Uber* which targets the existing park of underutilized cars and drivers. In both cases, the added value and the macro-economic impact are modest. For example, the value of *Aibnb* which doesn't own a single hotel room is about the same as the value of *Accor* ($13 billion) the French hospitality group [16], which owns 3700 hotels and hires 300 percent more people than *Airbnb*.

Probably the most widespread sharing-company practice to date involves unused real estate, but the sharing market for *intangible assets* – a company's brainpower, knowledge, and intellectual capital – shows just as much promise. In many companies, for example, technical expertise is severely underused, simply because the work of the R&D staff doesn't fit with the company's current strategic priorities. But, rather than divest its facilities, a company can share its staff.

---

[15] Airbnb Paris has more than 70 000 rental rooms or apartments in its portfolio.

[16] Accor S.A., using the brand name Accor Hotels, is a French multinational hotel group, part of the CAC 40 index which operates in 95 countries Headquartered in France, the group owns, operates and franchises 3,700 hotels (spanning all inhabited continents) representing several brands, from budget and economy lodgings to five-star hotels.

2.13. Positive impact of the sharing economy

The rise of the sharing economy is changing the face of European business – creating opportunities for new entrants, challenging incumbent players, and raising questions for all stakeholders. PWC's recent study (2016) for the European Commission [17] shows that activity in the sharing economy across Europe has accelerated over the past two years, expanding at roughly double the pace anticipated in 2014. PWC found that in 2015 alone, four key sectors of the sharing economy generated platform revenues of nearly €4bn and facilitated €28bn of transactions within Europe.

Uber, and similar services, are doing a historically unprecedented work of democratizing access to productive capital, an interesting challenge for anti-capitalists. Through them, the average car owner now owns capital that he can use to the same economic ends as any capitalist, and his property is recognized as equally valuable. His ownership is suddenly protected and encouraged by a system that was used to devalue it. The same goes for those who own any other property touched by Uberization. It now has to contend with the fact that the worker can buy property and use it as capital to value his labor freely. Uberization puts the traditional capitalist in competition with those who previously only had their labor to sell [18].

The collaborative economy provides new opportunities for citizens and innovative entrepreneurs to trade their under-utilized assets. But it has also created tensions between the new service providers and existing market operators. Uberization has also raised concerns over government regulations and taxation. The European Commission is looking at how it can encourage the development of new and innovative services, and the temporary use of assets, while ensuring adequate consumer and social protection. In many cases, this opportunity is exclusively only provided through collaborative platforms as the supply of goods and services through other channels is subject to licensing and other regulatory barriers.

The name sharing economy is now sometimes used in a broader sense to describe any sales transactions that are done via online market places, even ones that are business-to-business rather than peer-to-peer. For this reason Eckhard and Bardi [19] (2015) argue that *"when sharing is market-mediated,*

---

[17] Hawsworth J. and Vaughan R. (2016), *Sharing Benefits, How the sharing economy is reshaping business across Europe*, PWC, April.

[18] Hunter Charles (2016), *Why Marxists should support Uber and Airbnb*, BRUNOBERTEZ Block.

[19] Eckhard G. and Bard F. (2015), *The Sharing Economy isn't About Sharing at All*, Harvard Business Review, January 28.

..., it is no longer sharing at all" and the name sharing economy is a misnomer and should be called *"access economy"*. However, most commentators assert that the term is still valid as a means of describing a generally more democratized online marketplace, even when it's applied to a broader spectrum of services.

2.14. Environmental impact of the collaborative economy

To date, there has been little objective research done on the true environmental impacts of the collaborative economy, which takes into account not only direct and indirect environmental impacts, but also the rebound effect, that is increased consumption because of the extra money earned and saved from engaging in the collaborative economy instead of the traditional economy[20].

Hard data is hard to come by. Many green claims are anecdotal. *Airbnb* cites several studies that highlight how much energy, water and greenhouse gas emissions people save by staying in its properties, but the company does not **reveal** how these studies reached their conclusions. According to a study conducted by the Cleantech Group[21], for example, *Airbnb* claims that, in a year, its guests avoided greenhouse gas emissions comparable to 33,000 cars on North American roads, and saved the equivalent of enough water to fill 270 Olympic-sized swimming pools. One presumes that these savings are the result of traditional hotels operating less efficiently than individual homes. But *Airbnb*, which commissioned the study, has refused to allow its full study to be published online.

Numbers related to business-car use seem somewhat more reliable. The Transportation Sustainability Research Center (TSRC) estimated that 20% of users driving Zipcar vehicles for business (who joined through an employer) had sold a personal car after becoming a member, and another 20% avoided buying a car for the same reasons. The report said further that the business program as a whole had "eliminated the need for roughly 33,000 vehicles across North America.".

One quantifiable way to benefit the environment is to reduce traffic

---

[20] Rubicon (2015), *How Green is the sharing economy*, Knowledge and Wharton, December 1.

See also: Pickwell Jim (2016), *How the Sharing Economy Helps in the Fight Against Climate Change*, Huffington Post, The Block December 10.

[21] The Cleantech Group is a company that supports the development and marketability of clean technologies. The Cleantech Group provides members of its Cleantech network access to capital, investors, research and promotional opportunities.

congestion. A 2008 report by researchers at the University of California[22], "Traffic Congestion and Greenhouse Gases", studied a segment of Interstate 110 in Los Angeles during rush hour and calculated that "the congested traffic for this one-hour time period on this segment of freeway emits approximately 166 metric tons of CO2 [carbon dioxide]". If the traffic flow were improved so that cars were able to travel 20 miles per hour faster, said the report, CO2 emissions would drop 12%, "resulting in a reduction of 21 metric tons of CO2". Extrapolate that reduction to a full year, and easing congestion on just that one stretch of L.A. interstate would reduce CO2 emissions by 249,000 tons, the equivalent of taking 41,500 cars off the road.

2.15. Financial impact of the sharing economy

Referring to Petropolos[23],and to its more recent comprehensive review of the collaborative economy the following selected key findings are:

– Geron[24] estimated that the revenue flowing through the collaborative economy directly into people's wallets at $3.5 billion, and the value of the collaborative economy in the EU at €20 billion;

– Vaughan and Hawksworth[25] calculated that on a global basis the collaborative economy was worth $15 billion and could reach $335 billion by 2025;

– Barbezieux and Herody[26] estimated that in France, collaborative economy activities turn over $2.5 billion, involve about 15,000 firms (including self-employed micro-entrepreneurs), and generate 13,000 permanent jobs. This would amount to approximately 0.1 percent of French GDP generated by 0.5 percent of French companies for 0.05 percent of French total employment;

[22] Rubicon (2015), *How Green is the sharing economy*, Knowledge and Wharton, December 1.

[23] Petropoulose Giorgios (2017), *An Economic review of the collaborative economy*, Policy Contribution, Issue 5 Bruegel.

[24] Geron T. (2013), *Airbnb and the Unstoppable Rise of the Share Economy*, Forbes, January 23.

[25] Vaughan R. and Hawksworth J. (2014), *The Sharing economy: how will it disrupt your business? megatrends; the collisions' PWC*, PWC blogs.

[26] Barbezieux P. and Herody C. (2016), *Rapport au Premier Ministre sur l'économie collaborative*, Paris Republique Française.

– Goudin[27] (2016) approximated the potential economic gain from better use of capacities as a result of the collaborative economy to be €572 billion in annual consumption across in the EU if substantial associated regulatory barriers are removed;

– such barriers could reduce the value of potential increased use by up to €18 billion in the shorter term and by up to €134 billion in the medium and longer term, depending on the scale of the obstacles;

– from PWC research[28] of nine major European countries, it is estimated that at least 275 sharing economy organizations have been founded to date. The UK and France have led this start-up creation, with over 50 sharing economy organizations founded in each of these countries;

– Germany, Spain and the Netherlands have each contributed over 25 sharing economy organizations, while less than 25 have been established in each of Sweden, Italy, Poland and Belgium.

Most of these estimates, however, should be treated with caution as, because of the lack of reliable data and consolidated empirical evidence, they are inevitably based on questionable assumptions.

These findings in part reflect the efforts being made by the UK and France to establish themselves as hubs for innovation and growth in the sharing economy – including the creation of policy regimes that are conducive to sharing economy business models. For example, the UK's March 2016 Budget introduced two £1,000 tax-free allowances for property and trading income for any sole trader, a measure that was billed as the "world's first sharing economy tax break" by the sharing economy sector. And in France, peer-to-peer accommodation providers have lauded a new national housing law that enables every resident to rent out their home without having to ask for permission from their city hall.

To make further progress, collaborative economy members will need to collaborate with their stakeholders across a number of fronts. This will include investing in market-leading reputational scoring systems, working with policymakers to develop new forms of self-regulation and to reform existing regulations, and more actively support users in understanding and implementing their legal and tax obligations.

---

[27] Goudin (2016), *The cost of Non Europe in the Sharing Economy*, The European Parliament Research Service, European Parliament.

[28] PWC, *ibidem*.

2.16. European participation in the collaborative economy

The evidence points to a relatively small – but growing – participation in the collaborative economy in Europe. The ING's July 2015 study[29] is potentially the most comprehensive investigation to date of European consumer's participation in the collaborative economy. The findings from the study were:

– around one third of European consumers have heard of the collaborative economy; Around 5% of European consumers have declared having participated in the collaborative economy in the past year;

– participation is highest amongst younger generations (under 35) and well-educated; On average, a third of European consumers think their participation in the collaborative economy will increase over the next 12 months;

– cars were the most shared item, but holiday accommodation should overtake cars over the next year; The majority of sharers in Europe made €1,000 or less (the median of earnings for sharers in Europe was found to be around €300).

ING found the strongest awareness and adoption in Southern European member states of Spain and Italy, at roughly three times the participation rate seen in some of the Northern European member states such as Germany and Austria.

2.17. Guidelines for regulating the sharing economy

What is the right approach for local governments when it comes to regulating the sharing economy? The problem is difficult because almost every "sharing economy" business has a "non-sharing economy" equivalent. While the sharing economy revolutionized access to commerce for underutilized goods, the sharing economy seldom invents needs or markets. Most sharing economy businesses replicate existing service. The global proliferation of these collaborative platforms poses new challenges for regulators trying to keep pace with rapidly evolving business models The ease with which individuals can now connect, cooperate, share information, share assets and obtain services is truly transformative. At the same time,

---

[29] ING International (2015), *The European sharing economy set to grow by a third in the next 12 months.* [online] ING.com. Available at: http://www.ing.com/Newsroom/All-news/European-sharing-economy-to-grow-by-a-third-in-the-next-12-months.htm.

since we are at the infancy of this new era, the extent of transformation in the way we do business is difficult to grasp.

2.18. The EU Commission's views [30]

If the European Commission decides to proceed with a common set of rules, there are a number of pitfalls it should avoid:

– New regulations must not limit the options available to consumers and providers in the sharing economy. The sharing economy is already well-established in many Member States. EU regulation should not roll back the progress already made.

– Rules should reinforce the strengths of the sharing economy – flexibility, cost reductions, greater business employment and self-employment of workers otherwise excluded from labor markets – rather than undermine them. Onerous employment rules are likely to reduce employment opportunities and consumer welfare.

– The sharing economy shows the need for liberalization of existing rules and also the need for differentiated regulatory response. The sharing economy has not only put competitive pressure on incumbents, but it has also rendered price controls and regulations aiming to promote customer safety redundant.

An EU rulebook should emulate best practice across the EU. There are successful models of open and flexible labor markets, such as the UK, Poland and Denmark, with low unemployment and high levels of labor force participation. These models are better placed to take advantage of the benefits offered by the sharing economy.

Regulatory approaches: the case of Uber

Uber is a popular ride-sharing app and one of the most successful firms to date in the sharing economy. The firm, whose main business activity is to connect drivers with passengers, launched its app in San Francisco in 2011. Its first European market was Paris from late 2011, and it has spread across the EU since then. *Uber* is currently active in 52 EU cities across 22 of the 28 Member States. *Uber*'s impact on EU labor markets has been significant, with reports that the app was used by 20,000 French drivers – many of them from minorities and other groups often excluded from the mainstream labor market – before the courts placed restrictions on its service last year.

---

[30] Zuluaga Diego, *Regulatory approaches to the sharing economy*, IEA; Institute of Economic Affairs Epicenter, the pan-European think tank network.

The app's legal status varies considerably across the Union. The firm has been subject to court injunctions ordering it to suspend its operations in several countries, including Spain, Portugal and Bulgaria. The regulatory environments in the Member States can broadly be divided into three categories. In some countries Uber faces no restrictions, while in other countries the app is currently illegal, pending court rulings.

A majority of Member States allow Uber to operate, but its drivers have to meet licensing and other requirements. Significantly, this means that UberPOP, the app's most basic offering aimed at non-professional drivers, in some others countries is banned or unavailable. UberPOP's value proposition arguably makes it the most peertopeer of the app's various categories, so restrictions on its operations constitute a perceptible barrier to the growth of cheap ride-sharing options.

Source: Zuluaga Diego, (2016) *Regulatory approaches to the sharing Economy*, Institute of Economic Affairs

2.19. Guidelines for regulating the sharing economy[31]

Stephen Miller[32] has proposed ten guidelines or building blocks from which a future regulation could rest. These guideline are summarized here after:

1. A regulatory response to the sharing economy requires recognition that the types of transactions occurring differ substantially in how they affect the real world and thus require a *differentiated regulatory response*. Notably, the nature of the public health and safety concerns associated "ride sharing" and "apartment sharing" clearly differ. One size doesn't fit all.

2. The sharing economy must *be transparent*. Most sharing platforms often explicitly violate local government ordinances and state Statutes. When a growing portion of the economy is illegal, it forces that economic activity underground, where it is more difficult to understand the nature of the economic activity and to obtain investment capital.

3. Regulating the sharing economy requires the right kind of Information. Because many sharing economy companies operate in a manner contrary to law, their resistance to efforts to obtain information about their

---

[31] Katz Vanessa (2015), *Regulating the Sharing Economy?*, Berkeley Technology Law Journal, Vol. 3, Issue 4.

[32] Stephen R. Miller (2016), *First Principles For Regulating the Sharing Economy*, Harvard Journal on Legislation, Vol. 53, 147-172.

practices is not surprising. The governance of complex systems depends on good, *trustworthy information.*

4. Several cities have taken to banning certain sharing economy uses. These bans are strategies for addressing the sharing economy and are largely ineffective, because the sharing economy brings tremendous opportunities to individuals, businesses and local governments. For this reason, the sharing economy is unlikely to go away any time soon and that is good for everyone.

5. The sharing economy challenges established markets, sometimes referred to as the "incumbent" market participant[33]. Here again, the short term rental market (STR) proves a useful example of the major change the sharing economy is causing, for instance, to the established hotel industry.

6. In 2015, the sheer volume of *Airbnb* rentals far surpasses any loss in market share seen by hotels. Moreover, many vacation destination property managers use *Airbnb* and similar websites to advertise their properties, perhaps reaching a wider audience through the sites, generating more market demand, and increasing prices and profits for their rentals. This novel use of *Airbnb* shows that a new market has been created for a new type of travel beyond simply stealing or disrupting from the existing market.

7. Many of the short term rental market-sharing units are located in single-family residential zones that explicitly do not permit hotels, much less bed and breakfasts, and often do not permit even de minims home business uses that may result in increased traffic or business related vans parked on the street.

8. The short term rental market illustrates how the sharing economy has to reimagining the nature of commercial transactions and requires a regulatory response that transcends established codes that were written to regulate established industries. Established markets – such as hotels – exist primarily as brick-and mortar commercial institutions working within the confines of business regulation.

9. In the STR Market, who is harmed by a resident renting his or her home for the weekend to a stranger? Is the neighbor harmed by having a stranger next door even if, as in most cases, the stranger behaves and causes no actionable nuisance behavior? Perhaps the resident of the neighborhood is harmed because the resident's child is scared by sharing a public playground with the stranger's child. Perhaps the character of the neighborhood changes as more residents participate in the STR Market. Perhaps the cumulative effects of multiple STR Market rentals cause market rents to rise, as landlords start to incorporate STR Market rentals into the market rent of residential apartments.

---

[33] Hahn R. and Metcalfe (2017), *The Ridesharing Revolution: Economic Survey and Synthesis*, January.

10. The Sharing Economy implicates diverse parties, each of whom should be considered. The only way that the sharing economy will ever find resolution as a viable, legal business venture will be to engage all parties with an interest in the issue An approach that acknowledges the legitimate concerns of all of the affected parties is far more likely to yield a result that seems fair to all unity benefits.

The sharing economy is changing quickly, thus complicating a clear regulatory response. In major European cities, like Paris, Amsterdam, Rome or Brussels where *Airbnb* holds a very strong market penetration, the local civil authorities are recently reinforcing their control, (a) by requiring a compulsory prior registration for all room-sharing providers, (b) by reducing the duration of the granted authorizations and (c) by charging heavier fines to violators. In Paris, the average fine charged move from €10 000s in 2016 to €20 000 in 2017.

In the conclusion of his 2010 seminal article, Miller[34] reviews several major trends occurring in the sharing economy right now, and then evaluates how those changes will affect the future of regulatory responses. There is perhaps no bigger question in the sharing economy than how the established market participants will respond to the disrupting web platforms. In many industries, the importance of Internet platforms to established brick-and-mortar businesses is no well understood. These established market participants are now seeking ways to either retain existing market share by repositioning the purchase of their products through "sharing", or are trying to find ways to enter the new markets created by the sharing economy platforms.

Regarding the taxation policy, a consensus is slowly emerging in the EU – at least for Belgium, France, Italy and the UK – for a low tax rate (typically 10%) applied to services between individuals, as long as the registered platform's income does not exceed €5 000 (Belgium and France) or €10 000 (Italy), with the obligations for the platforms to withhold collected taxes at source and send the information to tax authorities.

---

[34] Ethan Miller (2010), *Solidarity Economy: Key Concepts and Issues*, in Emily Kawano, Thomas Neal Masterson and Jonathan Teller-Elsberg, *Solidarity Economy I: Building Alternatives for People and Planet*, Papers and Reports from the 2009 U.S. Forum on the Solidarity Economy.

2.20. The recent decision of the European Court of Justice

Europe's top court has ruled in November 2017 [35] that *Uber* should be regulated as a transportation company – and not a tech firm. The decision by the European Court of Justice (ECJ) is a potential setback for *Uber*, which has long insisted that it should be treated as technology service that connects drivers and riders. The court rejected that argument in its landmark decision, ruling that *Uber* is at its heart a transportation company and should be regulated as such. *Uber* could now be subjected to the stricter licensing requirements that apply to traditional taxi operators. The startup could also eventually be asked to collect new taxes from customers. The ruling, which cannot be appealed, could have major implications for other companies that operate in Europe's gig economy. The upstart firms have typically faced lighter regulation than their traditional rivals. What the judgment does show is that it's not a brave new world for the gig economy", said Rachel Farr, a senior employment lawyer at Taylor Wessing. "The law applies to them all". *Uber* said in a statement that the ruling would "not change things in most EU countries where we already operate under transportation law".

But it could limit the company's ability to use drivers who do not have professional licenses – a service currently offered in only a few European markets.

The Uber case was brought by professional taxi drivers in Spain who argued that the startup had an unfair advantage because drivers on its *UberPop* service didn't have the taxi licenses required by the city of Barcelona. A Spanish court referred the case to the European Court of Justice. Farr said the ruling could open the door to more expensive *Uber* rides in Europe, because the company could eventually be required to collect sales taxes from consumers. The taxes had previously gone uncollected because Uber drivers – who are classified as independent contractors – were too small to be registered for the tax. it's a fair presumption that as long as there's an *Uber*, there will be disagreement over whether the ride-hailing firm is a force for good or bad – or more precisely, good or bad for whom?

---

[35] CNN Money (London) First published December 20, 2017: 3:58 AM ET.

2.21. Conclusion

The collaborative economy is a major new development in the global economy: It matches people online who want to share assets and services on a temporary basis. There is evidence that Europe could enjoy major economic gains from the collaborative economy, especially if barriers are removed and if the regulatory framework is adjusted to better accommodate on line platforms. The technology is disruptive to many traditional businesses and smart regulation is required to give consumers protection and a safe and transparent environment for on line transactions. There is little doubt that the sharing economy can make a contribution to a more sustainable development, because Internet platforms allow people to share with anyone in society, thereby increasing the size of the market potential. This means that physical assets can be used more efficiently and that less energy and material are needed in the economy. Its is not clear today what will be the impact of the recent decision of ECL.

Chapter 3

CORPORATE GOVERNANCE, OWNERSHIP AND GLOBAL MARKETS

Daniela M. Salvioni

ABSTRACT: *The elimination of space and time barriers to the circulation of information and capital, the growing complexity and importance of business/stakeholder relationships, and the establishment of corporate social responsibility principles have changed the corporate governance approach of listed companies. Indeed, the prerequisites have been created to attenuate behavioural differences, which for a long time have characterized companies with wide ownership dispersion (outsider systems) and those with concentrated ownership or control (insider systems). This chapter analyses the conditions for the pervasive improvement of the corporate governance approach in a global perspective. The analysis shows that adhering to international principles and recommendations as well as establishing a social responsibility and sustainability approach facilitate the convergence between insider and outsider corporate governance systems. In particular, the shared medium- to long-term value orientation of top executives and investors is affirming regardless of the ownership structure of companies and the characteristics of risk capital markets.*

SUMMARY: 3.1. Corporate ownership and capital markets. – 3.2. Corporate governance and market relations. – 3.3. Competitive orientation towards the capital market. – 3.4. Corporate governance in a global perspective.

3.1. Corporate ownership and capital markets

The ownership and control structures of listed companies are influenced by the evolution of the capital market and have specific significance at the corporate governance level. The latter has often been associated with the principal-agent or agency theory, highlighting the relationship between the firm's owners and those developing its management processes (Denis, Denis and Sarin, 1999; Jensen and Chew, 2000; Hansmann and Kraakman, 2001; Daily, Dalton and Cannella, 2003).

Globally recognized corporate governance systems are based on the relationship between the shareholders' meeting and those in charge of implementing top management, administration and control activities. In this regard, the different systems take into account: the relations between the governing bodies distinguishing between monistic systems and dualistic systems; delegation in the nomination processes distinguishing between horizontal dualistic systems (where both the board of directors and the supervisory board are appointed by the shareholders' meeting) and vertical dualistic systems (where the shareholders' meeting, at times in conjunction with employees, appoints the supervisory board that subsequently appoints the administrative body).

The main systems in industrialized countries currently consist of those that allow the adoption of a single corporate governance system and those that allow choosing between monistic and dual systems, those that favour systems based on the administrative mandate (e.g., Great Britain, the United States, Canada, Spain, Greece, etc.) and those that emphasise the role of control at the level of governance bodies (e.g., Germany, Austria, Italy, etc.).

Beyond the various corporate governance structures adopted in different countries, an element of differentiation in the governance approach of listed firms is mainly associated with the characteristics of financial markets and the level of concentration of corporate ownership. In this respect, outsider systems are distinguished from insider systems (Salvioni, 2008; Salvioni and Gennari, 2014a).

Outsider systems, typical of Anglo-Saxon countries, are characterized by the dominance of large publicly traded firms, fractional and dispersed ownership (public company), and ownership and management separation. In the presence of truthful, correct, and transparent communications, the efficient functioning of capital markets determines consensus/control over the administration activities. The approval/disapproval of the actions of the governance bodies is therefore reflected in changes in the share value resulting from the dynamics of the demand and supply of ownership shares, and in turnover at the corporate governance mandate and shareholding level.

The dominant outsider system model is of a monist type, with governing bodies that generally have a short-term mandate (annual) and the high presence of non-executive and independent members. In such cases, the market directly exercises control over corporate governance based on information received on actual and prospective behaviours and results. The reporting system is consequently of relevance and emphasises the role of external controls to certify communications on the governance structure, goals, and performance achieved.

Outsider systems therefore require well-developed stock markets and high resource attraction potential. In such contexts, moving investments from one stock to another is relatively straightforward in light of the information available on the corporate governance and related performance, taking particular account of the interventions of institutional investors acting as market facilitators. In addition, investors are generally unconnected to the management and the business performance relationship, and therefore the degree of meeting expectations, consensus, and resource allocation take on particular importance.

Insider systems are typical of countries with poorly developed financial markets, concentrated and commonly stable shareholding, as in the case of most European countries, and majority shareholder involvement in management able to influence corporate decisions. In such cases, conflicts of interest may arise between majority and minority shareholders and therefore implementing effective supervisory activities within the corporate governance bodies takes on importance. The preferred governance system is therefore dualistic, although there are countries that despite high ownership concentration employ the monistic model (for example, Spain, Greece, and Canada).

In insider systems, the corporate governance mandate typically lasts several years with the high participation of majority shareholders in management and a lesser number of independent members in the governing body. Turnover on the corporate governance mandate level is frequently low, often associated with changes in the ownership structure, internal conflicts with the board of directors, independence requirements, and the participation of minority shareholders.

In insider systems, the competitive orientation towards the stock market is largely determined by the desire to maintain high share values and may at times be influenced by the shareholders' resolutions aimed at authorising the acquisition of own shares. In addition, often only a marginal part of capital is traded, thereby limiting the market's impact on corporate governance.

Countries with insider systems have different ways of assigning the corporate governance mandate, particularly:

• Systems where the corporate governance mandate is attributed exclusively by the owners, typically with the high involvement of majority shareholders (Latin-type insider system)

• Systems characterized by the active participation of shareholders as well as employees (Rhine-type insider system).

The first group includes countries such as Italy, underlining the economic risk associated with share capital participation. The capital market orientation is therefore emphasised in relation to the role attributed to the shareholders' meeting as sole mandator of the corporate governance bodies. The mandate may also be a direct or indirect expression of the shareholding, depending on which model is adopted: the monistic model (the shareholders' meeting appoints the board of directors which internally, where appropriate, appoints the members that will take charge of supervisory board), the horizontal dualistic model (the shareholders' meeting appoints both the board of directors and the supervisory board), or the vertical dualistic model (the shareholders' meeting appoints the supervisory board, which in turn names the administrative body).

The presence of one or more majority shareholders and the existence of a shareholders' agreement tend to affect the market orientation in insider systems, which at times have purely formal validity, or rather, are bound by rules and recommendations. This phenomenon is reflected in the characteristics of the corporate governance systems, both in terms of the preferred models and in terms of the composition and mandate duration.

For example, the analysis of corporate governance systems of Italian firms with greater capitalization highlights: ownership is often highly concentrated within a family, group or public entity, and protected by voting agreements and cross-shareholding; significant ownership participation in management, since shareholders play an important role in governance, often with co-ordination (e.g., board chair) and/or executive tasks. However, market supervision would seem to be transcended by the overwhelming prevalence of dualistic systems and the progressive development of rules and recommendations aimed at safeguarding minority shareholders, the qualitative composition of the governing bodies, and the transparency of information disclosure.

On the other hand, emphasised in Rhine-type insider systems are all primary resource conferrers (shareholders and workers), thus highlighting the role of workers and the relationship between owners, employees, and unions. In this case, the tendency is to balance the relations with capital markets and within the organization, commonly emphasising the role of credit institutions that in addition to providing interest-bearing funding participate in the shareholding. However, Rhine-centric systems enhance the interdependence between shareholder value creation and organizational behaviours, as well as co-ordination between top management and employees to optimize the resources, activities, and results relations.

The Rhine system is native to Germany and widespread in continental Europe and Scandinavia and has some similarities with the Japanese system (insider-type and open to collaboration with employees). In particular, the German economic system is oriented towards the co-management principle, with the direct participation of owners and workers in appointing the supervisory board within a vertical dualistic governance system. In this respect, larger firms are expected to involve employees in appointing 50% of the supervisory board members.

Beyond the different characteristics of stock markets and the composition of corporate shareholding, on a global level, shareholders have always had a significant role in conferring the corporate governance mandate. Indeed, the shareholders' meeting is often the only body that appoints the members of the governing bodies, and even in the presence of employee co-participation (as in the Rhine model) tends to significantly intervene in conferring the governance mandate. This has contributed on the one hand to affirming the shareholder view, which for a long time dominated the corporate governance orientation, emphasising economic performance and financial reporting, and on the other hand, producing divergences in governance orientation in relation to the ownership structure and stock market characteristics.

Globalisation and the emergence of the concepts of corporate social responsibility and sustainable development have undoubtedly underlined the need for greater convergence between the corporate governance systems and the limits inherent in over-focusing on the shareholder view.

Since the beginning of this century, the importance of greater attention to the corporate governance of public interest entities has been emphasised, particularly the ability to activate an ever-wider and more complex network of relationships correlated with:

– On the one hand, the need to achieving positive, lasting relationships with all relevant stakeholders and the importance of a competitive orientation towards the market with reference to all trading areas (Spitzeck and Hansen, 2010; Mason and Simmons, 2014).

– On the other hand, attention to the effectiveness, flexibility, and convergence of corporate governance principles in the various national realities to increase the opportunities for competition and comparison between firms (Gilson, 2004; Lellapalli, 2015; Clarke, 2016).

3.2. Corporate governance and market relations

In global markets, space and time barriers to the circulation of information and capital tend to disappear, firm/stakeholder relationships become more complex and emphasise the interdependencies between successful economic, competitive, and social conditions. Consequently, elements that take on greater importance include promoting the integrity of the corporate governance management function accompanied by national and supranational initiatives aimed at reducing the gap between global markets and the divergences in corporate governance systems and external supervision characterizing different countries (Cohen, C. Boyd and G. Boyd, 2000; Clarke and Dela Rama, 2007; Salvioni, 2008; Dignam and Galanis, 2009; Salvioni, and Gennari, 2014b).

The globalisation of information and the emergence of a broad concept of responsibility have significantly influenced the evolution of corporate governance; specifically, the partiality and limits inherent in the lack of correlation between meeting shareholder expectations and the overall effectiveness of the firm's market relationships, the need for greater corporate governance convergence based on structural and operational best practices to ensure adequate and widespread attraction of consensus and resources.

The potential to optimize results over time depends on valorising the expectations of all stakeholders with whom the firm interacts. Activating positive stakeholder engagement processes has increasingly become a prerequisite for the formation of virtuous circles, resources, activities, achievements and consensus, also in view of the greater risk factors influencing firm operations and the increasing complexity of direct and mediated relationships between firms and markets.

The above shows that market orientation is embodied in corporate governance whereas: the governance mandate is conferred by shareholders – in some cases even with the participation of workers (as in Germany and other European countries following the Rhine model) – and is appropriately implemented in aligning the expectations of all the firm's relevant stakeholders; the rules, standards and recommendations for administrative control and communication structures and procedures are designed to protect shareholders as well as all other stakeholders; corporate governance presuppose safeguarding the success potential, which results in optimizing the ability to create value over time.

The firm's knowledge and innovation capacity has become increasingly important to maintain the conditions of success, coupled with the affirmation of effective principles of responsible business conduct (RBC) (OECD, 2014).

Interaction with stakeholders ensures a better understanding of the firm's expectations, its priorities and related prospective changes, facilitating the adoption of social responsibility-oriented strategies and integrating economic, social, and environmental performance[1].

---

[1] "The board is not only accountable to the company and its shareholders but also has a duty to act in their best interests. In addition, boards are expected to take due

Under today's competitive conditions, creating the prerequisites for business success is therefore significantly influenced by behavioural correctness and competencies developed to understand the markets and emerging opportunities[2]. These conditions also entail the ability to set up effective information systems, make decisions based on carefully identifying the prospective risks, anticipate the moves of competitors, establish high-profile relationships in the firm's markets.

The complexity of the essential relationships for value creation emphasises the linkages between the ability to optimize economic performance, competitiveness, and the correct assumption of responsibility for all relevant stakeholders and the environment (Salvioni and Bosetti, 2009; Salvioni and Astori, 2013). The formation of joint stock companies, the consequent separation – at least partial – of ownership and management, and especially stock market listing, confer particular importance to the protection of shareholders who risk the financial resources granted and can affect the firm's market value.

Globalisation and the greater competition that listed firms encounter in acquiring the consensus of capital subscribers have undoubtedly also determined a clear competitive orientation for the stock market (Salvioni and Gennari, 2014b). The relationship between the results achieved, the capacity to meet expectations, demand/supply for a company's shares and related market value have thus gained increasing importance for successful corporate governance.

A firm's market value is in fact influenced by a number of external and internal factors. The former include general economic phenomena (for example, discount rates, inflation, unemployment, exchange rates, the development of capital market, etc.), political relations between countries, stock

---

regard of, and deal fairly with, other stakeholder interests including those of employees, creditors, customers, suppliers and local communities. Observance of environmental and social standards is relevant in this context", G20/OECD, *Principles of Corporate Governance*, OECD Publishing, Paris.

[2] "… global companies adopt closed innovation policies when they operate in sectors that are protected from competition (Utterback, Kim 1985; Mansfield et al. 1981; Abernathy, Utterback 1978). With closed innovation policies, the leading companies concentrate their expertise in governing innovation processes in internal structures, and intellectual property is defended against potential 'copying' and external appropriation. In conditions of global competition, closed innovation policies are distinguished by performance indices that refer to the generation of a 'theoretical' innovation potential, and typically regard: the costs met for R&D activities; the number of patents developed and owned; the number of new products and modified products", S.M. Brondoni (2015), *Global Networks, Outside-In Capabilities and Smart Innovation*, Symphonya. Emerging Issues in Management, n. 1, 6-21. http://dx.doi.org/10.4468/2015.1.02brondoni.

market development and transparency, the spread of the use of parallel markets, the manifestation of insolvency states, scandals, and situations of poor corporate governance, communications of competitors, trading partners, organisations and institutions, and the emergence of speculative tendencies among investors. The latter include the behaviours adopted, the achievements and conditions that characterize the evolution of the business (e.g., firm structure and the geographic scope of operations, supply markets, relations with employees and trade unions, investments, sales markets, supply agreements, sectoral dynamics of customer firms, etc.).

In addition, the elimination of space and time barriers in the dissemination of information, the growing importance and globality of institutional investors, and the role of financial analysts are all phenomena that produce greater competitiveness in resource acquisition, emphasing the need for transparency, and maintaining the trust and consensus of firm activities.

Therefore, for listed firms, the relevance of a competitive capital orientation is evident, both as a primary source of resources and in relation to the role of the demand/supply of capital shares to affirm the firm's value and to demonstrate consensus on the activities of the governance bodies due to the increasingly frequent need to counteract and/or mitigate the effects of speculative behaviours.

3.3. Competitive orientation towards the capital market

The main function of corporate governance is associated with the ability to create trusted relationships, act responsibly and transparently, ensure the firm's broad potential for resource acquisition, financial stability, and sustainable growth [3].

As noted, the stock market characteristics and the level of dispersion of capital shares tend to highlight different conditions of interaction between the firm and the risk capital market. Indeed, such conditions have for a long time determined differences in regulating corporate governance mandates and management choices.

The emergence of global market processes, the spread of corporate social responsibility principles (CSR) and the valorisation of the importance

---

[3] "The purpose of corporate governance is precisely to create an environment of trust, transparency and accountability necessary for obtaining long-term investment, financial stability and sustainable growth. If nothing is done, the very fabric and foundation of doing business in an effective and sustainable fashion is at risk", OECD (2015), *Corporate Governance and Business Integrity. A Stocktaking of Corporate Practices*, p. 13.

of the stakeholder view[4] have undoubtedly favoured convergence between different markets, emphasising the importance of governance with a clear competitive orientation towards the stock market based on broad benchmarks.

CSR and the valorisation of stakeholder relations effectively promote convergence between different corporate governance systems and are also the basis for regulatory measures and recommendations aimed at ensuring effective corporate governance. Equally, the progressive integration of major capital markets would seem to stimulate the pursuit of flexibility, efficiency, and convergence of principles and governance systems in search of the best practices with widespread validity[5].

The attention of international institutions and legislators has focused particularly on joint stock firms and, in this context, listed firms, given the extent of the interests involved and the priority role that corporate governance assumes in the protection and effectiveness of market relationships.

The globalisation of relations between stock markets, share issuers, and investors has therefore led to frequent revisions of national laws and regulations according to paths consistent with the culture, traditions, and market conditions of each country, but at the same time projected towards the application of international best practices.

Specifically, there has been an emphasis on generally accepted corporate governance principles, reflected in different governance models, whose

---

[4] "Stakeholder theory promotes a practical, efficient, effective, and ethical way to manage organizations in a highly complex and turbulent environment. It is a practical theory because all firms have to manage stakeholders – whether they are good at managing them is another issue. It is efficient because stakeholders that are treated well tend to reciprocate with positive attitudes and behaviors towards the organization, such as sharing valuable information (all stakeholders), buying more products or services (customers), providing tax breaks or other incentives (communities), providing better financial terms (financiers), buying more stock (shareholders), or working hard and remaining loyal to the organization, even during difficult times (employees). It is effective because it harnesses the energy of stakeholders towards the fulfillment of the organization's goals. It is useful in a complex and turbulent environment because firms that manage for stakeholders have better information upon which to base their decisions and, because they are attractive to other market participants, they have a degree of strategic flexibility that is not available to competitors that do not manage for stakeholders", Jeffrey S. Harrison, R. Edward Freeman, Mônica Cavalcanti Sá de Abreu (2015), *Stakeholder theory as an ethical approach to effective management: Applying the theory to multiple contexts*, Rev. Bus. Manag., São Paulo, Vol. 17, No. 55, pp. 858-869, Special Edition.

[5] In this regard, amongst others, the OECD principles are noted. Originally drafted in May 1999 and revised in 2004 and 2015, the G20/OECD Principles of Corporate Governance are one of the 12 key standards for international financial stability of the Financial Stability Board and form the basis for the corporate governance component of the Report on the Observance of Standards and Codes of the World Bank Group.

affiliation also relates to the firm's equity structure and to the evolutionary conditions of risk capital markets.

At the same time, CSR and sustainability principles have contributed to the modification of corporate governance variables, creating convergence conditions that transcend the traditional divergences linked to ownership and the different stock market characteristics.

Globalisation is particularly significant in the capital market, since the transition to electronic monetization and the fall of barriers to the transfer of information enable simultaneously meeting the planetary demand and supply of corporate shares.

Indeed, the electronic transferability of money and capital shares – coupled with the gradual reduction of differences between the spatial spheres, cultures, information and communication systems, traditions and institutions – is correlated to: broadening the number of relevant nations governing the world economy (in this regard, consider the transition from the G6 of 1975, to G7, to G8, to G20); the increasing number and importance of international regulatory bodies promoting corporate governance transparency and the related results; the tendency to standardize corporate governance approaches, even in the context of differences arising from historic, cultural, economic, and legal factors characterising different countries; changes in the behaviours of investors increasingly aimed at diversifying, also geographically, the share capital investment risk.

As noted, faced with the need for a discipline aimed at ensuring the overall fairness of transactions, the international comparison highlights differences between countries, especially with reference to listed companies, stock market characteristics, and the composition of corporate shareholding.

The evolution of economic systems, the dissemination of information and the affirmation of institutional investors point to the growing need to protect risk capital holders and the importance of greater attention to the capital market. However, this requires distinguishing those situations characterized by strong dependence on capital attractiveness from those where market consensus, albeit important, generally coincides with the existence of one or more majority shareholders.

In listed companies, capital market orientation is conditioned by the dominance of outsider or insider systems, by those appointing corporate governance bodies (owners only as in Anglo-Saxon and most industrialized countries; owners and employees in the German case, and generally, in the Rhine model), and by the stakeholders represented in the governing and control bodies[6].

---

[6] "One of the most striking differences between countries' corporate governance systems is the difference in the ownership and control of firms that exist across

Capital market orientation is undoubtedly more incisive in outsider systems, given the dispersion of shareholding and the growth potential offered by the market. In this context, firms compete for the acquisition of financial resources to determine their growth capacity and affirmation in the environment, while the efficiency and attractiveness of market investors tend to determine the capitalization of firms. This is reflected in the governance models and relevant variables to avoid conflicts of interest between firm shareholders and administrators. In particular, assuming equal attraction of market resources, the following take on importance: transparency, qualifying the firm image, the professional profile and past tasks of board members, and obtaining results that meet the investors' potential expectations better than other operators.

Insider systems, on the other hand, are affected by the existence of majority shareholdings that may, in the absence of pre-emptive protection provisions of minority and/or other relevant stakeholder classes, determine unbalanced governance systems. From this derives the need to emphasise control in the dual dimension of a dedicated body and the composition of the board of directors (e.g., by appointing representatives of minority shareholders and a significant percentage of non-executive and independent members).

The different role of the market in outsider and insider systems over time is reflected in the dominance of public companies and in the divergence of the capitalization values of listed firms. Beyond situations caused by economic and speculative crises, in outsider systems, public companies predominate, capitalization values tend to be higher, and stock trading is more frequent than in insider systems.

In the context of insider systems, the existence of governance mandates conferred solely by the shareholders' meeting (Latin system) or by the shareholders' meeting and workers (Rhine system), tends to highlight a different approach aimed at mitigating the imbalance of power in favour of minority shareholders. In this sense, the German type relationship-based system would seem to offer greater guarantees and protection of minority shareholders than the Latin type shareholder-oriented system.

---

countries. There are tradeoffs between ownership concentration and voting power concentration. Systems of corporate governance can be distinguished according to the degree of ownership and control and the identity of controlling shareholders. In 'outsider' systems (notably the US and UK) of corporate governance the basic conflict of interest is between strong managers and widely dispersed shareholders. In 'insider' systems (notably Continental Europe and Japan), on the other hand, the basic conflict is between controlling shareholders (or blockholders) and weak minority shareholders", M. Maher, T. Andersson (1999), *Corporate governance: Effect on firm performance and economic growth*, OECD.

However, the differences between insider and outsider systems are attenuated by the globalisation of markets and information that entail the activation of integration strategies between the different national stock exchanges, increasingly frequent shifts of investors from one market to another in consideration of convenience and risk reduction, the global impact of economically significant phenomena originating in specific geographic areas and markets, the dissemination of so-called 'out of market' operations[7].

Since the mid-1990s, international alliances between financial market operators began to form through the implementation of various strategies primarily related to: network strategies based on collaboration agreements involving several stock exchanges in a substantially federative project; participatory strategies involving ownership structures and preluding mergers between stock exchanges; segmentation strategies focusing on the activation of market segments aimed at obtaining foreign securities. At the same time, stock market regulation increased and measures have been taken to facilitate the listing of smaller firms.

In addition to the elimination of space and time barriers, the 2000s have seen more and more frequent movements of capital from one stock market to another, particularly by institutional investors, and the formation of sectoral alliances.

Lastly, the dissemination of information - with particular regard to disrupting situations and variables, and significant financial scandals - takes on a worldwide scope, varying the market dynamics of all industrialized countries, in the face of feared risks and changes in trusted relationships and agreements between issuers, stock exchanges, and investors. The dissemination of information in question sometimes also entails speculative behaviours that may distort the stock market trends.

---

[7] In this respect, the European Parliament approved Directive 2004/39 / EC of 21 April 2004 (MiFID - Markets in Financial Instruments Directive) – revised with the Directive 2014/65/UE (MiFID II) – which is an important step towards building an effective and competitive integrated financial market with the EU. The Directive abolishes the obligation to concentrate on regulated markets and introduces new forms of exchange, such as Multilateral Trading Systems (MTFs) and Systematic Internalisers. One of the main objectives of MiFID is to create a competitive and harmonized financial environment for regulated markets, investment firms, as well as strengthening investor protection, the efficiency and integrity of the financial markets themselves. The main market regulations are: the elimination of the obligation to concentrate trade on regulated markets; new trading venues, represented by regulated markets, multilateral trading facilities (MTFs) and internalisers; pre-trade and post-trade transparency rules of market information; specific provisions for the admission of financial instruments on regulated markets; the rules for admission of traders to regulated markets and MTFs; the regulation of transaction reporting to the competent authorities; the discipline applicable to clearing and settlement systems.

These phenomena seem to broaden the scenarios of reference, increasing the importance of information systems and risk management, requiring greater attention to transparency and reporting, valorising the role of financial analysts, and mitigating the different corporate governance market orientations of outsider and insider systems.

Modern corporate governance identifies the system by which firms are managed and controlled to effectively meet their stakeholders expectations over time. Corporate governance is therefore aimed at ensuring the long-term pursuit of the firm's mission, in accordance with financial effectiveness and sustainable development. The related implementation is based on decisions that entail considering the relationships with the various stakeholders and their expectations to define the timescales and modes of satisfaction compatible with the internal and external dynamics, and ensure the attainment of consensus and trust. In this regard, the establishment of effective relationships with stockholders has primary importance and, for listed firms, must take into account the relevant stock market variables, the other operators competing for capital, the expectations of investors, and the existence of potential facilitators and/or influencers of behaviour.

Broadening the relationship between stock markets, the emergence of parallel trading platforms, and the spread of electronic communications have undoubtedly resulted in the need for a comprehensive approach to obtaining consensus and financial resources. This approach should be aimed at improving market competition, increasing firm value, and maintaining appropriate stock enhancement capabilities. This in evidence of the proper development of the governing and control activities typical of corporate governance, but stressing the importance of: effective external control actions (information certification and activated by stock markets and specific institutions); consistent and transparent behaviours associated with clear, verifiable and truthful communications able to meet the cognitive and evaluative expectations of existing and potential investors.

The need to improve corporate governance occurred in all its evidence with the financial crisis that began in 2007/2008, which also questioned the efficiency of capital markets (OECD, 2009). In terms of a competitive stock market approach, the crisis particularly emphasised the prevalence of opacity in firm/environment relations and the lack of transparency in relations between manager, owners (any sub-components representative of majority and minority shareholders), and other stakeholder classes; the frequent dominance of personal interests of members of the governing bodies over the interests of the firm and frequent lack of attention to risk management systems, internal control, and environmental protection; the need to activate global market supervision and behavioural regulation systems consistent with the definitive fall of space barriers sanctioned precisely by the crisis.

In particular, the need for widespread improvement in corporate governance has affirmed according to the approach aimed at:

– Greater convergence between governance systems given the globality of confrontations for the acquisition of consensus and resources.
– Valorising the close relations between economic, competitive, and socio-environmental management variables and devoting greater attention to the risk management system.
– Developing strategies and reporting tools to facilitate stakeholder engagement and enhance transparency on overall performance.
– Attaching greater importance to the lasting involvement of shareholders in relation to appreciating value creation capabilities over time.

The above-mentioned phenomena are closely interconnected and call for greater attention to the principles and values dominating internal and external relationships, as well as the innovation of processes aimed at ensuring a systematic, coordinated, effective, and efficient approach to sustainable development. In this sense, international recommendations and numerous national regulatory policies have proliferated, promoting the increasing interest in the quality of governance and related reporting.

The affirmation and dissemination of corporate social responsibility principles facilitate primarily the global convergence of governance guidelines for growth and value creation in the long run (Salvioni and Gennari, 2017). Such condition would eliminate a substantial factor of divergence between insider and outsider corporate governance systems, a prerequisite to improving the movement of capital, greater stock market stability, and transcending a purely speculative investment approach.

3.4. Corporate governance in a global perspective

The integration of markets as a result of the globalisation phenomenon has started a gradual but steady path of improvement and convergence in governance structures, but especially in corporate governance processes.

The fall of barriers in capital markets, together with the numerous corporate scandals, have primarily increased the attention of international institutions, national regulations, and self-regulatory code of conduct towards implementing widely accepted and high-quality governance principles and standards (de jure or formal convergence)[8]. Attention has focused particu-

---

[8] "According to several scholars, globalisation of financial and product markets is

larly on: governance structures and the related qualitative composition, the internal committees of such structures, the transactions with related parties and market abuse, the protection of minority shareholders and relations with stakeholders, top management remuneration, control and transparency systems.

The dissemination of generally accepted principles, binding rules and self-regulatory standards have undoubtedly favoured the integration of financial markets and the efficient procurement of resources (Yoshikawa and Rasheed 2009; Lazarides and Drimpetas, 2010; Brondoni, 2014; Salvioni, Franzoni and Gennari, 2015). However, the sharing of principles and regulatory guidelines may be an element of nominal convergence, without promoting significant and substantial convergence. Compliance with a standard or a guiding principle does not effectively guarantee the expected results when exclusively qualifying compliance activities in form.

A significant boost to the effective convergence of corporate governance systems (substantial or de facto convergence) is undoubtedly associated with the dissemination of the concepts of corporate social responsibility and sustainability.

Given the primary role of shareholders, corporate governance choices have long favoured profit maximization (Berle and Means, 1932; Friedman, 1962; Jensen and Meckling, 1976), with a partial vision considering financial performance as the firm's only responsibility. Although such behaviour

---

encouraging a gradual path of convergence of corporate governance systems. The convergence between outsider and insider systems can be observed as convergence "in form" or "de jure" and convergence "in function" or "de facto".

Convergence in form or de jure refers to the convergence of rules at an international level. The growing wish of both investors and issuers to operate in global capital markets requires some degree of acceptance of high common values and standards. International bodies encourage convergence in both corporate governance principles and sustainability, considering the latter as a condition for sound governance in terms of risk management, cost reduction and access to capital markets. At the same time, good governance encourages trust in the economic system, because it is a condition for the development of the entire society and the environment. In this regard, the most significant principles and guidelines are contained in the UN Global Compact publications, the ILO *Tripartite Declaration of Principles Concerning Multinational Enterprises and Social Policy* (2014), the G20/OECD *Principles of Corporate Governance* (2015), the ISO 26000 (2010), the green paper on *The EU Corporate Governance Framework* (2011) and many other EU recommendations, directives and papers. Good governance is also required by a number of country-based codes and regulations. In particular, the national regulators are expected to adopt principles and rules in accordance with those suggested and shared internationally. This explains why the rules and recommendations for effective corporate governance are similar in countries with significant differences in corporate governance structures", D.M. Salvioni, F. Gennari, L. Bosetti (2016), *Sustainability and convergence: The future of corporate governance systems?*, Sustainability, 8, 1203; doi:10.3390/su8111203.

has been particularly evident in outsider systems, it has dominated the majority of businesses in industrialized countries.

For listed firms, shareholder-oriented governance tended to result in significant operational differences between outsider and insider systems in relation to the different characteristics of the stock markets, the different degree of separation between ownership and management, and the related implications in terms of capitalization value and control.

In outsider systems, the high dispersion of share capital and the short duration of the governance mandate tended to correlate business success to short-term profit maximization. In such situations, annual financial performance largely ensured positive market feedback on the activities of managers with high independence. Thus shareholders evaluated, usually annually, the effectiveness of governance with respect to short-term return expectations and their consensus was reflected in renewing the mandates of the board members and in the market value of shares.

However, in insider systems, the high concentration of capital and the frequent involvement of majority shareholders in management, often with executive roles, tended to be reflected in the governance approach towards maximizing value creation potential over time. Governance was in fact strongly influenced by the behaviour of majority shareholders whose long-term involvement in ownership determined the prevalence of maximizing financial performance objectives in the long run.

The role of firms in society has changed with the emergence of the new concepts of social responsibility, sustainability, and constantly improving the effectiveness of relations with all firm stakeholders (Brondoni, 2010). This has prompted a review of the governance approach, according to a logic focused on enhancing the close relationship between competitive, economic, and socio-environmental success[9].

CSR does not imply a loss in the importance of value creation and adequate returns on risk capital, and instead emphasises the interdepend-

---

[9] "High Sustainability Firms in contrast, not only pay attention to externalities but in fact, such firms are characterized by distinct governance mechanisms which directly involve the board in sustainability issues and link executive compensation to sustainability objectives; a much higher level of and deeper stakeholder engagement, coupled with mechanisms for making it as effective as possible, including reporting; a longer-term time horizon in their external communications which is matched by a larger proportion of long-term investors; greater attention to nonfinancial measures regarding employees; a greater emphasis on external environmental and social standards for selecting, monitoring and measuring the performance of their suppliers; and a higher level of transparency in their disclosure of nonfinancial information", R. Eccles, I. Ioannou, G. Serafeim (2014), *The impact of corporate sustainability on organizational processes and performance*, Manag. Sci., 60, 2835-2857.

ence between stakeholder relationship management, economic, social and environmental responsibility, results (economic and otherwise), the ability to obtain consensus and resources[10]. This affirms a governance approach aimed at increasing the shareholder value creation potential over time through exploiting opportunities and managing the economic, social, and environmental risks that firms face (Salvioni, Gennari and Bosetti, 2016).

Firm oriented towards sustainable development are clearly aware of their responsibilities towards their various stakeholders and adopt governance methods and tools to improve their economic, social, and ecological performances. In such situations, corporate governance requires an approach based on a broad understanding of responsibility, on a modern interpretation of the links between long-term success and the equitable balance of all stakeholder interests (Salvioni, 2003).

The affirmation and dissemination of the principles of responsible governance facilitate the global convergence of governance guidelines for growth and value creation in the long run. This is capable of eliminating the substantial corporate governance divergence between outsider and insider systems, a prerequisite to improving the movement of capital and transcending a purely speculative investment approach often marked by high shareholder turnover. As a result, the relevant evaluation variables also change that define the strategic approach to corporate governance and that of investors who turn to the stock market.

Firms that adopt a socially responsible strategy devote specific attention to the equitable composition of stakeholder expectations to reducing the impact of their activities on the environment. This contributes to improving: lasting competitive success, the internal working environment necessarily correlated to the greater sharing of objectives and to progressively increasing the levels of operating efficiency, and qualifying the corporate image and brand (Salvioni, Franzoni and Cassano, 2017).

Investors who understand the importance and greater guarantees offered by socially responsible firms in terms of reducing financial risk make their own investment decisions based on remuneration and longer-

---

[10] "Perhaps the most important intellectual breakthrough regarding modern conceptions of CSR is that socially responsible activities can, and should, be used to enhance the bottom line. The corollary is that most, if not all, economic decisions should also be screened for their social impact. Economic returns and social returns should not remain quarantined in isolated units. Firms that successfully pursue a strategy of seeking profits while solving social needs may well earn better reputations with their employees, customers, governments, media, etc. This can, in turn, lead to higher profits for the firms' shareholders", P.L. Cochran (2007), *The evolution of corporate social responsibility*, Business Horizons, 50, 449-454.

term capitalization expectations. In this sense, consider the statements contained in the letter sent in March 2014 by Larry Fink, Chairman and CEO of investment firm BlackRock, to the Chairman or CEO of companies in which their clients are shareholders: *"To meet our clients' needs, we believe the companies we invest in should similarly be focused on achieving sustainable returns over the longer term. Good corporate governance is critical to that goal. That is why, two years ago, I wrote to the CEOs of the companies in which BlackRock held significant investments on behalf of our clients urging them to engage with us on issues of corporate governance. While important work remains to be done, good progress has been made on company-shareholder engagement. I write today re-iterating our call for engagement with a particular focus on companies' strategies to drive longer term growth"*.

This assertion is confirmed in BlackRock's Annual Letter to Shareholders of 16 April 2015, *"This annual report highlights how the platform we've created over time translates into long-term value for clients and shareholders even in the face of global market upheaval. But it also gives us a chance to look toward the future. BlackRock has stayed ahead of the competition over time by thinking long term: building the technology, talent and investment solutions that our clients and shareholders can build on, and that will pay dividends for decades, not just quarters"*.

The dissemination of a broad concept of responsibility, principles of sustainability and the change in the approach of investors have undoubtedly fostered a review of the relevant performances of firms, helping to create significant corporate governance operational convergence between outsider and insider systems (Salvioni, Franzoni and Gennari, 2018).

Thus, in successful firms, corporate governance leads to the progressive broadening of objectives, taking an interest in the entire network of internal and external relations, in an approach based on the exchange of information and the optimization of behaviours in relation to stakeholders expectations.

Regardless of stock market characteristics and ownership concentration, socially responsible firms have thus changed their corporate policies, attaching importance to the creation of sustainable value as a condition of growth and development in the medium-long term, thereby attenuating one of the main differences between insider and outsider corporate governance systems given the different timescales in affirming results.

Nonetheless, to be consider is that globalisation – accompanied by the gradual reduction of differences between spatial environments, cultures, information systems, traditions and institutions – tends to require greater uniformity in corporate governance approaches worldwide. In addition, the fall of barriers between markets and the movement of capital, although increasing the alternatives for investors, has highlighted that the long-term value creation approach could be a significant factor in reducing investment risks.

The change in the governance approach also stresses the importance of corporate communications, promoting informational content and dissemination choices that are ever more responsive to the cognitive and evaluative expectations of stakeholders. In this regard, in addition to financial performance, the stock markets advocate a range of social and environmental indicators. Likewise, the emphasis is on the concepts of transparency, accountability, and web communications, underlining the importance of integration between financial and non-financial reporting.

References

Berle A.A., Means G.C., *The Modern Corporation and Private Property*, Harcourt, Brace World Inc., San Diego, CA, USA, 1932.

Borgonovi E., *Sustainable Economic Growth in the Global Society*, Symphonya. Emerging Issues in Management (symphonya.unimib.it), (2), 50-63, 2007. http://dx.doi.org/10.4468/2007.2.06borgonovi.

Brondoni S.M., *Intangibles, Global Networks & Corporate Social Responsibility*, Symphonya. Emerging Issues in Management (symphonya.unimib.it), (2), 6-24, 2010. http://dx.doi.org/10.4468/2010.2.02brondoni.

Brondoni S.M., *Global Capitalism and Sustainable Growth. From Global Products to Network Globalisation*, Symphonya. Emerging Issues in Management (symphonya.unimib.it), (1), 10-31, 2014. http://dx.doi.org/10.4468/2014.1.02 brondoni.

Brondoni S.M., *Global Networks, Outside-In Capabilities and Smart Innovation*, Symphonya. Emerging Issues in Management (symphonya.unimib.it), (1), 6-21, 2015. http://dx.doi.org/10.4468/2015.1.02brondoni.

Clarke T., *The Continuing Diversity of Corporate Governance: Theories of Convergence and Variety*, Ephemera (16) 1, 19-52, 2016.

Clarke T., Dela Rama M., *Managing in Turbulent Times*, New York, Harper & Row, 2007.

Cochran P.L., *The Evolution of Corporate Social Responsibility*, Business Horizons, (50), 449-454, 2007. doi:10.1016/j.bushor.2007.06.004.

Cohen S.S., Boyd C., Boyd G., *Corporate Governance and Globalization*, UK: Edgar Elgar Publishing, 2000.

Daily C., Dalton D., Cannella A., *Corporate Governance: Decades of Dialogue and Data*, Academy of Management Review, (28) 3, 371-382, 2003.

Denis D.J., Denis D.K., Sarin A., *Agency Theory and the Influence of Equity Ownership Structure on Corporate Diversification Strategies*, Strategic Management Journal, (20), 1071-1076, 1999.

Dignam A.J., Galanis M., *The Globalization of Corporate Governance: Assessing the Impact of Globalization on Corporate Governance Systems*, UK: Ashgate, 2009.

Eccles R., Ioannou I., Serafeim G., *The Impact of Corporate Sustainability on Organizational Processes and Performance*, Management Science, (60) 11, 2835-2857, 2014.

Freeman R.E., Dmytriyev S., *Corporate Social Responsibility and Stakeholder Theory: Learning From Each Other*, Symphonya. Emerging Issues in Management (symphonya.unimib.it), (2), 7-15, 2017. http://dx.doi.org/10.4468/2017.2.02freeman.dmytriyev.

Freeman R.E., Wicks A., Harrison J., Parmar B., De Colle S., *Stakeholder Theory: The State of The Art*, Cambridge University Press, 2010.

Friedman M., *Capitalism and freedom*, Chicago, University of Chicago Press, 1962.

Garriga E., Mele D., *Corporate Social Responsibility Theories: Mapping the Territory*, Journal of Business Ethics, (53), 51-71, 2004. https://doi.org/10.1023/B:BUSI.0000039399.90587.34

Gilson R.J., *Globalizing Corporate Governance: Convergence in Form or Function*, in Gordon J.N., Roe M.J. (eds.), Convergence and persistence in corporate governance, Cambridge University Press, Cambridge, 2004.

G20/OECD, *Principles of Corporate Governance*, OECD Publishing, Paris, 2015.

Hansmann H., Kraakman R., *The End of History for Corporate Law*, Georgetown Law Journal, (89), 439-468, 2001.

Harrison J.S., Freeman R.E., Cavalcanti Sá de Abreu M., *Stakeholder Theory as an Ethical Approach to Effective Management: Applying the Theory to Multiple Contexts*, Review of Business Management, São Paulo, Vol. 17, (55) 858-869, Special Edition, 2015.

Jensen M.C., Chew D., *A theory of the Firm: Governance, Residual Claims and Organizational Forms*, Cambridge, MA: Harvard University Press, 2000.

Jensen M.C., Meckling W., *Theory of the Firm: Managerial Behavior, Agency Costs and Ownership Structure*, Journal of Financial Economis, (3), 305-360, 1976.

Lazarides T., Drimpetas E., *Corporate Governance Regulatory Convergence: A*

Remedy for the Wrong Problem, International Journal of Law and Management, 52(3): 182-192, 2010.

Maher M., Andersson T., *Corporate Governance: Effect on Firm Performance and Economic Growth*, OECD, 1999.

Mason C., Simmons J., *Embedding Corporate Social Responsibility in Corporate Governance: A Stakeholder Systems Approach*, Journal of Business Ethics, (119), 77-86, 2014. https://doi.org/10.1007/s10551-012-1615-9.

OECD, *Corporate Governance and Business Integrity. A stocktaking of Corporate Practices*, 2015.

OECD, *Global Forum on Responsible Business Conduct*, 26-27 June 2014, Summary Report, 2014. Available at http://mneguidelines.oecd.org/globalforumon responsiblebusinessconduct/2014GFRBC_Summary.pdf.

OECD, *Corporate Governance and the Financial Crisis: Key Findings and Main Messages*, 2009.

Salvioni D.M., *Corporate Governance and Global Responsibility*, Symphonya. Emerging Issues in Management (symphonya.unimib.it), 1, 44-54, 2003. http://dx.doi.org/10.4468/2003.1.05salvioni.

Salvioni D.M., *Market-Driven Management and Corporate Governance*, Symphonya. Emerging Issues in Management (symphonya.unimib.it), (2), 13-27, 2008. http://dx.doi.org/10.4468/2008.2.02salvioni.

Salvioni D.M., Astori R., *Sustainable Development and Global Responsibility in Corporate Governance*, Symphonya. Emerging Issues in Management, (1), 28-52, 2013. http://dx.doi.org/10.4468/2013.1.03salvioni.astori.

Salvioni D.M., Bosetti L., *Corporate Responsibility, Ethics and Management Control. Some Evidence from Italian Public Utilities*, in D.A. Frenkel-C. Gerner-Beuerle (eds.), Challenges of the Law in a Permeable World, Atiner, Athens, 2009.

Salvioni D.M., Gennari F., *Corporate Governance in Listed Companies and Market-Driven Management*, in Tipuric D., Raguz I., Podrug N. (eds.), *Rethinking Corporate Governance*, Essex: Pearson, 136-145, 2014a.

Salvioni D.M., Gennari F., *Corporate Governance, Sustainability and Capital Markets Orientation*, International Journal Of Management and Sustainability, (3), 469-483, 2014b.

Salvioni D.M., Gennari F., *CSR, Sustainable Value Creation and Shareholder Relations*, Symphonya. Emerging Issues in Management (symphonya.unimib.it), (1), 36-49, 2017. http://dx.doi.org/10.4468/2017.1.04salvioni.gennari.

Salvioni D.M., Gennari F., Bosetti L., *Sustainability and Convergence: The Future of Corporate Governance Systems?*, Sustainability, (8), 1203, 1-25, 2016. http://dx.doi.org/10.3390/su8111203.

Salvioni D.M., Franzoni S., Cassano R., *Sustainability in the Higher Education System: An Opportunity to Improve Quality and Image*, Sustainability, 9, 914, 1-27, 2017. http://www.mdpi.com/2071-1050/9/6/914.

Salvioni D.M., Franzoni S., Gennari F., *Social Responsibility as a Factor of Convergence in Corporate Governance*, in Gal G., Akisik O., Wooldridge W. (eds.) Sustainability and Social Responsibility: Regulation and Reporting. Accounting, Finance, Sustainability, Governance & Fraud: Theory and Application, Springer, Singapore, 2018.

Spitzeck H., Hansen E.G., *Stakeholder Governance: How Stakeholders Influence Corporate Decision Making*, Corporate Governance: An International Review, 10(4): 378-391, 2010. http://dx.doi.org/10.1108/14720701011069623.

Yoshikawa T., Rasheed A.A., *Convergence of Corporate Governance: Critical Review and Future Directions*, Corporate Governance: An International Review, 17(3), 2010.

Chapter 4

GLOBAL MANAGEMENT
AND "ECONOMIC PATRIOTISM"

Nicola Bellini

ABSTRACT: *The resurgence of economic nationalism is creating a new political scenario confronting corporate strategies in their management of global businesses. Some elements of contemporary economic nationalism, e.g., trade barriers, are expected to entail a merely short-lived revival of old-fashioned protectionism inescapably inconsistent with established global value chains. However, both governments and multinational corporations are mandated to "re-invent" a credible relation between the collective interests (national, regional, local) and the economy's structure in an interdependent world. This conceptual essay discusses to what extent conventional management science wisdom (based on well-rooted myths on globalisation) is challenged by these changes and how the economic language of mercantilism (Magnusson, 1994) may help us redefine such relation in the 21st century economy.*

SUMMARY: 4.1. The "protectionist turn". – 4.2. Making sense of the new scenario: the language of mercantilism. – 4.3. Economic patriotism and territorial loyalty.

4.1. The "protectionist turn"

The year 2017 apparently marked a dramatic change on the stage of international economic relations. More than anyone else, Donald Trump made it clear in his Inaugural Speech the nature of that change: "From this day forward, a new vision will govern our land. From this day forward, it's going to be only America first, America first." As a consequence (and as announced in Trump's successful presidential campaign), the new administration has attempted to rebuild American competitiveness on a mix of financial and environmental deregulation and of active "protectionist" support to American vs. foreign interests.

This major shift in the US economic policy has been the object of critical comments by a large majority of world leaders, in a fierce defense of open market policies, as they had been multilaterally coordinated and developed in recent years. According to German Chancellor, Angela Merkel, "anyone who tries to withdraw from international competition can perhaps deliver short-term advantages. But over the medium and long-term, their own capacity to innovate will be weakened". Even the Chinese President, Xi Jinping, stated that "pursuing protectionism is like locking yourself in a dark room, which would seem to escape the wind and rain, but also block out the sunshine and air". With less imaginative, but equally explicit words, the ECB president, Mario Draghi, warned that "a turn towards protectionism would pose a serious risk for continued productivity growth and potential growth in the global economy".

And yet the "protectionist turn" cannot be limited to the Trump phenomenon or to the threatening "populism" of some European political leaders. Italians witnessed the French government's opposition to the agreement for the acquisition of the naval shipyards of Saint-Nazaire by Fincantieri with sincere surprise. This opposition went up to the point of considering the nationalization option in order to safeguard French sovereignty on that strategic industrial activity. This contrasted sharply with a hands-off attitude that, on the contrary, had characterized Italian policies in recent years with basically no opposition to several foreign (including, in particular, French and Chinese) acquisitions of flagship brands of the national economy and with only instrumental debates around some more controversial cases of attempted acquisition (Alitalia, TIM, Mediaset, FCA) (Bellini, 2018).

In the Saint-Nazaire case, the surprise originated from the fact that the newly elected President, Emmanuel Macron, had been widely perceived as favoring open and pro-European economic policies. As some commentators pointed out, the purely political need to "show" the willingness to intervene explained more than the actual substance of the specific case and yet this was signaling that France, although on the way to deep reforms, would not abandon its characterization as a specific variant of "coordinated-market economy", as widely discussed in the literature (Clift, 2012). It would have been enough to read the Macron's campaign book. Although opposed to old-fashioned nationalism in economic matters, he would never renounce to the "more than two hundred years old ambition" of France and to "reconnect with the productive dream that is at the heart of our history and of our identity" (Macron, 2017, 79 – author's translation). In this paper we do not intend to investigate the reasons of this turn that are left to the still fuzzy interpretations provided by economists, sociologists and political scientists. Rather we attempt to question, although in a very preliminary and tentative way, its implications for corporate strategists and management scholars.

4.2. Making sense of the new scenario: the language of mercantilism

The resurgence of economic "nationalism" is creating a new political scenario confronting corporate strategies in their management of global businesses. Some elements of it, e.g., trade barriers, are expected to entail a revival of old-fashioned protectionism, but this is likely to be short-lived: trade protectionism contradicts global value chains that require numerous border crossings of intermediate products.

However, "international flows of finance, investment, goods, services and people will continue to be mediated institutionally, politically and ideologically – perhaps more so in an age when borders are being rebuilt" (Pike et al., 2017). Within the global interdependent economy, both governments and corporations are mandated to re-invent a credible relation between the collective interests (supranational, national, regional, local) and the individual interests of profit-making actors economy's structure.

Within this scenario, management scholars and practitioners see their view of the State – industry relationship severely challenged. So far, authors have overwhelmingly supported the idea of the inescapable obsolescence of industrial policies as traditionally designed and managed within the framework of Nation-States and of territorially limited political mandates.

Ten years ago, "Symphonya" asked me to discuss the policy implications of the Market-Driven Management approach. I argued that we should not underestimate the governments' ability to change and adapt to the globalization scenario, especially at a time when the financial crisis had dramatically increased the demand for state intervention. What seemed especially noticeable was the emergence of governance-based "pragmatic" policies as a result of the coordination of public and private actors, in a context – however – that is characterized by an inherently high risk of "policy failure". Pragmatism was combined with the search for alternative ways of managing industrial development, like place-based and urban policies. Still there was no doubt about the weakening of the Nation-State and of its developmental role (Bellini, 2008).

A decisive challenge to traditional industrial policies has been provided also by the new patterns of innovation. One can hardly deny the role that the State has historically played in sustaining and driving innovations (Mazzuccato, 2014) and yet the traditional conceptual framework fails to deal effectively with open innovation. The focus itself of policy makers must change: as Brondoni (2015) points out, "in open markets (...) innovation (...) loses its role of 'ideological hierarchy' over imitation. (...) With open innovation the capacity to exploit the competition acquires prime importance, while the capacity to accumulate know-how becomes less important". In fact, "the relationship between spatial and non-spatial logic in innovation systems is, more than ever, an unresolved one" and requires from policies to be "outward looking" (Bellini et al., 2012; Bellini, 2015).

But what if governments are not "weak" anymore? Is it possible to integrate within that framework the resurgence of economic nationalism and protectionism or is there an unresolvable divide and opposition between those political attitudes and the neo-liberal, global-minded world order? Should management scholars and practitioners disregard that resurgence as a disturbance and a regressive, but passing phenomenon or should they rather assume that there are some longer-term trends that diverge from the neo-liberal expectations and that we need to take them seriously?

The first step – we suggest – should be the re-appropriation of the mercantilist logic in the strategic management discourse that is now culturally dominated by the neo-liberal vision, ideologically trapped in the juxtaposition about "how much" State and "how much" market – most often implying that there is "too much" State and "not enough" market (Bellini, 2000). In the classical Porter model, "government is not best understood as a sixth (competitive) force because government involvement is neither inherently good nor bad for industry profitability. The best way to understand the influence of government on competition is to analyze how specific government policies affect the five competitive forces" (Porter, 2008, 86).

In the economic literature mercantilism has been many times undergone intellectual defeat, starting by Adam Smith, and many times has come back, in policy practice more often than in academia. During the last decades neo-mercantilism had a similar fate, being linked to an inherently conflictual (zero-sum) view of international trade relations (Tyson, 1992) and simplified into the obsessive and malevolent pursuit of a persistent current account surplus (Guerrieri and Padoan, 1986).

However, the scope of the economic language of mercantilism (Magnusson, 1994) is wider. In particular, mercantilism raises the attention around the long-term "harmony" between economic performance ("plenty") and political power (Viner, 1948): on the one hand, it questions the impact of competitiveness and innovation on power in international relations; on the other hand, it reflects also the concern about maintaining social cohesion in phases of societal changes. In the absence of "invisible hands", mercantilist thinking is also about countering centrifugal individual interests by explicitly relating individual profits to a superior collective interest (Roll, 1938, 42ff.). This seems especially relevant today, with the co-existence of winners and losers of globalization and the political risks we all are now quite aware of.

Mercantilism is not just about building a defensive approach to external challenges. It is also a way to deal with the positioning of a country with respect to emerging opportunities deriving from a dynamic technological scenario, as we are witnessing now with the potential revolution induced by new manufacturing technologies (the so-called "Industy 4.0") and the global reallocation of productive capacities that is its consequence. "In the 'playing field' conceived by evolutionary theory, where finance, technology, and competition are always pushing towards unexpected outcomes and unpredictable possibilities, (…) government policies to assist structural transformation are a permanent necessity dictated by the market's behavior rather than by its failures" (Burlamaqui, 2000).

4.3. Economic patriotism and territorial loyalty

Adopting the mercantilist logic and language legitimizes the (re)introduction in our management toolbox of two concepts: economic patriotism and territorial loyalty.

The expression "*economic patriotism*" has been around for several years. Reference is often made to a 2005 statement by then Prime Minister of France, Dominique de Villepin, commenting the need to regulate tender offers: "I know that this is not part of the usual language, but when the situation is difficult, when the world changes, it is a question of gathering our forces around a true economic patriotism and defending France and what is French"[1]. A few years earlier a French official report on the State's "economic intelligence" had first made such reference. According to this report, "economic intelligence is an economic patriotism. I guess the reader's smile to discover these words. Whether our tropism is our region, our country or Europe, it is this economic patriotism that will be the guarantor of our social cohesion" (Carayon, 2003, 11 – author's translation). At that time, in the US, public debates had brought up economic patriotism already for some years, at least since the 1980s, with a variety of meanings: the economic facet of political and military patriotism; as a way to recognize the distinctive role of the US in the world economy; as a slogan to convey the need to strengthen the middle class and protect domestic jobs; as "buying American"; as opposed to opportunistic self-interest. e.g. going international to avoid paying domestic taxes; etc. (Bump, 2014).

The economic and political economy literature has framed this idea in more consistent terms only later. Reich (1992) identified, between "zero-

---

[1] http://www.lemonde.fr/societe/article/2005/07/27/plaidoyer-de-dominique-de-villepin-en-faveur-d-un-patriotisme-economique_675859_3224.html (author's translation).

sum nationalism" and "laissez-faire cosmopolitanism", a "positive economic nationalism, in which each nation's citizens take primary responsibility
for enhancing the capacities of their countrymen for full and productive
lives, but who also work with other nations to ensure that these improvements do not come at others' expense" (Reich, 1992, 311). More accurate-
ly, economic patriotism has been defined as "economic choices which seek
to discriminate in favour of particular social groups, firms or sectors understood by the decision-makers as insiders because of their territorial status.
Economic patriotism entails a form of economic partiality: a desire to shape
market outcomes to privilege the position of certain actors" (Clift and
Woll, 2013).

Economic patriotism should not be confused with protectionism. Economic patriotism can be "liberal" in the sense of actively and creatively
promoting liberalization of key sectors, supranational integration and the
emergence of national and transnational "champions" (Clift and Woll,
2013). In the case of the European Union, we witness the "Europeanasa-
tion" of the notion of economic patriotism (Trouille 2014). This is done
especially by suggesting the need for European champions as un update
version of the national champions and also through the more traditional
advocacy of a protective "fortress Europe". Economic patriotism may thus
"anticipate" a *patrie* that is not yet established as political jurisdiction (Rosamond, 2013).

Economic patriotism is also not the same as economic nationalism in the
meaning of Friedrich List, because "economic patriotism is agnostic about
the precise nature of the unit claimed as *patrie*: it can also refer to supranational or sub-national economic citizenship" and patriotisms with different
economic references can overlap (Clift and Woll, 2013).

At the same time, the definition of who are the insiders and therefore
deserving positive discrimination is not automatically based on "nationali-
ty" but on a wider idea of "citizenship". In his seminal work of 1992, Rob-
ert Reich advocated a shift in the idea of nation that refocuses on labor
away from corporations, breaking the link between the nation's prosperity
and the success of the nation's core corporations: "As corporations of all
nations are transformed into global webs, the important question – from
the standpoint of national wealth – is not which nation's citizen own what,
but which nation's citizen learn how to do what, so they are capable of adding more value to the world economy" (Reich, 1992, 137).

This approach is fully consistent with the mercantilist logic. Also two
centuries earlier, the mercantilist Alexander Hamilton, in his 1791 "Report
on Manufactures", had considered that the role of governments was to ex-
cite the "confidence of cautious, sagacious capitalists, *both citizens and for-*

eigners". In fact, a partially overlooked aspect of Donald Trump's rhetoric is that he repeatedly praised foreign companies investing in the US, such as FCA or Samsung ("Thank you, @Samsung! We would love to have you!"). Good citizen behavior then becomes an essential aspect of a corporate strategy, possibly also with positive effect on the company's image on the local markets that can more than offset the weakening phenomenon of the "buying national" programs. Being loyal to a place, even if foreigner can, pay off.

Territorial loyalty can be defined as the propensity to territorially embed innovation and investments within a specific territorial context. Barriers to exit increase loyalty: the need to re-start a costly learning process may be higher than the benefits of moving to a different place (Calafati, 2009, 29 ff.). In a sense, territorial loyalty stresses that the individual compliance with the collective needs can be based on a sort of enlightened self-interest. This was already clearly stated by Tocqueville and brilliantly summarized one century later by Calvin Coolidge in the 1930s (as quoted by Reich, 1992): "Patriotism is easy to understand in America; it means looking out for yourself by looking out for your country".

The importance of loyalty derives from the possibility of "exit" (Hirschman, 1978), a possibility that we must assume being increased in an era of globalization. In a framework of growing internationalization, corporations are constantly in search of a (more) convenient relational context. This implies a learning process that is reversible, negotiated and dependent both on "objective" factors and on symbolic ones (that are the object of place branding and marketing). This makes territorial loyalty "contingent" (Calafati, 2009, 19).

Territorial loyalty will then result from a mutual exchange of stability conditions. Corporations give stability to economic development by renouncing to or postponing opportunistic mobility and by embedding value-creating activities. Governments invest in the "attractiveness" of the territory, offering stability of rules and conditions, a reliable knowledge base, symbolic contributions to the image of the corporate brand, and of course selective policies targeted at individual companies, industries and the territorial contexts where they work.

References

Bellini N., *The Decline of State-Owned Enterprise and the New Foundations of State-Industry Relationship*, in F. Amatori, P. Toninelli (eds.), *The Rise and Fall of State Owned Enterprise in the Western World*, Cambridge University Press, Cambridge, 2000, 25-48.

Bellini N., *Market-Driven Management: the Policy Implications*, Symphonya. Emerging Issues in Management, (1), 34-44, 2008. http://dx.doi.org/ 10.4468/2008.1.04bellini.

Bellini N., *Smart specialisation in Europe: Looking beyond regional borders*, Symphonya. Emerging Issues in Management, (1), 22-29, 2015. http://dx.doi.org/ 10.4468/2015.1.03bellini.

Bellini N., *Industry Modernisation and Beyond*, in A. Grasse, M. Grimm, J. Labitzke (eds.), *Italien zwischen Krise und Aufbruch*, Springer VS, Wiesbaden, 2018, 297-312.

Bellini N., Teräs J., Ylinenpää H., *Science and Technology Parks in the Age of Open Innovation. The Finnish Case*, Symphonya. Emerging Issues in Management, (1), 25-44, 2012. http://dx.doi.org/10.4468/2012.1.03bellini.teras.ylinenpaa.

Brondoni S. M., *Global Networks, Outside-In Capabilities and Smart Innovation*, Symphonya. Emerging Issues in Management, (1), 6-21, 2015. http://dx.doi. org/10.4468/2012.1.03bellini.teras.ylinenpaa.

Bump P., *'Economic patriotism': Explaining the vague, finger-wagging, immortal phrase*, The Washington Post, July 17, 2014.

Burlamaqui L., *Evolutionary economics and the economic role of the State,* in Burlamaqui L. et al. (eds.), *Institutions and the Role of the State*, Edward Elgar, Cheltenham, 2000, 27-52.

Calafati A., *Economie in cerca di città. La questione urbana in Italia*, Donzelli, Roma, 2009.

Carayon B., *Intelligence économique, compétitivité et cohésion sociale*, La Documentation Française, Paris, 2003.

Clift B., *Economic patriotism, the clash of capitalisms, and state aid in the European Union*, Journal of Industry, Competition and Trade, 13(1), 101-117, 2013. DOI: 10.1007/s10842-012-0138-5.

Clift B., Woll C. (2013), *Economic patriotism: reinventing control over open markets*, in Clift B., Woll C. (eds.), *Economic Patriotism in Open Economies*. Routledge, Abingdon, 2013.

Guerrieri P., Padoan P.C., *Neomercantilism and international economic stability*, International Organization, 40(1), 29-42, 1986.

Hirschman A.O., *Exit, voice, and the state*, World Politics, 31(1), 90-107, 1978.

Macron E., *Révolution*, Éditions Pocket, Paris, 2017.

Mazzucato M., *The Entrepreneurial State. Debunking Public vs. Private Sector Myths*, Anthem Press, London, 2014.

Porter M.E., *The five competitive forces that shape strategy*, Harvard Business Review, 86(1), 25-40, 2008.

Rosamond B. (2013), *Supranational governance as economic patriotism? The European union, legitimacy and the reconstruction of state space*, in Clift B., Woll C. (eds.), Economic Patriotism in Open Economies, Routledge, Abingdon, Oxon, 2013.

Trouille J.M., *Industrial Nationalism versus European Partnerships: An Analysis of State-Led Franco-German Interfirm Linkages*, Environment and Planning C: Government and Policy, 32(6), 1059-1082, 2014. DOI:10.1068/c0916b.

Tyson L. D. A., *Who's bashing whom?: trade conflict in high-technology industries*, Institute for International Economics, Washington, D.C., 1993.

Viner J., *Power versus plenty as objectives of foreign policy in the seventeenth and eighteenth centuries*, World Politics, 1(1), 1-29, 1948.

Chapter 5

OUTSIDE-IN OPEN INNOVATION
IN COMPETITIVE BUSINESS MANAGEMENT

Elisa Arrigo

ABSTRACT: *The growing complexity of the external environment and the globalisation of markets have led companies across many industries to expand their activities and processes in the global landscape. This chapter provides an in-depth analysis on how global companies manage innovation in an open way through developing network relations to anticipate and satisfy customers while seizing new business opportunities. By adopting an outside-in management approach, companies are able to develop a global scale learning platform by strengthening their ability to gain insights from the outside. In fact, the network configuration promotes market knowledge and learning from every periphery in the competitive scenario and allows companies to participate in partnerships and collaborations with stakeholders to more efficiently manage their innovation processes.*

5.1. Introduction

Market saturation, convergence of many industries, speed characterizing changing competitive dynamics, combined with strong competitive rivalry, have generated a situation of hyper-competition (D'Aveni, 2010) and over-supply in many industries (Brondoni, 2005, 2014).

As the external environment becomes more dynamic, corporate strategy is conceived as constantly evolving, and is based on three key principles: all actions are actually interactions (due to the interdependence existing among firms); are relative, since they need to be assessed in relation to the competitors' moves; and, finally, need to be projected in the long term to interpret their evolutionary dynamics. However, acquiring a better competitive position, can only be temporary, since hyper-competition implies a continuous disruption of the existing competitive status quo, and every competitive advantage gained over competitors is rapidly imitated and sur-passed (D'Aveni, 1994).

Therefore, each firm is focused on creating a continuous series of tem-porary advantages by reacting rapidly to competitors' moves and being bet-ter at satisfying customers than other firms. In a similar competitive scenar-io, it becomes relevant to understand how organizations can successfully compete, evolve, and survive when firm-specific advantages are not sus-tainable, but temporary in nature (D'Aveni, Dagnino and Smith, 2010).

One solution may be to focus on innovation by handling it in an open way (Chesbrought, 2006, 2014; Van de Vrande et al., 2009; Brondoni, 2015) through adopting an outside-in management approach (Day, 2011, 2013; Arrigo, 2012). This is in line with the view of corporate strategy as dynamic maneuvering in which the interchange with the outside environ-ment represents a key element for the development of each firm, as in the monitoring and analysis of its evolution (Mintzberg, Ahlstrand and Lampel, 1998).

The aim of the present chapter is to provide an overview on how global companies manage innovation in an open way through developing network relations to anticipate and satisfy customers while seizing new business op-portunities due to an outside-in management approach.

To achieve this goal, the remainder of the chapter is organized as fol-lows. Firstly, a description of the competitive scenario faced by firms in the global market is offered by deepening the relevance of network relations and adopting an outside-in perspective in competitive business manage-ment. Secondly, the notion of open innovation is dealt with, by emphasiz-ing the relevance of capturing knowledge from the external environment and converting it into innovative processes, products or services. Finally, the conclusions are reported.

5.2. Network relations and outside-in perspective in competitive business management

The hyper-competitive environment, which currently characterizes several business-to-consumer markets, has made it progressively impossible for a single firm to hold and exploit all relevant resources to compete in the global marketplace. As a result, many firms have undertaken plans to ex-tend their activities worldwide, creating mega-organisations with global networks of companies (Brondoni, 2008) whose nodal points are globally dispersed but closely connected (Holm, Eriksson and Johanson, 1999).

This network structure is flexible and responsive to market changes and promotes a learning process (Mintzberg, Ahlstrand and Lampel, 1998) from each periphery of the competitive scenario. The larger the firm, the more touch points the business will have at the periphery of its global market. Corporate activities can be located in different geographical areas selected according to the best available conditions for firms. The market space is no longer conceived as a stable and fixed element, but becomes a critical competitive driver (Brondoni, 2008) chosen on the basis of threats and opportunities provided by multiple potential locations. For example, manufacturing can be spread over different sites or partners that are geographically distant where workers labour costs or technical skills held are more advantageous than in the country of origin.

Strategic alliances (Gulati, 1998; Larsson et al., 1998; Das and Teng, 2000) have become very popular, particularly cross-border strategic ones, in order to help firms expand more easily in the global market, by leveraging their core competencies, and acquiring from their partners, information and knowledge on local customer preferences and legal/fiscal procedures. In being dynamic, this type of corporate strategy doesn't exclude analysing the external environment and interacting with customers, suppliers, distributors, competitors and other market players. In fact, if a firm remains closed, it will be unable to survive in the long term.

As stated previously, intense competitive rivalry means that firms cannot simply wait and react to competitors' moves or customers' requests but must try to anticipate them by adopting an outside-in approach (Day, 2011, 2013) that represents a winning strategy. This management approach calls for the formulation of a corporate strategy beginning with an analysis of the external competitive environment. Thus, adopting an outside-in management approach goes far beyond simple observation of competitive rivals and customer desires, it also requires supply chain restructuring (Arrigo, 2012a).

Traditionally, firms that adopted an inside-out approach defined their corporate strategy internally, only then looking externally, which was typical of a market situation of controlled competition (Brondoni, 2005) where the preservation of the existing status quo was the key purpose. With this aim in mind, firms built and integrated their skills from an informed vantage point, on the alert for the opportunities and threats present within their external environment. In such a scenario, monitoring and scanning activities were crucial. However, an inside-out management limits a firm's ability to anticipate market changes and to modify the system of competitive relationships existing in the marketplace (Arrigo, 2012a).

In contrast, in open markets, corporate decisions are driven by analysing current and potential customers' requests and by studying competitors' competitive strategies. Specifically, market-driven firms are recognized as being able to develop a global scale learning platform in gathering and examining large quantities of information. To gain insight into the external environment, they set up appropriate channels of internal information sharing (Baker and Sinkula, 1999).

In global markets, acquiring a position of competitive advantage depends on a firm's ability to obtain, integrate, reconfigure and share knowledge across its organization and to its partners quickly and efficiently. Market knowledge flows in multiple directions and, by having multiple dispersed locations, a firm with an established global network can gather data and local knowledge by collaborating with business partners using clearly defined information flows and channels. Depending on market conditions, certain partners can be eliminated, while new partners are added, or assigned tasks given to each partner can change in order to improve competitiveness of the entire global network (Jaworsky, Kohli, and Sahay, 2000; Tuominem, Rajala, and Möller, 2004).

An outside-in management approach combined with an orientation focused on its competitors enables a firm to achieve two key results: firstly, acquiring better knowledge of the competitive environment and, secondly, making the market periphery (Saka-Helmhout, 2011) clearer. By analysing every market signal as either a new competitive offer, or a reflection of latent customer need, as a means of creating strategic alliances is likely to prove decisive to corporate success. Corporate processes can be dispersed across several offshore destinations, benefitting from the convenience of developing global knowledge, one means for firms to remain competitive.

A global network alliance can promote not only the innovativeness of each firm, but also that of its entire network.

5.2.1. Outside-in capabilities

To anticipate market dynamics and manage the growing volatility and instability, firms need to develop specific dynamic capabilities (Eisenhardt and Martin, 2000; Teece, 2007). Capabilities are recognized among the main sources of a firm's competitive advantage and reflect the ability of managers to renew them over the course of time (Vorhies, Harker and Rao, 1999).

In particular, dynamic capabilities involve higher-level activities that empower a firm to produce goods and services in high demand and enable it to integrate, build, and reconfigure internal and external resources to address and shape rapidly changing business environments (Teece and Lehin, 2016). In the global market, they have two main components: developing a coherent global system in which the unique features of each local environment are considered in order to facilitate customization of country strategies, and the adaptation, integration and reconfiguring of internal and external assets to seize opportunities in open markets (Griffith and Harvey, 2001). In fact, dynamic capabilities serve many functions: sensing opportunities or threats deriving from environmental trends; responding to modifications in the competitive scenario by combining in different ways or externally acquiring new resources; and choosing the best internal configuration in order to deliver the greatest customer value in relation to other competitors' offers (Teece, 2007).

However, only those dynamic capabilities that lead a firm to outperform the competition, according to Day (1994), represent *'distinctive capabilities'* of a firm. Market-driven firms have a strong capacity to learn from the acquisition, interpretation and incorporation of knowledge generated through interaction with other market players. It has been, in fact, proven that processing marketing information can be related to a firm's degree of market orientation; the more a firm focuses on studying its market, the greater its inclination to process this wealth of information and the higher its learning orientation (Baker and Sinkula, 2002).

Generally, market-driven firms possess distinctive capabilities (Day, 1994) across the following corporate processes allowing them to coordinate their activities on a global scale:

– *Inside-out capabilities*: internal capabilities stimulated by market requirements, competitive challenges and external opportunities such as specific skills developed in manufacturing, logistics, technological development and human resources management;

– *Outside-in capabilities*: their focus is outside the organization and they define corporate strategies in relation to the analysis and interpretation of the external environment so as to allow the firm to compete successfully in the market; and

– *Spanning capabilities*: required to integrate *inside-out* and *outside-in* capabilities and apply both an internal and external analysis. This is the case with strategy development, new product development, pricing, purchasing, and customer service delivery.

Specifically, outside-in capabilities are those that allow a firm to anticipate and be responsive in satisfying customers, and grasping new business opportunities more effectively than their competitors. Firms pay increasing care in developing such capabilities because market dynamics and competitive pressures erode each competitive advantage acquired over their rivals. Indeed, under these circumstances, firms are forced to rethink their customer value creation strategies (Martens, Matthyssens and Vandenbempt, 2012) and can revitalize their market strategies due to *outside-in* capabilities that allow them to gather fresh knowledge from the market and define new actions to satisfy their customers.

The starting point for the development of *outside-in* capabilities lies in individual firms recognizing the enormous gap existing between the complexity and dynamism of the global market and having the ability to both understand and manage it (Arrigo, 2012b).

Market-driven firms outclass their competitors using two important and distinctive *outside-in* capabilities allowing them to anticipate and rapidly reconfigure their corporate activities. These can be identified as their market sensing and customer linking capabilities (Day, 1994). Customer linking capability involves the ability to create and manage collaborative relationships; while a successful market sensing can be performed through two interrelated learning processes that act as dynamic sub-capabilities. They are peripheral vision (for recognising weak signals from the business's periphery) and vigilant learning (in order to properly interpret the implications of such weak signals) (Day and Schoemaker, 2016). The latter skill also enables firms to adapt their behaviour from being reactive to a sense-and-respond approach (Day, 2011).

In fact, a vigilant firm is characterized by curiosity, attentiveness and the idea of acting on partial information from the *outside-in*. Thus, vigilant market learning involves a willingness to be immersed in customers' lives and competitors' strategies with an open-minded approach to latent needs and an ability to sense and act on weak signals from the market.

5.3. Outside-in open innovation

In the management literature, innovation has been frequently considered as the source of firms' competitiveness (Utterback, 1994; Hurley and Hult 1998; Baker and Sinkula, 1999; Knight and Cavusgil, 2004; Gassmann, Enkel and Chesbrough, 2010; Christensen 2013; Drucker, 2014). An innovation process can be identified in many aspects of corporate strategy, for example, by distinguishing radical, incremental, new, discontinuous, and imitative innovations (Garcia and Calantone, 2002). However, while in noncompetitive markets innovations can be developed and commercialized mainly within the company's boundaries and are often associated with technological innovations, in open markets the closed innovation model based on full control of a self-reliant firm is superseded by an open innovation one (Chesbrough, 2003; Chesbrough and Brunswicker, 2014).

Open innovation expressly refers to 'the use of purposive inflows and outflows of knowledge to accelerate internal innovation, and expand the markets for external use of innovation, respectively' (Chesbrough,

Vanhaverbeke and West, 2006, p. 1). The first process is called 'inbound open innovation', referring to the internal exploitation of external knowledge, while the second is called 'outbound open innovation' and denotes the external exploitation of internal knowledge. In fact, exploration aims at new discoveries and experimentation in order to find innovative business options, procedures, or products. In contrast, exploitation involves the use of existing knowledge, resources, and capabilities to reach a better understanding of existing markets, products, or processes by improving relationships with customers, competitors, and partners (Aspara et al., 2011).

Firms implementing an outside-in management approach try to maintain a balance between exploration and exploitation and embrace the idea of treating innovation in an open way based on the assumption that innovation sources may also lie outside the companies' boundaries (Arrigo, 2012a). Therefore, firms need to look outside for new paths to innovations (Gassmann, Enkel and Chesbrough 2010), adopting a holistic view of the innovation management process is required to seize new opportunities (Inauen and Schenker-Wicky, 2011).

Based on this assumption, firms have to reorganize themselves to enable collaboration with numerous stakeholders including customers, suppliers, retailers, universities and research centers. Innovation processes may be the result of skills developed internally, or activated by customer requests and interactions with partners who are involved in the manufacturing of new products or processes. In fact, cooperation with partners, customers, competitors, and suppliers is recognized as an essential factor enhancing a firm's performance and innovativeness (Von Hippel, 2005). For example, customer co-creation enables the establishment of an active, creative and social collaboration process between firms and customers in the context of new product development and determines a paradigm shift from a manufacturer-active paradigm to a customer-active one (Piller, Vossen and Ihl, 2012). However, external networking and co-creation require strong relational capabilities in order to fully access the resources of many partners (Day and Schoemaker, 2016).

Simultaneously, within the global market, firms need to choose carefully where to place the receptive points for potential new sources of innovation so as to capture new insights through an outside-in approach (Arrigo, 2012a). In markets where competition is particularly fierce, leading firms' behaviour reveals the crucial importance of open innovation policies where imitation and innovation processes become a primary condition in responding to global competition (Brondoni, 2015).

Nevertheless, in certain circumstances, innovation may originate from imitation of competitors precisely when a firm successfully and rapidly re-produces an innovation that other companies have conceived and launched at an earlier date onto the market. Imitation does not entail only mindless repetition of others' processes or products but becomes 'creative imita-tion' (Zhou, 2006) when companies make incremental innovations based on radical innovations of others ideas. Sometimes, imitation can become even more important than simply innovation for business growth (Shenkar, 2010b).

To emphasize the relevance of imitative policies, the term 'imovators' (from the fusion of imitator and innovator) has been proposed to indicate those firms that appreciate the value of imitation and do not see it as an impediment but, on the contrary, as a supportive driver to innovation (Shenkar, 2010b). Global markets and technological advances have ex-panded the ranks of imovators and have made imitative processes more feasible, cost effective and faster. In reality, through using an imitative pro-cess, firms can save in R&D investment and, in the case of me-too products can also save on marketing expenditure since customers are already aware of product usage and specifications and therefore do not need be informed through marketing communications (Shenkar, 2010a). Moreover, imova-tors can modify the original product in order to better fit customers' tastes. Thus, both technological risk of failure of imitative processes or commer-cial risk are low for imitator firms (Zhou, 2006; Luo, Sun and Lu Wang, 2011).

The learning process from competitors can be easier for firms within a global network's alliance because the network configuration allows identi-fying and utilizing, for learning purposes, all the available channels: supply chain, distribution and marketing, production, etc. Furthermore, since firms share resources and knowledge inside a global network, it is more likely they acquire a good understanding of their partners and, through the outside-in absorption (Cohen and Levinthal, 1990) of external knowledge, can also gain access to other innovation projects.

Within open innovation management, three core processes can be iden-tified (Gassmann and Enkel, 2004). Outside-in processes involve the activi-ties of sourcing knowledge and technologies from stakeholders (consumers, suppliers, etc.) and licensing intellectual property from other firms. Inside-out processes include external technology transfers for the commercializa-tion of in-house technology and the coupled processes combine outside-in and inside-out processes by working together with complementary partners or participating in other companies.

By focusing on outside-in processes, Inauen and Schenker-Wicky (2011) demonstrated a positive relationship between the openness of outside-in processes in R&D management and the competitiveness and innovation performance of firms. More precisely, greater openness towards customers and universities led firms to increase their product innovations, while, greater openness towards competitors, suppliers, and universities led to more process innovations.

Nevertheless, companies engaged in open innovation must balance the need to promote openness among partners whilst taking proactive steps to protect their core competences (Muller, Hutchins and Cardoso Pinto, 2012). Having access to several collaborators can promote both innovative and imitative processes. In reinforcing the stated aim of open innovation being to acquire and combine external sources of knowledge in order to accelerate internal innovative processes, it is relevant here to highlight two main issues that could arise: how to become the owner of attractive resources and how to prevent others from copying them (Chesbrough and Appleyard, 2007).

In order to overcome the problems of innovation ownership and protection, a firm involved in an innovative process should be able to quickly recognize the created value and safeguard it through intellectual property (IP) management. However, this is not always simple as frequently a company's disclosure of many internal processes and data may cause a loss of control over internal goals and, at the same time, promote external innovation. Companies specifically engaged in strategic alliances with competitors have to find both formal (such as patent, trademark, or copyright protection) and informal methods (such as shorter lead time or first mover advantages) in order to defend their competitive advantage while they are absorbing knowledge from the outside (Arrigo, 2015). One consequence is that new business models of IP aggregators and IP brokers, where IP is mutual and shared, are spreading as part of this evolution (Gasmann, Enkel and Chesbrough, 2010).

5.4. Conclusions

The chapter has illustrated how in hyper-competitive markets companies can find convenient ways to manage innovation in an open way through developing network relations. The ability of firms to understand and quickly recognize new business opportunities depends on the development of distinctive capabilities and on the adoption of an outside-in approach in their competitive business management.

The state of hyper-competition characterizing the competitive landscape puts an end to the sustainability of a competitive advantage for a long-term. Firms are thus focused on creating a continuous series of temporary advantages to persist over the long term by being able to rapidly react to competitors' moves and to satisfy customers.

Similarly, the relevance of developing dynamic distinctive capabilities is emphasized to try to govern the uncertainty and turbulence of global markets and, innovation policies appear central in the drive to develop temporary competitive advantages. It is acknowledging that low cost and high quality represent those competitive drivers necessary to operate on the global markets but are not sufficient to acquire pre-eminence over the competitors. Thus, the strategic focus of firms should shift from striving only for the lowest cost or the best quality to improving the capacity to innovate by using all available sources of innovation.

Effective and efficient management of innovation results from a firm's ability to monitor the external environment by collecting data and information, useful in generating learning and developing new knowledge. The chapter has highlighted how an outside-in management aproach stresses the significance of capturing knowledge from the outside and converting it into innovative processes, products or services. As a result, firms can enter into strategic alliances with several business partners in order to deal better with the competition and take advantage of market opportunities, thereby outperforming their competitors and managing the uncertainty and instability of global markets.

Adopting an outside-in management approach and by being open, firms are able to draw on insights from multiple and diverse geographical locations, increasing their potential to develop innovative processes necessary to their survival. Outside-in open innovation, thus, emerges as a fundamental competitive driver to achieve success in hyper-competitive markets, enabling companies to increase their competitive advantage over other firms.

References

Arora A., Athreye S., Huang C., *The Paradox of Openness Revisited: Collaborative Innovation and Patenting by UK Innovators*, Research Policy, 45(7), 1352-1361, 2016. http://doi.org/10.1016/j.respol.2016.03.019.

Arrigo E., *Alliances, Open Innovation and Outside-In Management*, Symphonya. Emerging Issues in Management (symphonya.unimib.it), (2), 53-65, 2012a. http://dx.doi.org/10.4468/2012.2.05arrigo.

Arrigo E., *Market-Driven Management and Outside-In Capabilities*. In S.M. Brondoni (ed.), *Managerial Economics and Global Corporations*, (26), Giappichelli, Torino, 43-56, 2012b.

Arrigo E., *Open Innovation and Market Orientation: An Analysis of the Relationship*, Journal of the Knowledge Economy, 9(1), 150-161, 2018. http://doi.org/10.1007/s13132-015-0327-7.

Aspara J., Tikkanen H., Pontiskoski E., Jarvensivu P., *Exploration and Exploitation across Three Resources Classes: Market/Customer Intelligence, Brands/Bonds and Technologies/Processes*, European Journal of Marketing, 45(4), 596-630, 2011. http://doi.org/10.1108/03090561111111352.

Baker W.E., Sinkula J.M., *Learning Orientation, Market Orientation, and Innovation: Integrating and Extending Models of Organizational Performance*, Journal of Market-Focused Management, 4(4), 295-308, 1999. http://doi.org/10.1023/A:1009830402395.

Baker W.E., Sinkula J.M., *Market Orientation, Learning Orientation and Product Innovation: Delving into the Organization's Black Box,* Journal of Market-Focused Management, 5(1), 5-23, 2002. http://doi.org/10.1023/A:1012543911149.

Barney J.B., *Gaining and Sustaining Competitive Advantage*, Pearson Higher Ed, 2014.

Brondoni S.M., *Managerial Economics and Global Competition*, Symphonya. Emerging Issues in Management (symphonya.unimib.it), (1), 14-38, 2005. http://dx.doi.org/10.4468/2005.1.02brondoni.

Brondoni S.M., *Market-Driven Management, Competitive Space and Global Networks*, Symphonya. Emerging Issues in Management (symphonya. unimib.it), (1), 14-27, 2008. http://dx.doi.org/10.4468/2008.1.02brondoni.

Brondoni S.M., *Global Capitalism and Sustainable Growth. From Global Products to Network Globalisation*, Symphonya. Emerging Issues in Management (symphonya.unimib.it), (1), 10-31, 2014. http://dx.doi.org/10.4468/2014.1.02 brondoni.

Brondoni S.M., *Global Networks, Outside-In Capabilities and Smart Innovation*, Symphonya. Emerging Issues in Management (symphonya.unimib.it), (1), 6-21, 2015. http://dx.doi.org/10.4468/2015.1.02brondoni

Chesbrough H., *Business Model Innovation: It Is Not Just About Technology Anymore*, Strategy & Leadership, 35(6), 12-17, 2007. http://doi.org/10.1108/10878570710833714.

Chesbrough H., Appleyard M.M., *Open Innovation and Strategy*, California Management Review, 50(1), 57-76, 2007. http://doi.org/10.2307/41166416.

Chesbrough H., Brunswicker S., *A Fad or a Phenomenon?: The Adoption of Open Innovation Practices in Large Firms*, Research-Technology Management, 57(2), 16-25, 2014. http://dx.doi.org/10.5437/08956308X5702196.

Chesbrough H., Vanhaverbeke W., West J. (eds.), *Open Innovation: Researching a New Paradigm,* Oxford University Press on Demand, 2006.

Christensen C.M., *The Innovator's Dilemma: When New Technologies Cause Great Firms to Fail*, Harvard Business Review Press, 2013.

Cohen W.M., Levinthal D.A., *Absorptive Capacity: A New Perspective on Learning and Innovation*, Administrative Science Quarterly, 128-152, 1990. http://doi.org/10.2307/2393553.

Das T.K., Teng B.S., *A Resource-Based Theory of Strategic Alliances,* Journal of Management, 26(1), 31-61, 2000. http://doi.org/10.1016/S0149-2063(99)00037-9.

D'Aveni R.A., *Hypercompetition: Managing the Dynamics of Strategic Management*, New York, 1994.

D'Aveni R.A., *Hypercompetition*, Simon and Schuster, 2010.

D'Aveni R.A., Dagnino G.B., Smith K.G., *The Age of Temporary Advantage*, Strategic Management Journal, 31(13), 1371-1385, 2010. http://doi.org/10.1002/smj.897.

Day G.S., *The Capabilities of Market-Driven Organizations*, The Journal of Marketing, 37-52, 1994. http://doi.org/10.2307/1251915.

Day G.S., *Closing the Marketing Capabilities Gap*, Journal of Marketing, 75(4), 183-195, 2011. http://doi.org/10.1509/jmkg.75.4.183.

Day G.S., Moorman C., *Regaining Customer Relevance: The Outside-In Turnaround*, Strategy & Leadership, 41(4), 17-23, 2013. http://doi.org/10.1108/SL-04-2013-0021.

Day G.S., Schoemaker P.J., *Adapting to Fast-Changing Markets and Technologies*, California Management Review, 58(4), 59-77, 2016. http://doi.org/10.1525/cmr.2016.58.4.59.

Drucker P., *Innovation and Entrepreneurship*, Routledge, 2014.

Eisenhardt K.M., Martin J.A., *Dynamic Capabilities: What Are They?*, Strategic Management Journal, 1105-1121, 2000.

Enkel E., Gassmann O., Chesbrough H., *Open R&D and Open Innovation: Exploring the Phenomenon*, R&D Management, 39(4), 311-316, 2009. http://doi.org/10.1111/j.1467-9310.2009.00570.x.

Garcia R., Calantone R., *A Critical Look at Technological Innovation Typology and Innovativeness Terminology: A Literature Review*, Journal of Product Innovation Management, 19(2), 110-132, 2002. http://doi.org/10.1016/S0737-6782(01)00132-1.

Gassmann O., Enkel E., *Towards a Theory of Open Innovation: Three Core Process Archetypes*, R&D Management Conference (RADMA), Lissabon, 2004.

Gassmann O., Enkel E., Chesbrough H., *The Future of Open Innovation*, R&D Management, 40(3), 213-221, 2010. http://doi.org/10.1111/j.1467-9310.2010.00605.x.

Griffith D.A., Harvey M.G., *A Resource Perspective of Global Dynamic Capabilities*, Journal of International Business Studies, 32(3), 597-606, 2001. http://doi.org/10.1057/palgrave.jibs.8490987.

Gulati R., *Alliances and Networks*, Strategic Management Journal, 19(4), 293-317, 1998.

Holm D.B., Eriksson K., Johanson J., *Creating Value through Mutual Commitment to Business Network Relationships*, Strategic Management Journal, 20(5), 467-486, 1999. http://www.jstor.org/stable/3094165.

Hurley R.F., Hult G.T.M., *Innovation, Market Orientation, and Organizational*

Learning: An Integration and Empirical Examination, The Journal of Marketing, 42-54, 1998. http://doi.org/doi:10.2307/1251742.

Inauen M., Schenker-Wicki A., *The Impact of Outside-In Open Innovation on Innovation Performance*, European Journal of Innovation Management, 14(4), 496-520, 2011. http://doi.org/10.1108/14601061111174934.

Jaworski B., Kohli A.K., Sahay A., *Market-Driven versus Driving Markets*, Journal of the Academy of Marketing Science, 28(1), 45-54, 2000. http://doi.org/10.1177/0092070300281005.

Knight G.A., Cavusgil S.T., *Innovation, Organizational Capabilities, and the Born-Global Firm*, Journal of International Business Studies, 35(2), 124-141, 2004. http://doi.org/10.1057/palgrave.jibs.8400071.

Larsson R., Bengtsson L., Henriksson K., Sparks J., *The Interorganizational Learning Dilemma: Collective Knowledge Development in Strategic Alliances*, Organization Science, 9(3), 285-305, 1998. http://doi.org/10.1287/orsc.9.3.285.
Luo Y., Sun J., Lu Wang S., *Emerging Economy Copycats: Capability, Environment and Strategy*, Academy of Management Perspectives, May, 37-56, 2011.

Martens R., Matthyssens P., Vandenbempt K., *Market Strategy Renewal as a Dynamic Incremental Process*, Journal of Business Research, 65(6), 720-728, 2012. http://doi.org/10.1016/j.jbusres.2010.12.008.
Muller A., Hutchins N., Cardoso Pinto M., *Applying Open Innovation where Your Company Needs It Most*, Strategy and Leadership, 40(2), 35-42, 2012. http://doi.org/10.1108/10878571211209332.

Piller F.T., Vossen A., Ihl C., *From Social Media to Social Product Development: The Impact of Social Media on Co-Creation of Innovation*, Die Unternehmung, 65(1), 1-22, 2012.

Saka-Helmhout A., *Learning from the Periphery: Beyond the Transnational Model*, Critical Perspectives on International Business, 7(1), 48-65, 2011. http://doi.org/10.1108/17422041111103831.
Shenkar O., *Copycats: How Smart Companies Use Imitation to Gain a Strategic Edge*, Strategic Direction, 26(10), 3-5, 2010a. http://doi.org/10.1108/02580541011080474.
Shenkar O., *Imitation is more Valuable than Innovation*, Harvard Business Review, April, 28-29, 2010b.

Teece D., *Explicating Dynamic Capabilities: The Nature and Microfoundations of (Sustainable) Enterprise Performance*, Strategic Management Journal, 28(13), 1319-1350, 2007. http://doi.org/10.1002/smj.640.
Teece D., Leih S., *Uncertainty, Innovation, and Dynamic Capabilities*, California

Management Review, 58(4), 5-12, 2016. http://doi.org/10.1525/cmr.2016.58.4.5.

Tuominen M., Rajala A., Möller K., *Market-Driving versus Market-Driven: Divergent Roles of Market Orientation Business Relationships*, Industrial Marketing Management, 33(3), 207-217, 2004. http://doi.org/10.1016/j.indmarman.2003.10.010.

Utterback J., *Mastering the Dynamics of Innovation: How Companies can Seize Opportunities in The Face of Technological Change*, Harvard Business School Press, Boston, MA, 1994.

Van de Vrande V., De Jong J.P., Vanhaverbeke W., De Rochemont M., *Open Innovation in SMEs: Trends, Motives and Management Challenges*, Technovation, 29(6), 423-437, 2009. http://doi.org/10.1016/j.technovation.2008.10.001.

Von Hippel E., *Democratizing Innovation*, MIT Press, 2005.

Vorhies D.W., Harker M., Rao C.P., *The Capabilities and Performance Advantages of Market-Driven Firms*, European Journal of Marketing, 33(11/12), 1171-1202, 1999. http://doi.org/10.1108/03090569910292339

Zhou K.Z., *Innovation, Imitation, and New Product Performance: The Case of China*, Industrial Marketing Management, 35(3), 394-402, 2006. http://doi.org/10.1016/j.indmarman.2005.10.006.

Chapter 6

HYBRID INNOVATION
IN GLOBAL BUSINESS MANAGEMENT

Paolo Rizzi

ABSTRACT: *An important opportunity for manufacturing firms to strengthen their competitiveness in the global market is modernizing their business model to enable developing hybrid innovation processes. In particular, companies must develop new business models in which both value creation and value capture occur in a value network that can include suppliers, partners, distribution channels, and coalitions. Thus, value networks strive for product innovation, but also for production system innovation to achieve greater flexibility in global business management.*

SUMMARY: 6.1. Introduction. – 6.2. Market structure, enterprise dimension and innovation. – 6.3. Drivers of innovative product and hybrid innovation. – 6.4. Social innovation and sharing economy. – 6.5. Innovation, enterprise and territory.

6.1. Introduction

Questions and challenges related to innovation, enterprise and economic development are diverse and complex. Are innovations derived from large companies that tend to monopolize or from small and medium-sized enterprises that emphasize creativity and the introduction of new products and services?

Is innovation driven by technology or do demand and the new trends of consumption prevail? Which innovation forms are actually more important, the innovations of product or process and organizational ones? Is it technological and innovative development that drives the growth of businesses and economies or vice versa is innovation favoured by the context and therefore by the levels of productivity and profitability of businesses and territories? Finally, does the central role in the development of innovative processes derive from the skills and the capabilities of entrepreneurs and enterprises or the strength of regional and national innovation systems?

To answer these questions, we will refer both to the theoretical and empirical literature on these issues, and to the observation of some recent trends in the development of countries and regions and the change of business in some productive sectors such as the information and communication technology, the tourism and the instrumental goods branch such as the machine tools.

6.2. Market structure, enterprise dimension and innovation

According to the seminal work of Schumpeter (1912, 1942), which introduced the concept of economic development and change, there are two different innovative activity patterns.

In the first, he put the figure of the entrepreneur and the company at the center of attention, where the innovative entrepreneur represents the main actor in the innovative process, and the drivers are many small businesses which offer new products or services and reduce their cost in a market characterized by ease of entry and perfect competition with clearing of over profit.

If before the research of the Austrian economist, innovation was considered as an exogenous and freely accessible element and economic science was focused on the incorporation of technological progress in allocation of resources, with the "first Schumpeter" the innovative phenomenon becomes endogenous, produced by individual operators, and the concept of innovation is affirmed as a "trilogy" process: invention as expression of knowledge and pre-economic fact of individual nature (scientific creativity); innovation, that is the application of the invention to the production process (economic creativity); diffusion as a process by which innovation is communicated and disseminated to members of the economy and spreads among enterprises and production sectors.

In the second pattern (neo-Schumpeter), the innovative phenomenon is the result of the efforts in R&S of large enterprises, the relationship between profit and innovation is overturned, because the domain of large companies is the price to be paid to have a high rate of innovation. Concentrated industrial structures are in this view more encouraged to innovate and the monopoly should therefore be the form of market that ensures more rapid and incisive technological progress. On the contrary, the Arrow hypothesis (1962) assumes that the introduction of innovation in a competitive environment ensures that innovative enterprise has greater profitability and greater competitiveness towards competing companies.

While not allowing generalizations, the results of the theoretical and empirical analysis lead to believing that, within some limits, monopoly has a positive role in stimulating innovative investment and is therefore characterized by "dynamic efficiency" (Vivarelli and Piva, 2005). However, the intrinsic static inefficiency of the monopoly has given rise to antitrust regulations that punish anti-competitive behaviours related to the monopoly or joint exercise of market power. On the other hand, the activities of individual R&S, dispersed over numerous companies, can undergo tight budgetary constraints and generate duplication, thus damaging social welfare. There are therefore desirable agreements between undertakings that share their innovative efforts and emulate the advantages of scale and access to the capital of large enterprises.

The recent dynamics of the large multinationals of information technology demonstrate on the one hand that main innovations today are associated with large size, and on the other hand that the huge profits that these companies record make have determined many antitrust policy interventions. Among the top 10 companies in the world by capitalisation, we find Google, Microsoft, Facebook and Amazon, which derive their value on the market from the innovative quality of their products (mobile phones, computers, e-commerce, search engines, social networks) and the enormous number of customers in the world. But almost all of these companies are also subject to severe interventions and sanctions for the abuse of their market power.

The European Commission fined Google €2.4 billion in 2017 for manipulating search results to favor its own shopping services over those offered by competitors (Toplensky and Ram, 2017). This action stems from a 2010 complaint filed by rival online shopping services, which claimed that Google's search engine unfairly promoted its shopping comparison product, Google Shopping, over their own. The European Commission said that Google abused its market dominance in giving an illegal advantage under EU antitrust rules. Google is also facing antitrust probes in Brazil, and has been under investigation by antitrust regulators in South Korea.

Facebook was accused by the EU Commission of violating the antitrust rules by providing misleading information when assessing the merger with Whatsapp about the ties between the accounts of the two communications systems. If confirmed, the accusation could lead to a fine on Facebook up to 1% of its global turnover (Lashinsky, 2017).

Microsoft has also been sanctioned in the past for antitrust rules both in the United States and Europe. In 2001 Microsoft Corporation was accused, by United States Department of Justice and 20 states, of engaging in anti-competitive practices and abusing its monopoly power on personal computers in its handling of operating system and web browser sales. Bundling its Internet Explorer web browser software with Windows operating system, Microsoft obtained significant advantages in browser competition, restricting the market for competing web browsers (Netscape Navigator and

Opera).The European Commission also fined Microsoft in 2004 for abuse of its dominant position in the market, ordering them to pay €497 million and divulge certain information about their server products and release a version of Microsoft Windows without Windows Media Player (Hines, 2004).

Some authors argue that giants of new technologies should be stopped because, apart from their radical innovations that respond to growing consumer demand, their monopolistic tendency and the consequences of their market power would lead to restrictions on competition and even to the democracy. Amazon would destroy competition in retail, Google and Facebook would endanger the news industry, generally the big 4 radically develop artificial intelligence without considering the adverse effects on employment because new technologies are job-killing. (Taplin, 2017). Antitrust agencies should hinder the power of these corporations, just as they did with AT&T and IBM in the past or Bayer-Monsanto today.

6.3. Drivers of innovative product and hybrid innovation

In addition to the market structure and enterprise size, the economic and managerial studies sought to identify what other factors are capable of stimulating innovative activity in the strategic choices of businesses and in general of countries and regions.

There are four different approaches that have been proposed over the years: scarcity push, demand pull, technology push and endogenous skill bias (Piva and Vivarelli 2005; Christensen et al., 2006; Di Stefano et al., 2011).

The incentive to innovate in the first case (scarcity push) would be justified by the shortage of productive input that becomes more expensive and thus represents a constraint on the expansion of the company's production capacity. Replacing the poor factor with more abundant (or less expensive) inputs would be the first innovative boost, even for the effect on the price of the productive factor. This is the case for oil products and, in general, the production of carbon-based energy, whose physical shortage has caused the dramatic rise in renewable sources and their technologies (solar, wind, biomass) in recent decades.

In the second case, demand sets the direction and the speed of development of the new products or services, which arise from the emergence of new needs to meet. Businesses build their competitive edge by anticipating trends market, that is the expected demand. A classic example of this kind of innovation market-drives is the miniaturization of digital cameras and photo editing software.

Within the hypothesis of technology-push is the offer of firms that find in direct and indirect investment innovative activities to present on the market. The company becomes a promoter of innovation in this case, because the type of inventions/innovations that are introduced are linked to the level of scientific and technological competence achieved by the firm. The Tablet is an obvious example of the technology push approach since it was not designed to meet needs but to create new ones by reconciling Smartphone technology with Notebook technology. In the same perspective Samsung Galaxy in 2012 joined the touchscreen technology and the tablet one to meet the new demands of digital consumers.

The latest explanation (endogenous skill bias) identifies in human capital the decisive element of innovative business choice. The relative growth of skilled workers, which characterized the manufacturing and services sectors in many developed countries in the last decades, stimulate technological progress and the adoption of innovations complementary to the high qualified workers available on the labor market (Piva and Vivarelli, 2005). The role of the "creative class" is central in this view, and the key to economic growth lies in the ability to attract knowledge workers (science and technology employees, architects and engineers, but also art, design and media workers) and to translate that underlying advantage into creative economic outcomes in the form of new ideas, new high-tech businesses and city or country growth (Florida, 2002).

If the first type of innovation (scarcity push) refers to the quantitative constraints on productive inputs, the determinants driven by demand or technology often result as a complementary explanation in the innovative business process, so that the two approaches are therefore not mutually exclusive. So much so that today we introduce the concept of "hybrid" innovation (Rizzi et al., 2012).

In the machine tool industry for example, the innovation process has a threefold hybrid characterization: it is a fundamentally market pull branch, given the decisive stimuli from major international customers and because the industrial users openly ask their own suppliers to intervene on components and machineries, but it also shows technology push features, as highlighted by high R&D expenditure in these producers of instrumental goods (Rizzi et al., 2012). The machine tool firms, given their particular focus on customization, do mainly incremental/continue innovation (Porter 1986), in particular market pull ones (Corniani 2012). The typical case, in fact, is the one of a customer asking for a machine tool with a better performance than the previous ones,thus stimulating the producer to innovate. However, in this industrial sector innovation can be made only by resorting to the so-called technological one, which involves R&D and engineering, explaining the existing network with universities, public research institutes and private laboratories (Germany, North of Italy).

The second hybrid connotation in this sector is connected with the nature of the industries that compete at a global level, thus oriented towards open innovation and imitation and that spread knowledge along with figures about partnerships for innovation activities as suggested by Brondoni (2012), but, at the same time, it shows some characteristics attributable to businesses focused on local competition, such as defensive intellectual property (i.e. confidentiality agreements, patents, R&D expenditure). A possible explanation for this apparent dichotomy could be found in the small dimensions of this kind of firm and the particular nature of this industrial branch, which is a capital goods supplier. In fact, the tendency to protect, as far as possible, every competitive technological advantage that could emerge from the innovation activity is evident but at the same time the source of innovation derives from thick strong networks of partnerships in particular with clients and suppliers. The imitation becomes in this perspective a frequent mode of innovation.

The third, and last, hybrid feature of innovation processes in the machine tool industry is about the propensity for both product innovations (the single machine) and production systems innovations, given the particular flexibility and re-configurability of the machines for industrial automation (Rizzi et.al. 2012). The same new ICT goods are becoming more and more a mix of product or service and process innovations, if not even organizational, as the Amazon case demonstrates widely, having radically transformed commercial sales processes around the world.

The last distinction to mention is that between Blue Ocean versus Red Ocean strategy of innovation (Kim and Mauborgne, 2005). In the first case innovation allows businesses to create new ones in areas where competition does not exist (Smartphone or Bla-bla car) instead of pushing them to fight for the market share in existing sectors. The Cirque du Soleil's case is emblematic in this respect, because it redefines the circus show placing it in a new entertainment segment, blending opera and ballet with circus format and eliminating star performer and animals. The other well-known case is Starbucks, which entered the saturated market of coffee shops by combining differentiation, low cost, strong branding focus and creating a comfortable environment which increases customer time in store.

6.4. Social innovation and sharing economy

Social innovation can be defined as the development and implementation of new ideas (products, services and models) to meet social needs and create new social relationships or collaborations (European Commission 2013).

It represents new responses to pressing social demands, and its object is human well-being both at an individual and collective level. The notion has spread widely in the last years in literature and political agenda, because it may represent a new model of business, but also a model of governance in order to develop and provide new services (Zamagni, 2015).

In advanced economies we still have a tayloristic model of organization that does not allow for a true exploitation of the potential of the digital revolution, while social innovation can be the new model of management, more suited to the dynamics of the post-tayloristic world in which for example intrinsic motivations do play a much greater role than in the previous era.

In general, social innovation could help to solve the current democratic problems of countries which need to combine economic development and well-being with social equity and environmental equilibrium, but also political representativeness and the promotion of civil society, which can support the creation and strengthening of social capital.

In particular in order to overcome the limits of the welfare state (paternalism, economic unsustainability, low respect for differences and identities), social innovation can favor the shift to the welfare society, in which the governance model is driven by the principle of circular subsidiarity (government-economic actors-civil society) and single actors become protagonists in a sort of "generative" welfare (Donati, Magatti). The case of "social street" in Italy is a good example of this form of social innovation: it originates from the experience of the Facebook (FB) group "Residents in Fondazza street – Bologna" started in September 2013 with the purpose of promoting socialization between neighbors resident in the same street in order to build relationships, to share expertise and knowledge, to implement common interest projects, with common benefits from a closer social interaction.

In this perspective, social innovation is closely linked to the development of the sharing economy, which today constitutes a truly evolving galaxy. The first category is sharing in the strict sense, as the common use of resources (physical goods, digital products, space, time or skills). It is the case of couchsurfing.org, a platform that allows itself to be hosted by homeowners, Blablacar, to offer car or passages, Insegnalo to share knowledge. The second form is bartering, that is multilateral exchange of goods and services among individuals - thanks to platforms like Reoose - or companies, such as the Sardex credit trading circuit. Sardex is a complementary currency, able to coexist with the traditional one and create a circuit where Sardinia companies, using a digital billing unit, have the opportunity to support each other, funding mutually without interest. The third category is crowding, a connective action of ideas – thanks to crowdsourcing platforms like Zooppa – or economic resources, with crowdfunding platforms like Kickstarter or Gofundme or Indiegogo. This is participatory financing with groups of people who use their common money to support the efforts of other people or organizations, generally non-profit. There are several forms of crowdfunding: crowd equity or investing in return for equity/securities; crowd lending or investing in return for repayment at some agreed upon rate of interest; crowd patronage or investing in return for benefits from a proposed product/service; crowd charity or investing without expectation of additional material or financial returns (Gleasure and Feller, 2016).

A latest category of sharing economy is "making" and includes all forms of network production, by informal groups of enthusiasts dedicated to building or repairing objects without the help of experts (Do It Yourself With Others) to the most organized forms of manufacture digital (Hackerspaces and FabLab).

The effects of these new forms of social innovation and sharing economy in the model of management and business or sector performance are extremely pervasive.

Considering the tourism market (Montargot, 2016; Brondoni, 2016), the diffusion of services provided on a peer-to-peer or shared usage basis, creates competitive alternatives to traditional touristic activities. The spread of digital distribution platforms and access through mobile media, and the new channels of private accommodation (Airbnb and Couchsurfing), transportation (Uber and Blablacar), dining (EatWith and Feastly), travel planning (Vayable and VoomaGo) represents a sort of progressive disintermediation of the traditional industrial structure of the tourism sector , pushed by the current more autonomous approach to travel consumptions but also by structural reasons, both economic (low cost) and technological (easy access and simpler forms of mobility and accomodation). The result is the drastic downsizing of traditional travel agencies and tour operators, in favour of on-line agencies and low-cost providers selling their product on the Internet, and non-professionals who decide to rent out their house/apartment or rooms/beds to supplement their main income.

On one hand, the opportunities deriving from this new forms of sharing economy for tourism nowadays allow for enlarging the market to less visited destinations, more users and suppliers, more consumer options and tourism experiences. On the other hand , the impact in terms of entrepreneurship and innovation should not hide the spread of new risks in terms of minor protection of consumers, loss of tax revenue and in general the insurgence of unfair competition for traditional more regulated firms and operators (Salvioni, 2016; Rizzi and Graziano, 2017).

6.5. Innovation, enterprise and territory

According to a large economic and management literature, innovation has a key role in improving businesses' performances in terms of profitability, efficiency and market share (Rosenberg, 1991; Chen et al., 2009; Hall et al., 2008 and 2009; Huang, 2011). But the single firm needs new forms of "networking" for survival and competitiveness, mainly regarding R&D and innovative process. In fact, cooperation in innovation and product development fields turns out to be very effective (Valle and Vázquez-Bustelo, 2009), in particular in industrial districts (Chiarvesio et al., 2004), and in medium-tech and high-tech productions.

Obviously, these paths of collaboration depend on many factors, such as the size of the business, its geographical location, the spillovers of the territorial system.

First of all, the firm dimensions affects the kind of technological innovation, which can be distinguished into product innovation and technology acquisition (Conte and Vivarelli, 2005), the former strictly bonded to formal R&D (made mainly by big enterprises, which carry it out internally), while the latter is primarily linked to process innovation, and achieved through technology acquisition or cooperation agreements.

A second factor is geographical location, primarily at a regional level, which includes elements such as infrastructures, business environment, clusters and public services that could determine significant differences between the performances of firms from different regions (Piva and Vivarelli 2005).

Finally, innovation, especially if characterized as internal formal R&D, allows for the creation of products more capable of meeting market needs, and also produces highly positive spillovers and synergies (Valle and Vázquez-Bustelo, 2009), also from the point of view of employee numbers and qualifications (Piva and Vivarelli, 2009). Therefore, human capital turns out to be one of the most important hallmarks of firms in innovative processes, significantly determining performances, in terms of turnover, profitability and productivity (Bottazzi et al. 2008); at the same time, also the business organization can benefit from innovation (Azadegan and Wagner, 2011; Oke, 2013), which helps in giving birth to the so-called "competitive triangle" (human capital development, R&D, and business organization) that can generate a virtuous circle for the businesses.

The relationship between innovation, technical progress and economic (regional or national) development is increasingly bi-directional, because if the role of innovation on the territory is clear and confirmed by a huge series of empirical studies, the effect of competitiveness of local/national systems on the innovative business performance appears in the same way consolidated (Rizzi et al., 2015, Ciciotti, 2009).

In this second perspective, the regional systems of innovation represents the other side of the coin, focusing on the role that territories can have in the innovation process. Technological districts and platforms, innovative milieu, regional innovation systems become the most effective incubators in the current globalized economy that help businesses cultivate and fertilize their innovative processes (Ciciotti, 2009). The success of innovative districts in some areas such as Silicon Valley, Baden-Wurttemberg and Emilia Romagna shows the relevance of a systemic approach to innovation (Etzkowitz and Etzkowitz, 2015), for which enterprise and their clusters represent only one of the explanations for (local) development, recognizing the positive role played in the process of technology and skill transfer by geographical proximity and the consequent possibilities that both static and dynamic external economies may be generated.

In this perspective, the concept of the Triple Helix of university-industry-government relationships initiated in the 1990s by Etzkowitz, explains the shift from a dominating industry-government model to a growing triadic relationship in the contemporary knowledge economy. This thesis also confirms the growing hybridisation of elements from business, research center and university, and public intervention to generate new institutional and social formats for the production, transfer and application of knowledge. Territorial innovation systems are in this view capable of efficiently integrating skills at firm level and the supporting infrastructures and other intermediate innovative institutions which in general characterise innovative clustering in which the individual operators form tight and interdependent connections. Concepts like collective learning, learning regional, social capital become the main factors that drive and promote enterprises in the complex effort of innovation.

But it should not be forgotten that the central role in tackling the new forms of hybridization of contemporary innovative processes, between social innovation and sharing economy, technology push and demand pull, product and process innovation, small enterprise and multinational, is always attributable to entrepreneurs and their creative and competitive capacity.

References

Azadegan A., Wagner S., *Industrial Upgrading, Exploitative Innovations and Explorative Innovations*, International Journal of Production Economics, 130 (1), 2011. https://doi.org/10.1016/j.ijpe.2010.11.007.

Bottazzi G., Secchi A., Tamagni F., *Productivity, Profitability and Financial Performance*, Industrial and Corporate Change. Oxford University Press, 2008. https://doi.org/10.1093/icc/dtn027.

Brondoni, S.M., *Innovation, Imitation and Global Competition*. Paper presented at the 33rd AISRe Conference, Rome 13th -15th September 2012.

Brondoni S.M., *Global Tourism Management. Mass, Experience and Sensations Tourism*, Symphonya. Emerging Issues in Management, n. 1, 2016. http://dx.doi.org/10.4468/2016.1.02brondoni.

Chen Y.-S., Lin M.-J.J., Chang C.-H., *The Positive Effects of Relationship Learning and Absorptive Capacity on Innovation Performance and Competitive Advantage in Industrial Markets*, Industrial Marketing Management, 38(2): 152-158, 2009. https://doi.org/10.1016/j.indmarman.2008.12.003.

Chiarvesio M., Di Maria E., Micelli S., *From Local Networks of SMEs to Virtual Districts? Evidence from Recent Trends in Italy*, Research Policy, Elsevier, 2004. doi:10.1016/j.respol.2004.08.009.

Christensen C.M., Bower J.L., *Customer Power, Strategic Investment, and the Failure of Leading Firms*, Strategic Management Journal 17: 197-218 1996. www.jstor.org/stable/2486845.

Christensen C.M., Cook S., Hall T., *What Customers Want from Your Products*, Harvard Business Review, 2006.

Ciciotti E., *Innovation, Technological Diffusion and Regional* Development, in Scienze Regionali, 3, 2009.

Conte A., Vivarelli M., *One or Many Knowledge Production Function? Mapping Innovative Activity Using Microdata*, IZA DP No. 1878, 2005.

Corniani M., *Global Innovation and Competitive Value Analysis*, Paper presented at the 33rd AISRe Conference, Rome, 13th-15th September 2012.

Di Stefano G., Gambardella A., Verona G., *Technology Push and Demand Pull Perspectives in Innovation Studies: Current Findings and Future Directions*, Working Paper, KITeS Bocconi University, 2011.

Etzkowitz H. and Etzkowitz A., *Beyond Austerity: A Neo-Schumpeterian Regional Innovation Strategy*, RSA Conference, Piacenza, 25-27 May 2015.

European Commission, *Guide to Social Innovation, Regional and Urban Policy*, February, Bruxelles, 2013.

Florida R., *The Rise of the Creative Class*, Basic Books, New York, 2002.

Gleasure R., Feller J., *Emerging Technologies and the Democratisation of Financial Services: A Metatriangulation of Crowdfunding Research*, Information and Organization, 26(4), 2016. http://dx.doi.org/10.1016/j.infoandorg.2016.09.001.

Hall B.H., Lotti F., Mairesse J., *Employment, Innovation and Productivity: Evidence from Italian Microdata*, Industrial and Corporate Change, 17, 813-839, 2008. doi:10.1093/icc/dtn022.

Hines M., *Microsoft Pays EU in Full*, CNET News.com, July 2, 2004.

Huang K.-F., *Technology Competencies in Competitive Environment*, Journal of Business Research, 64(2): 172-179, 2011. https://doi.org/10.1016/j.jbusres.2010.02.003.

Kim W.C., Mauborgne R., *Blue Ocean Strategy: How to Create Uncontested Market Space and Make the Competition Irrelevant*, Boston: Harvard Business School Press, 2005.

Lashinsky A., *Should We Use Antitrust Law Against Google or Facebook?*, Fortune, July 17, 2017.

Montargot N., *Digitalisation Advances and Hospitality Service Encounters*, Symphonya. Emerging Issues in Management, n. 1, 2016. http://dx.doi.org/10.4468/2016.1.07montargot.

Oke A., *Linking Manufacturing Flexibility to Innovation Performance in Manufacturing Plants*, International Journal of Production Economics, 143(2) June 2013. doi:10.1016/j.ijpe.2011.09.014.

Piva M., Vivarelli M., *Innovation and Employment: Evidence from Italian Microdata*, Journal of Economics, 2005. doi 10.1007/s00712-005-0140-z.

Piva M., Vivarelli M., *The Role of Skills as a Major Driver of Corporate R&D*, International Journal of Manpower, 30, 835-52, 2009.

Porter M.E., *Competition in Global Industries*, Harvard Business School Press, Boston, MA, 1986.

Rizzi P., *The Role of Innovation in the Firms Performance: the South Italy Case*, AIV Associazione Italiana di Valutazione Conference, Genova 17-18 aprile 2015.

Rizzi P., Graziano P., *Regional Perspective on Tourism Global Trend*, Symphonya. Emerging Issues in Management, Special Issue, n. 3, 11-26, 2017 DOI: http://dx.doi.org/10.4468/2017.3.02rizzi.graziano.

Rizzi P., Campanini F., Costa S., *Hybrid Innovation: the Case of The Italian Machine Tool Industry*, Symphonya. Emerging Issues in Management, n. 1, 2012. http://dx.doi.org/10.4468/2012.1.04rizzi.campanini.costa.

Rizzi P., Graziano P., Dallara A., *The Regional Competitiveness: an Alternative Approach*, in Riss Rivista Internazionale di Scienze Sociali, International Review of Social Sciences, 307-336, 3/2015.

Rosenberg N., *Technology and the Pursuit of Economic Growth*, Cambridge University Press, 1991.

Salvioni D.M., *Hotel Chains and the Sharing Economy in Global Tourism*, Symphonya. Emerging Issues in Management, n. 1, 31-44, 2016. http://dx.doi.org/10.4468/2016.1.04salvioni.

Schumpeter J.A., *The Theory of Economic Development*, Harvard University Press, Cambridge, 1934 (first edition 1912).

Schumpeter J.A., *Capitalism, Socialism and Democracy*, George Allen & Unwin London, 1942.

Taplin J., *Can the Tech Giants Be Stopped?*, The Wall Street Journal, July 15-16, 2016.

Toplensky R. and Ram A., *What the EU's €2.4bn Antitrust Fine Means for Google*, Financial Times, June 27, 2017.

Toplensky R., *Google Faces Big Fine in First EU Case Against Search Practices*, Financial Times, June 16, 2017.

Valle S., Vázquez-Bustelo D., *Concurrent Engineering Performance: Incremental versus Radical Innovation*, International Journal of Production Economics, 119 (1), 2009. doi:10.1016/j.ijpe.2009.02.002.

Zamagni S., *Social Innovation and Inclusive Development: The Specific Role of Territory*, RSA Conference, Piacenza, 25-27 May 2015.

Chapter 7
GLOBAL FIRMS AND CROSS-CULTURAL MANAGEMENT

Federica Codignola

ABSTRACT: *Cross-cultural and multinational challenges in global business management have become a fundamental theme in recent times. As firms continue to expand across borders and the global marketplace becomes progressively more reachable for small and large businesses alike, the current scenario offers increasing opportunities to working globally. Nevertheless, numerous cases of failure exist linked to the management's incapacity to identify cross-cultural issues and to appropriately and effectively deal with these. As the current global scenario is becoming increasingly complex, global managers will have to become more perceptive and responsive to the challenges and risks deriving from the multicultural backgrounds of countries they deal with or work in. Disregarding cultural complexities whilst managing global firms can be perilous. Embracing a county's cultural diversity may or may not be a factor of success for a firm. However, not understanding and not exploiting such diversity will undoubtedly increase the possibility of failure or stagnation.*

SUMMARY: 7.1. Global firms and cultural environment. – 7.2. Cultural environment and cross-cultural management. – 7.3. The role of Hofstede's organizational culture dimensions on corporate culture. – 7.4. National culture and corporate culture. – 7.5. Conclusion.

7.1. Global firms and cultural environment

Cross-cultural and multinational challenges in global business management have become a fundamental theme in recent times. As firms continue to expand across borders and the global marketplace becomes progressively more reachable for small and large businesses alike, the current scenario offers increasing opportunities to working globally. Nevertheless, numerous cases of failure exist linked to the management's incapacity to identify cross-cultural issues and to appropriately and effectively deal with these. As the current global scenario is becoming increasingly complex, global managers will have to become more perceptive and responsive to the challenges and risks deriving from the multicultural backgrounds of countries they deal with or work in. Disregarding cultural complexities whilst managing global firms can be perilous. Embracing a county's cultural diversity may or may not be a factor of success for a firm. However, not understanding and not exploiting such diversity will undoubtedly increase the possibility of failure or stagnation.

Firms dealing with the progression of globalisation must face unstable environmental context. Each of them requires a definite approach and system of interaction. This said, habitually one does not take into account that amongst the different variables that identify the environmental context it is the dominating culture that plays a primary, decisive role. Therefore, a study of the cultural variable could be an effective tool that sustains strategic analyses carried out by businesses today. An in-depth knowledge of the dominant cultures featuring in diverse environmental contexts can in fact help businesses decrease the prevalence of uncertainties originating in approaches to unfamiliar markets. Additionally, it can facilitate the identification of the most appropriate solutions in the resolution or simplification of conflicts that occur during inter-organizational relations. The relevance of cultural differences is normally more evident during the implementation phase of international alliances, namely, when different cultures first meet and cultural shock may ensue. When the cultural orientation of the subjects involved varies widely, this shock might have a wide-ranging impact including negative consequences for the firm's involvement, the business environment, and the performance of the partners.

In fact, being competitive in a globalized background means – even from a merely managerial perspective – that one can no longer center exclusively on earning capability and profitability. Instead, one must also focus on knowledge and research. In order to implement significant changes on the one hand while attaining better competitiveness on the other, one must be capable to *know*. This means knowing not only how to obtain information, but also how to interpret and manage it optimally, especially in a global environment. Knowledge and profitability are therefore two interdependent variables – knowledge produces the foundation that permits one to reach a higher level of efficacy and efficiency on an entrepreneurial scale; profitability increases and in so doing acquires a gainful position in terms of the business' competition.

On the basis of three factors embedded in the process of the globalisation of companies and industries, external environment must be viewed as an unstable factor that is exposed to variations over the course of time. The first factor consists of new technologies (technological breakthroughs in robotics, sensors and high-performance computing, social media, etc.)

which on the one hand have reduced the initial obstacle; on the other they have improved competition between businesses, and in so doing – in terms of volume and intensity – demand. The second factor concerns the creation and the exploitation of new materials (i.e., natural polymers, etc.) and the high level of customization on offer. In this case the results can also be identified by taking note of the increasing number of equivalent or rival products. Lastly, the third factor concerns the growing number of export markets, their distance, their financial difficulties and exchange rate complications (see for example the 2007 banking crisis, the 2009 financial crisis in the United States and those of 2010 and 2015 in Spain, Ireland, and Greece). The combination of variables such as these has enlarged the existing number of barriers between firms working at the international level. These barriers can only grow when cultural asymmetries prevail between nations and important organizations.

In sum, globalisation may alter the role of culture and cultural evolution within society. Yet, while some literature speaks of *conflict between cultures* (Harrison, 2006; Harrison and Huntington, 2000), one should focus instead on how cultures can learn one from the other, or even offer inspiration so as to render these differences productive (Sodeberg and Holden, 2002). Other researchers have investigated whether the emergence of a *worldwide culture* (Lechner and Boli, 2005) or *global culture* (Bird and Stevens, 2003) is not slowly cancelling out, or at very least changing, the existence of national cultures.

The fact to use the cross-cultural management theoretical framework in order to better observe a globalized background in which the businesses operating are *market-driven oriented* (Brondoni, 2002; Lambin, 2000) makes the subject of cultural environment very significant, in particular in relation to business culture.

7.2. Cultural environment and cross-cultural management

Cross-cultural management analyses the behavior of individuals from different cultural origins in firms; it also compares and evaluates cultural disparities that exist between firms from differing cultural backgrounds.

Research on the topic of cross-cultural management originates in process of globalisation in markets, businesses, and competitive advancements. For instance, at a managerial level globalisation has brought top level firms players to face and interact with individuals from differing cultures. They must constantly strive to increase their personal skill and strategic capability in order to relate with individuals whose behavior is conditioned by different cultural priorities. According to Peterson, business culture in a globalized context requires executive figures able to maneuver in this reality. Yet, Peterson also emphasizes the limits of a merely theoretical training as opposed to the true value of experience and knowledge gained *in the field* – or by working in close contact with individuals from different cultures and above all by learning to recognize or tolerate the other party's priorities when common objectives are set (Peterson, 2004). In fact, forcing individuals from different cultural contexts to conform to one's own standard is not only complicated but above all counterproductive. By using the history of colonialism as an example, Griswold shows how all great powers attempted to inflict their own behavioral norms on existing standards, and how this approach ended up in constant failure. Similarly, a business or organizational culture that attempts to force its own cultural rules on its employees, *co-makers* or stakeholders who already have their own norms could easily meet with critical difficulties (Griswold, 2008).

Studies on the subject of cross-cultural management consequently show a kind of insurgence against the technological paradigms that dominated until the end of the Seventies and have since been directed towards the understanding of the features that affect the responses of a definite social group to external factors. To be more accurate, in terms of business management cross-cultural management studies help illustrate the behavior of individuals hailing from diverse cultural contexts within the internal background of a firm, and cultural discrepancies that subsist between organizations from different cultural backgrounds.

Nevertheless, in order better to observe the effects of culture on business and commercial interaction with the global markets, one must take a step back and examine the progression of theories on culture. In the 19th century Galton observed how *cultural groups* could not consider themselves independent one from another because the process of *cultural transfusion* between groups produced significant, enduring relations (Lindridge, 2005). Afterwards, researchers focused on the paradigm of a more polarized but far broader culture, even though a strongly comparative approach to diverse cultures was maintained. In the Fifties one spoke of *cultural ecology* in a conceptualization of culture as a phenomenon that has evolved in relation to the natural setting (Steward, 1955). During the Seventies the most important theoretical developments in cultural research took into account the studies of Geertz – according to whom culture should be anchored to the definite context of *social life* (Geertz, 1973) – and those of Keesing, who distinguished between the *ecological theory of culture* (according to which cultures are understood as adaptable systems), and the theory of *ideational culture* (according to which cultures are viewed as cognitive, structural and symbolic systems) (Keesing, 1974). In the Eighties

Hofstede's preeminent study *Culture's Consequences* gave great impetus to empirical analyses of the concept of culture and its variables (Hofstede, 1980). In 2001 the same Hofstede realized a second phase of his study, on which several authors subsequently based their research (Hofstede, 2001).

First, one finds the significance of Hofstede's observations in the fact that the concept of culture was studied in terms of straightforward, easily measurable features that assume the nation-state and national culture as the key units of analysis. Secondly, Hofstede defined the main strategic significance of cultural values in terms of a logic based on the optimal management of managerial behavior. Finally, the author undoubtedly contributed to enhancing a consciousness and understanding of cultural diversities. He delineates culture as the "*collective psychological programming of people in a certain environment. Culture is not an individual characteristic; it involves a certain number of people who have been conditioned through the same education and the same life experiences*" (Hofstede, Hofstede, Minkov, 1991, p. 4). In the United States, for instance, notwithstanding the fact that there is manifest heterogeneity between the genetic origins of the population, the *psychological programming* – of which the author speaks – of the population is a common denominator and is visible in the phenomenon of the *melting pot,* in which originally different cultures amalgamate – and in this case, under the influence of the education system (Hofstede, Hofstede, Minkov, 1991).

As a result, if individuals with different genes get the same education and are subjected to the same cultural rules, they will mostly feature the same ideas, values, and behavioral patterns. The collective component therefore becomes a tool that is crucial to the dissemination of a sort of subconscious conditioning to which individuals are subjected.

Culture could appear as a process that is invisible from the outside and is consequently difficult to describe. Yet the author shows that this arises through specific categories, and states that the capacity to communicate between cultures comes from knowledge, awareness, and personal experience (Hofstede, Hofstede, Minkov, 1991).

The examination of these phenomena is a relatively complex exercise, first of all because many of the essential *values* are absorbed by individuals in a subconscious manner, and secondly because of the difficulties encountered in the understanding of that which is reported by different subjects. One of the key functions of culture consists in its aptitude to act as a filter between individuals and the external world, thereby affecting decisions, the majority of which can thus be traced to a specific background. In this sense, alongside Hofstede's classification of the *five dimensions*, is Hall's classification that differentiate the cultural context according to the *high-low context* (Hall, 1977).

7.3. The role of Hofstede's organizational culture dimensions on corporate culture

The process linked to the above-mentioned preferences and values directs all individuals to realize a personal system that aims to evaluate situations in a different way or give different elements more weight than others. The way in which each individual creates this system is strongly affected by five dimensions (Hofstede, 1980, 1991) that are based on four fundamental problems which society faces: social inequality; the relationship between the individual and the group; social implications of gender; and managing of uncertainty inherent in economic and social processes. Through these dimensions, Hofstede discloses the differences between cultures.

The first dimension is that of the *power distance*: here one determines the degree of acceptance of power in institutions or organizations. The acceptance is widespread when the subjects composing an organization accept the implementation of power even if it is not evenly distributed. Circumstances of this sort are more recurrent in countries where a strong middle class has created stable conditions (i.e., Italy) or in some African countries, in which the ruling power is passively accepted. In Germany and the United States the power distance in terms of authoritarian power is low if we consider the value given to the ideal of equality (everyone can attain a position of authority). Transferring this hypothesis to the precise context of a business, in a typical hierarchical system the distance from authority between a superior and his subordinate becomes the difference between the scale to which the subject with a greater level of authority can affect the behavior of the subordinate worker and *vice versa* (Mulder, 1971). Mulder defined authority as *"the potential to determine or direct the behavior of other people"* and *power distance* or *distance from authority* as the *"degree of inequality between subjects with greater or lesser powers within the same social system"* (Mulder, 1971, p. 31). The evaluation of power distance is not only shaped by the social environment of the two subjects, but also by their respective national cultures. The propensity of the stronger subject to uphold or increase distances and the inclination of the less powerful subject to reduce them thus produce a kind of balance. Generally speaking, this occurs in a forced impact on the work environment and consequently, on the firm's performance.

Firms are in fact represented by their business culture: organizations with dramatic hierarchical pyramids and polarized authority structures, in which managerial policies and the exchange of information is limited to a privileged few or is characterized by discriminatory divisions in the staff body, are representative of cultures in which there is a greater distance from power. At the opposite extreme, however, there are those firms in which the leadership management is flexible and open to discussion, information is accessible to all, and the decision-making structure is decentralized. For instance, in cultures where there is a greater distance from authority, if a subordinate subject is victim to an incidence of a superior's abuse of authority, the subordinate party would not even take into account the option of resolving the issue, whereas, in instances where there is less distance between authority and subordinate subjects, the latter contemplate the option of using definite institutional tools to protest, even within the firm.

The second dimension relates to the *uncertainty avoidance* (Cyert and March, 1992). In this case how an organization or a firm perceives threats originating in external situations or factors, and the manner in which it tries to avoid them, are measured. Uncertainty about the future is a representative factor that affects business organizations, and if exaggerated, can develop high levels of anxiety. For this reason individuals try to connect forces through the field of *technology, law* and *religion*. By means of technology one is able to limit uncertainties originated by nature; through laws one can control unforeseeable behavior on the part of other subjects; in religion one gets the moral support that helps one accept the very same uncertainties.

The condition of *poor uncertainty management* is often seen in contexts in which there is a greater tendency to take risks and there is a strong, direct connection between risk and performance (i.e., Scandinavian and English-speaking nations, the United States and developing countries). At the other extreme, situations of *strong uncertainty management* are recurrent in contexts that are not characterized by a tendency towards risk taking, and in which rules play an important role in a complete irrefutable vision (i.e., Japan and Latin America). Distancing oneself from uncertainties leads to the realization of a greater degree of separation from the factor of ambiguity. In fact, those cultures sited furthest from the influence of uncertainty are formed of institutions, organizational structures, and relations that focus on making future events foreseeable and easy to understand. On the contrary, cultures with a lower tolerance of uncertainty are usually characterized by a weaker sense of urgency. In a mirror image replication of the social concept of defending itself from uncertainties with the tools of technology, law, and religion, these organizations make use of *technology, rules*, and *rituals* (Cyert and March, 1992). More specifically, if technology assists us to get easily foreseeable short term results, rules can help reduce the uncertainty caused by the unforeseeable nature of *stakeholders*. Nevertheless, such rules only make sense when they are respected and are consistent with the values of the individuals whose behavior is subject to this form of conditioning. If similar conditions are not respected, the distance between those who create the rules and those who are obliged to follow them can only increase.

Lastly, *rituals* are used in order to stay away from the feeling of uncertainty when considering the future. In business these rituals are represented by integration courses for managers, meetings and their ceremonious aspects, language, reports, planning and control systems, the inclusion of expert consultants, computer simulations, etc. (Bocock, 1974).

The third dimension, or that of *individualism/collectivism*, quantifies the level of interaction between individuals and an organization. Those belonging to individualistic societies (i.e., English-speaking nations) show greater reticence towards the construction of relationships, because individuals originally from these nations are inclined to give more value to their own personal time and consequently they pursue a merely opportunistic logic. For example, when they begin a relationship with an external partner, they almost invariably do so with the purpose of obtaining these partners' knowledge. Conversely, in a collectivist context a strong inclination towards team work, exchange, and interaction triumphs. A most typical example of this attitude is the Japanese concept of collectivity, in which individuals learn from one another. A person who has received an education and cultural or social imprint of a traditionalist nature will hence experience great difficulty in thinking of himself as an isolated element. Whereas Western culture considers an individual as something that is entirely separate from society and culture, the Chinese tradition (Fang, 2006; Ghauri and Fang, 2001) associates the concept of the individual to the social and cultural environment in terms of an inclusive logic, so that it is such environment that gives meaning to the existence of an individual (Riesmann, Glazer, Denney, 2001).

Business logic then is extremely important in regard to group decision. In Western nations, where all enjoy the privilege to express themselves, individuals try to condition the decision to be taken by emphasizing their personal opinion. According to Confucian philosophy – which still dominates in Japan (Ock, 1988; Tipton, 2009) –, the majority has to concur on each phase of the discussion during the decision-making process, until a final consensus is achieved.

The fourth dimension (*masculinity/femininity*) follows a number of behavioral models and managerial styles adopted in some organizations. Countries with a *feminine* culture (Sweden, Norway, Finland and the Netherlands) show a number of features, such as a minimal difference between men and women's salaries, many women in top level executive positions, decisions made by the group, employees who do not tolerate their companies meddling in their private lives and are more oriented towards a diminution of work hours than towards a salary rise. These nations have then a marked competitive advantage in particular fields such as the bio-chemistry, consulting, and service industry sectors. Conversely, nations with a *male* culture (United States, England, Germany, Japan and Italy), place far more emphasis on decisions taken by the individual, firms strong-ly interfere in the private lives of employees on the part of firms and their competitive strength emerges predominantly in a high degree of specializa-tion in heavy industry.

Finally, the fifth dimension is that of *short* and *long-term orientation*. Firms belonging to the first category are characterized by a strong tendency towards personal stability, respect for tradition, and the defense of reputa-tion, where organizations from the latter category show features such as perseverance, moderation, and a strong sense of respect for hierarchical orders.

Today Hofstede's work is perceived as pertaining to an early cross-cultural research stage essentially aimed to show that culture matters in all in organization and managerial studies. Yet the contexts wherein cross-cultural management takes places have become even more variegated and complicated. As a substitute of the expatriate manager acting as the bump-er for a firm or department, workers nowadays deal with swapping, com-municating virtually across the world, or interrelating in multinational and detached work teams. Cross-cultural management has then become a standard component of a firm's daily reality. In fact, the growth of Internet usage have truly changed overall circumstances – intercultural communica-tion barriers caused by differences in norms, values, etc., expressions and behavioral patterns (i.e., attitudes, communicational forms, languages, etc.) (Spencer-Rodgersa and McGovern, 2002), dissimilar interpretations of so-cial and power roles, stereotypes, etc. (Delecta and Raman, 2015), the cir-cumstances have truly changed. Cross-cultural management, along with globalisation – has recently highlighted a need for a global culture where anyone could effortlessly access and reach information that permits her or him to recognize and comprehend the socio-cultural background of his co-workers (Canavilhas, 2015).

7.4. National culture and corporate culture

Alongside with a critical and significant turn in managerial literature (Al-vesson and Deetz, 2000), the specific framework of cross-cultural manage-ment has also experienced a critical turn. For instance, *critical cross-cultural management* has specifically focused on interpersonal micro-levels (i.e., *sta-*

tus differences, degrees of power, etc.) (Primecz, Mahadevan and Romani, 2016).

However, at a more general level, in order better to examine *cross-cultural management* theory, an interesting approach distinguishes *cross-cultural research* from *cross-national research*. The first analytical branch – which we have dealt with so far – focuses on the recognition of similarities and differences of cultures in environmental areas of greater or smaller dimensions. The branch of cross-national research is instead explicitly oriented towards an observation of cultures in Western nations. In this case particular weight is given to the theory that expounds the existence of a close relation between organizations' orientations and the culture of the environment in which they operate. Also included in the theoretical field of cross-national research are those studies aimed at the analysis and identification of those variables that can contribute to the production of levels of competitive advantage that are typical of all national contexts. One of these variables is culture itself.

Porter showed that an avoidance of uncertainty or risk taking – as mentioned above with regard to Hofstede's dimensions – could correspond to a major obstacle to the growth of certain sectors in the economy of a nation (Porter, 1990). In Switzerland, for instance, this avoidance to uncertainty has prevented the development of investments in activities that required a greater propensity toward risk taking (i.e., biotechnologies). However, if in contexts such as these an orientation towards collectivity prevails, individuals tend towards a consolidation of those relations formed in their own environment (i.e., Japan). In this way the interaction between individuals produces the foundation for a greater degree of open-mindedness towards the concept of progress and a greater impetus towards innovation, a fundamental step that allows a nation to set up a position of competitive advantage over others. Furthermore, van den Bosch and van Prooijen examined national culture by integrating Porter's diamond model into Hofstede's dimensional model. They showed how national culture is a variable that has the ability to affect a nation's competitive advantage, since the level of uncertainty management and the drive towards collectivity – both variables that depend on culture – can define the degree of openness to change and a nation's aptitude for inter-national relations (van den Bosch, van Prooijen, Porter, 1992).

In the past, the relation between national and corporate culture was mostly ignored. For instance, Hickson (et al.) showed that corporate culture could affirm itself in any cultural context (Horváth, McMillan, Azumi, Hickson, 1976). However, in 1980 – as previously mentioned – Hofstede identified a clear predominance of national culture over that of corporate culture. For his part, in 1986 Adler asserted that national culture did not often emerge in corporate organizations, because the culture of a corporate body filtered, modified or even cancelled out traits of national culture, thereby rendering all interested subjects homogenous, despite their different cultural origins (Adler, 1986). Only afterwards – thanks to several theoretical and empirical analyses supported by Hofstede's results – did cultural factors deriving from the nations in which businesses had established themselves assume a position of greater importance. In order to reach these conclusions, the preliminary hypothesis maintained that both national culture and corporate culture affect the behavior of subjects belonging to a firm or organization in an interdependent manner. As a result a corporate body must not be viewed as a simple receptor for external stimuli, but rather as an entity that develops its own culture within and together with that of the environmental context, interacting with the latter and influencing its creation and adaptation. From this perspective, a business is no longer merely a constituent element within the environmental context. Rather, it represents an essential factor in the characterization of development in a specific area or country.

Furthermore, a re-conceptualization of *localism* must also be taken into account. This relies to a firm's motivations for establishing itself in a certain area, not with the aim of taking advantage of factorial benefits, but with the objective of taking advantage of the opportunities that arise from the circularity process, that is, the circulation of knowledge and the chance to learn from it. In order to achieve conditions such as these, known as *economies of agglomeration*, businesses operating in these areas employ collective investments to build up truly collective centers designed for specific activities in the values chain. The concept of *neo-localism* is therefore developed through the capability of the firm itself to interact with the culture of the relating context. The nature of the resources that the firm intends to acquire when a situation of this type occurs therefore refers to an increase in existing degrees of awareness and knowledge. For this reason the firm cannot appropriate these resources through traditional means; rather, it must establish and manage a valid process of interaction with the adjacent environment. For this reason, one can employ of the notion of *grounding*, an idea inherent in the process in hand, and can produce technical opportunities such as joint ventures. In this case the degree and amount of interaction between partners originating in diverse cultures is of primary significance.

Obviously, cultural diversities can produce conflict when interactions and collaborations between subjects belonging to culturally different contexts come into being. Yet, such variations should be regarded as essential elements for a significant foundation in change management.

7.5. Conclusion

In conclusion, some of the early theoretical approaches to cross-cultural relations explained the concept of *culture* generally as a communicational obstacle that can cause difficulties to business. Diverse approaches, attitudes, languages, values, etc., can indeed represent a vast barrier in a multicultural business environment. Nevertheless, more recent literature viewed cultural diversity should be viewed as an opportunity that provides rooms for innovative solutions (Hoecklin, 1995). These opportunities in fact lead to a privileged entrance to new markets, open to knowledge exchange, help develop innovative marketing and managerial strategies. From then onwards, global firms have interpreted cultural diversities as a competitive advantage (Luo, 2016).

Holden and Søderberg have best captured the essence of these substantial changes that have affected the global business context, when they describe cross-cultural management as a tool that can *"facilitate and direct synergetic interaction and learning at interfaces, where knowledge, values and experience are transferred into multicultural domains of implementation"* (Holden and Søderberg, 2002).

References

Adler N.J., *From the Atlantic to the Pacific Century: Cross-Cultural Management Reviewed*, Journal of Management, 12, 1986. http://dx.doi.org/10.1177/014920638601200210.

Alvesson M., Deetz S., *Doing Critical Management Research*, Sage, London, 2000.

Arnett J.J, *The Psychology of Globalization*, American Psychologist, 57 (10), 2002. http://dx.doi.org/10.1037//0003-066X.57.10.774.

Bird A., Fang T., *Editorial: Cross-Cultural Management in the Age of Globalization*, International Journal of Cross-Cultural Management, 9 (139), 2009. http://dx.doi.org/10.1177/1470595809335713.

Bird A., Stevens M.J., *Toward an Emergent Global Culture and the Effects of Globalization on Obsolescing National Cultures*, Journal of International Management, 9 (4), 2003. http://dx.doi.org/10.1016%2Fj.intman.2003.08.003.

Bocock R., *Ritual in Industrial Society*, Allen&Unwin, London, 1974.

Brondoni S.M., *Global Markets and Market-Space Competition*, Symphonya. Emerging Issues in Management (symphonya.unimib.it), 1, 28-42, 2002. http://dx.doi.org/10.4468/2002.1.03brondoni.

Brondoni S.M., *Managerial Economics and Global Competition*, in Symphonya. Emerging Issues in Management (symphonya.unimib.it), 1, 14-38, 2005. http://dx.doi.org/10.4468/2005.1.02brondoni.

Brondoni S.M., *Market-Driven Management, Competitive Space and Global Networks*, Symphonya. Emerging Issues in Management (symphonya.unimib.it), 1, 14-27, 2008. http://dx.doi.org/10.4468/2008.1.02brondoni.

Brondoni S.M., *Intangibles, Global Networks & Corporate Social Responsibility*, Symphonya. Emerging Issues in Management (symphonya.unimib.it), 2, 6-24, 2010. http://dx.doi.org/10.4468/2010.2.02brondoni.

Cairns G., Sliwa M., *A Very Short, Reasonably Cheap and Fairly Interesting Book about International Business*, Sage, London, 2008.

Canavilhas J., *Nuevos Medios, Nuevo Eco-Sistema*, El Profesional de la Información, 24 (4), 2015. https://doi.org/10.3145/epi.2015.nov.09.

Cyert R.M., March J.G., *A Behavioral Theory of the Firm*, 2nd ed., Blackwell Publishers, Oxford, 1992.

Delecta J., Raman C., *Cultural Communication Barriers in Workplace*, International Journal of Management, 6 (1), 2015. no doi.

Fang T., *Negotiation: the Chinese Style*, Journal of Business & Industrial Marketing, 21 (1), 2006. http://dx.doi.org/10.1108/08858620610643175.

Geertz C., *The Interpretation of Culture*, Basic Books, New York, 1973.

Ghauri P., Fang T., *Negotiating with the Chinese: A Socio-Cultural Analysis*, Journal of World Business, 36 (3), 2001. http://dx.doi.org/10.1016/S1090-9516(01)00057-8.

Griswold W., *Cultures and Societies in a Changing World*, SAGE, Thousand Oaks, 2008.

Hall E.T., *Beyond Culture*, Anchor Books, New York, 1977.

Harrison L.E., *The Central Liberal Truth: How Politics Can Change a Culture and Save It from Itself*, Oxford University Press, New York, 2006.

Harrison L.E., Huntington S.P., *Culture Matters: How Values Shape Human Progress*, Basic Books, New York, 2000.

Hoecklin L., *Managing Cultural Differences: Strategies for Competitive Advantage*, Economist Intelligence Unit, Addison Wesley, London, 1995.

Hofstede G., *Culture's Consequences: Comparing Values, Behaviors, Institutions and Organizations across Nations*, 2nd edn., SAGE, Los Angeles, CA, 2001.

Hofstede G., *Culture's Consequences: International Differences in Work-Related Values*, SAGE, Los Angeles, CA, 1980.

Hofstede G., Hofstede G.J., Minkov M., *Cultures and Organizations: Software of the Mind*, McGraw-Hill, London, 1991.

Horváth D., McMillan C.J., Azumi K., Hickson D.J., *The Cultural Context of Organizational Control: An International Comparison*, International Studies of Management & Organizations, 6 (3), 1976. no doi.

Keesing R.M., *Theories of Culture*, in Annual Review of Anthropology, 3, 1974. http://dx.doi.org/10.1146/annurev.an.03.100174.000445.

Lambin J.-J., *Market Driven Management, Strategic and Operational Marketing*, Mac Millan, London, 2000.
Lechner, F., Boli J., *World Culture: Origins and Consequences*, Blackwell, Malden, MA, 2005.
Lindridge A., *Galton's Problem*, The Blackwell Encyclopedia of Management, IV, 2005.
Luo Y., *Toward a Reverse Adaptation View in Cross-Cultural Management*, Cross Cultural & Strategic Management, 23 (1), 2016. https://doi.org/10.1108/CCSM-08-2015-0102

Mulder M., *Power Equalization Through Participation?*, Administrative Science Quarterly, 1971. http://dx.doi.org/10.2307/2391284.

Ock Y.J., *The Impact of Confucianism in Interpersonal Relationships and Communication Patterns in East Asia*, Communication Monographs, 55 (4), December, 1988. http://dx.doi.org/10.1080/03637758809376178

Peterson B., *Cultural Intelligence: A Guide to Working with People from Other Cultures*, Intercultural Press, Boston, 2004.
Porter M., *The Competitive Advantage of Nations*, Mac Millan, London, 1990.
Primecz H., Mahadevan J., Romani L., *Editorial. Why is Cross-Cultural Management Scholarship Blind to Power Relations? Investigating Ethnicity, Language, Gender and Religion in Power-Laden Contexts*, International Journal of Cross-Cultural Management, 16 (2), 2016. https://doi.org/10.1177/1470595816666154.

Riesman D., Glazer N., Denney R., *The Lonely Crowd*, Yale University Press, New Haven, 2001.

Salvioni D., *Intangible Assets and Internal Controls in Global Companies*, in Symphonya. Emerging Issues in Management (symphonya.unimib.it), n. 2, 39-51, 2010. http://dx.doi.org/10.4468/2010.2.4salvioni.
Soderberg A.M., Holden N., *Rethinking Cross-Cultural Management in a Globalizing Business World*, International Journal of Cross-cultural Management, 2, (1), 2002. http://dx.doi.org/10.1177/1470595802002001091.
Spencer-Rodgersa J., McGovern T., *Attitudes Toward the Culturally Different: The Role of Intercultural Communication Barriers, Affective Responses, Consensual Stereotypes, and Perceived Threat*, International Journal of Intercultural Relations 26, 2002. https://doi.org/10.1016/S0147-1767(02)00038-X.
Steward J.H., *Theory of Culture Change: The Methodology of Multilinear Evolution*, University of Illinois Press, Urbana, IL, 1955.

Tipton F., *Modeling National Identities and Cultural Change: The Western European, Japanese, and United States Experiences Compared*, International Journal of Cross-cultural Management, 9 (145), 2009. http://dx.doi.org/ 10.1177/1470595809335722.

van den Bosch F., van Prooijen A., Porter M., *The Competitive Advantage of European Nations: The Impact of National Culture - A Missing Element in Porter's Analysis? A Note on Culture and Competitive Advantage: Response to van den Bosch and van Prooijen*, European Management Journal, 10 (2), 1992. http://dx. doi.org/10.1016/0263-2373(92)90066-D.

Part 2
MANAGERIAL ISSUES

Chapter 8

DESTRUCTURING OF MARKETING CHANNELS AND GROWTH OF MULTICHANNELLING. IN SEARCH OF A NEW MODEL FOR DISTRIBUTION SYSTEMS

Fabio Musso

ABSTRACT: *The emerging web revolution entails managing multichannel strategies by experimenting with new organizational solutions in search of a new reference model. Logistics have also begun to change dramatically, disrupting the classic configurations where logistics actors played a functional role in bringing efficiency to a process where a large number of producers offered goods to a myriad of consumers. In the coming years, many of the theories on distribution systems and the role of business actors at the production, distribution, and service levels will have to be rewritten.*

SUMMARY: 8.1. Introduction. – 8.2. Overview of marketing channels. – 8.3. Innovation and changes in marketing channels. – 8.4. The challenge of multichannelling. – 8.5. The functional shifting within channels. – 8.6. Conclusions.

8.1. Introduction

Since the end of the nineties, and as a consequence of the emerging web revolution, a process of reviewing the traditional models of organizing marketing channels has begun, with new emerging issues, in addition to those of disintermediation/reintermediation in the relationships between producers and trade intermediaries. What happened in the following years revealed a much more articulated picture, where multichannelling has come to dominate and where the boundaries between the various channel roles have quickly blurred. As a result, companies have been engaged in managing multichannel strategies by experimenting new organizational solutions in search for a new reference model. This issue involved both producers and retailers, with overlapping roles that contributed to making the framework more complex. In addition, also logistics started to change dramatically, breaking the classic patterns where logistic actors played a functional role in bringing efficiency to a process where a large number of producers offered goods to a myriad of consumers. Nowadays, logistics solutions adopted by larger e-commerce marketplaces are making possible a return to a direct producer-consumer relationship that develops itself on a global perspective.

The implications are numerous and relevant, including the way in which consumers buying behavior is changing, and the different role that retailers are intended to assume.

In the coming years much of the theories on distribution systems and the role of business actors at the production, distribution and service level will have to be rewritten.

8.2. Overview of marketing channels

Marketing channels provide the institutional structure that connects companies to the markets they serve. Marketing channels have been originally studied with reference to models based on the market structure and competition, and focused on the type of specialisation of the different channel mambers (Mallen, 1973), according to the Smithian-Stiglerian paradigm (Stigler, 1951), which explains the existence of commercial intermediaries with their ability to obtain economies of specialization.

Linked to the principles of microeconomics, the institutional perspective (Artle and Berglund, 1959; Bucklin, 1966) pointed out the attention on channel members as a sequence of institutions that transfer goods from the producer to the final customer, by activating various types of flows.

Similarly to the institutional perspective, the functional approach analyzed marketing channels in the light of the roles played by their members (Alderson, 1957). The functional approach takes these roles back to the fundamental activities of assortment composition (sorting), and assuming duties and risks connected to the function of stocking (postponement).

Marketing channels have also been described as vertical marketing systems (VMS) (McCammon, 1970) in those cases when a coordinating leader emerges. A VMS is a formally or informally coordinated distribution channel where channel members co-operate to achieve higher levels of efficiency and scale economies, and to eliminate channel conflicts arising out of diverse individual objectives.

There are three major types of VMS, and each uses different means for setting up leadership and power in the system: i) administered, where leadership is assumed by one dominant member that is large and powerful enough to control and coordinate the other members, even if out of a hierarchical realtionship; ii) contractual, where coordination and conflict management are attained through contractual agreements among members of the system; iii) corporate, where coordination and conflict management are controlled by common ownership.

All traditional perspectives assumed that a marketing channel can be seen as a whole structure, vertically integrated, which links the retailer to the manufacturer through a series of intermediaries (Davies, 1984). This is no longer an appropriate conceptualisation of the structure of distribution channels in most of retailing systems. In the last decade, power relations between agents within channels have been changed fundamentally by the actions of manufacturers and large retailers which, thanks to vertical integration strategies, extendied the scope of their activities, particularly at the expense of wholesalerers (Musso, 2010). Distribution channels have also been made more complex by the horizontal incorporation of additional actors who, while interacting directly with retailers, are not always engaged in the physical distribution: franchise organisations, voluntary chains, trade associations and buying gropups have become increasingly prominent agents within distribution channels.

In more recent years, global marketing emerged as a common area of action for an increasing number of companies (Cateora and Graham, 2007). Not only large multinationals – which are following a global perspective since several decades – are involved in international operations, also medium sized companies and even small firms are increasingly entering international markets in order to achieve better performances (Czinkota et al, 1995). The growth of e-commerce has fostered this trend by providing the ability to easily connect firms from around the world in a wide electronic marketplace (Kalakota and Whinston, 1996).

As a consequence, channel structures and marketing strategies need to be re-formulated in the context of globalisation (Rosenbloom and Larsen, 2008). Thus, the development and management of marketing channels that make products and services available to billions of customers around the world is facing a more complex challenge.

8.3. Innovation and changes in marketing channels

In recent years, innovation in marketing channels has manifested itself with high intensity and very fast, especially as a result of technology-related changes, which have allowed companies more efficient organizational solutions. As a result of technological change, new forms of distribution have emerged, with new and additional customer services. In most cases, innovation has involved channel partners upstream and downstream of the network they belong to, with the involvement of the entire vertical network rather than individual companies.

A key factor that stimulated innovation was the process of retail modernization, with a stronger role for retailers. Social changes and new patterns of end-use behavioral stimuli have also stimulated innovations to meet consumer goods and distribution systems (eg traceability and respect for social, ecological and ethical values in production processes).

Innovation types in marketing channels can be distinguished between tecnology-based, based on the opportunities offered by innovation in information and communication technologies (ICTs) and market-based (Musso, 2010). Market-based factors may, in turn, be distinguished in demand-driven factors, linked to variations in the characteristics and behaviors of customers that companies seek to comply with (Kaufman-Scarborough, Forsythe, 2009) and competitive factors, with reference to a differentiation and a rapid response to changes in the final demand. These criteria are often based on time-based competition (Hum, Sim, 1996, Brondoni, 2002, 2005), underlining the value of the time variable to pursue a competitive advantage and plan marketing policies.

Among the the major consequences of changes within marketing channels, two issues are emerging as particularly relavant. The first is related to the development of e-commerce, which has led to a change in consumer buying behavior and is hijacking an increasing share of sales on on-line channels, at the expense of physical stores. This points out the multichannel issue, which actually is the main challenge for all manufacturers.

The second issue arises from the functional shifting in the roles played by channel actors. Disintermediation can bring to exclude middlemen, but not the functions they perform. Functions and distribution tasks that need to be performed to consummate transactions between buyers and sellers cannot be eliminated from the distribution channel but only shifted within it. Of course, the multichannel issue and the functional shifting issue are strictly interrelated.

8.4. The challenge of multichannelling

The arising of new channels – as a consequence of structural innovation developed both by manufacturers retailers – leads to the phenomenon of multi-channelling, especially after the development of e-commerce, which enables the integration of online sales with a portfolio of multiple alternative distribution channels.

This development is fed from two sides. On the one side, many manufacturers and traditional retailers have added an online channel to their distribution strategies. On the other side, 'pure-play' Internet retailers are opening physical stores or are collaborating with traditional retailers (Agatz et al., 2008). The scope of multi-channel retailing has been broadened by considering issues such as the management of customers across channels and the integration of the retail mix across channels (Neslin et al., 2014).

From a marketing perspective, different channels differ in their abilities to perform various service outputs. The internet channel is particularly powerful in providing information to the customer, thereby reducing the buyer's search costs. Another advantage of the internet is the ability to provide a very large range of products. On the other hand, an advantage of the traditional channel is the proximity to customers. Offering multiple complementary channels provides a greater and deeper mix of customer service, thereby enhancing the seller's overall value proposition (Wallace et al., 2004).

For manufacturers, major marketing-related concerns in multichannelling include cannibalization and channel conflicts (Webb, 2002). With an increase of the number of channels carrying the product, the sales derived from each channel are reduced making it difficult for a company to recover its costs. Conflicts may arise between different divisions that manage a company's different channels, but even more so between different supply chain members, for example a manufacturer competing with its own resellers through a customer-direct internet channel (Tsay et al., 2004).

Consequently, managing the overall portfolio, rather than individual channels, as a key strategy in a multichannel organization (Rosenbloom, 2007) is necessary. For vendors, it is important to manage customer interactions across different channels using a common set of information and processes, and leveraging information learned on any channel to provide better services or more targeted offers on other channels. From an operations management perspective, economies of scale from the integration of multiple channels need to be weighed against specific requirements of each individual channel. Thus, companies need to make trade-offs when deciding which processes to integrate across channels and which processes to separate (Gulati and Garino, 2000).

The emergence of multichannelling contrasts with the phenomenon of disintermediation, which was foreseen when the internet began to emerge. Intermediaires, both retail and wholesale, as well as a myriad of agents and brokers, continue to operate along a broad spectrum of distribution channels. The survival of so many intermediaries in the face of the potential of e-commerce can be explained by looking at the basic economy. In particular, intermediaries affirm themselves in distribution channels because they are able to carry out distribution tasks and related services more efficiently than producers or consumers could do. Intermediaries are often low-cost distribution services producers, because as specialists in the delivery of these services, they can leverage economies of scale and scope (Stigler, 1951). In the long run, if intermediaries are unable to fulfill this role they are destined to disappear from the channel. If this is the case, their distribution activities are not taken over by producers or consumers, but by other types of intermediaries that are able to provide distribution services more efficiently (Anderson and Anderson, 2002). In recent years, this type of metamorphosis in distribution channels has been named as reintermediation, that is, a reconfiguration of intermediaries' roles within the channels, rather than eliminating intermediaries.

A wide range of international intermediaries, ranging from traditional wholesalers and retailers to import-export operators, sales agents, resident buyers, export houses and many more, are not likely to be disintermediate in a short time. Rather, a reconfiguration or re-intermediation based on the laws of the economy is the change that most likely will occur. Consequently, companies, rather than focusing on eliminating intermediaries, should target a channel redesign in which they can understand the optimal mix of subjects that can increase their overall efficiency.

Multichannelling, however, puts the danger of conflict between channels that are used at the same time. Interchannel conflict (Rosenbloom, 2010) occurs when parallel channel structures compete against each other within the same company. The typical case is when a manufacturer uses the on-line channel to make direct sales to final customers, thus competing with his distributors. In this case, the conflict is between the online channel and indirect channel (Rosenbloom, 2007).

In general, interchannel conflict reduces channel efficiency. In some cases, however, conflict can be positive if it provides the incentive for a more appropriate division of tasks between members of the channel itself.

With the development of online channels, as a direct relationship with end consumers, the potential for interchannel conflict has greatly increased. Although this conflict should be considered an intrinsic dimension in the behavioral dynamics of subjects along marketing channels, it can nevertheless be managed. This management can take place on two levels: in the phase of designing the channel structure, and in the management of existing channels.

In designing marketing channels, the issue of potential conflicts must be considered as part of the analysis and evaluation of solutions to be included in the channel strategy. Therefore, it is important to develop some mechanisms of cooperation between the manufacturer and the traditional retailer. For example, if the company plans to use both on-line and traditional channels, through independent intermediaries, it should make choices that avoid channel overlaps at the territorial level. Or, if both channels are used in the same territories, cooperation can be made objective through differentiated branding and profit-sharing strategies. By strategically implementing the differentiated branding and profit-sharing strategies, both the manufacturer and the retailer can achieve the full channel coordination and improve their individual profits (Yan, 2011).

When channels are already established and no radical redesign of channel strategies is planned, choices must be, at least in the short term, of gradual change and adaptation of existing structures to ongoing changes. Therefore, potential conflicts must be addressed during normal channel management. This can be managed in three distinct phases: the identification of conflict, the assessment of the potential effects of the conflict, and conflict resolution (Rosenbloom, 2010).

As regard the identification of the conflict, it is not obvious, since conflicts can occur in a underhand way. Therefore, being vigilant to identify a conflict from the earliest signs before it appears is necessary. In global channels, where distances are relevant and channel structures can be long and complex, the commitment to monitor emerging conflicts can be difficult. Formal surveys and direct audits with channel partners can be the tools to be activated to detect and counter conflicts from the initial stages (Rosenbloom, 2011).

With regard to the assessment of the potential effects of the conflict, it is necessary to check whether the conflict is likely to have a negative impact on the objectives of the company and also on the counterparty's interests, and appropriate action must be taken to counter the emergence of the conflict.

Finally, options for resolving conflicts may vary from meetings between parties, possibily in informal circumstances such as lunch or dinner, to the more formal solutions, including legal actions (Dant and Schul, 1992). Of course, early detection of a channel conflict and an appropriate plan to deal with it can make it possible to avoid the most complex and costly roads, like legal actions are.

8.5. The functional shifting within channels

Marketing functions that are typically performed by channel intermediaires, such as transport, storage, risk-taking, order processing, buying, selling and numerous others, can be transformed in many ways, but ultimately they still must be performed. Therefore, the question is not whether marketing functions or distribution tasks need to be performed but who should perform them (Mallen, 1973).

Actually, since distribution channels extend beyond the borders of individual countries and often extend globally, the concept of functional shifting is even more important to ensure speed, cost reduction and efficiency in channel relationships. To accomplish this condition, three fundamental issues must be defined (Rosenbloom, 2007).

The first issue concerns the assessment of what is the most cost-effective channel structure for distributing functions. Even with the advent of the Internet and the emergence of global markets, the laws of the economy have not changed. Channel structures and strategies to reach global markets must be economically efficient to be profitable. In many cases, Internet-based technologies can drastically reduce costs of selling, especially for digital products such as books, music, and financial services. For other heavy and bulky products, therefore with a high incidence of shipping costs, or having a low unit value, the online channel may be much less efficient. Therefore, in designing marketing channels the idea that the internet can change everything should be avoided. Economic feasibility is still the foundation upon which the channel structure must be built and physical constraints due to transport costs stil remain a limit to the excessive fragmentation of interactions.

The second question concerns the degree of control that the company expects. A classic marketing axiom is that the longer the channel and the less the degree of control for the producer, and vice versa. So if the company seeks the maximum control on how its products are marketed, the channel structure should be as short as possible, making direct the distribution from the producer to the final customer. Conversely, if control is not a critical condition for competitiveness, the optimum choice may be that of longer channels, using a number of intermediaries to reach markets with a minimum investment and low risk. However, here too, similarly to the economic considerations, the issue of control does not disappear with the introduction of online technologies. If the way that products are made available to end customers can affect brand value, market positioning or customer service, channel control can remain a crucial factor.

The third question related to functional shifting concerns channel management and how much it is part of the company's core competencies. Long-term profitability of a company is closely tied to what the company can do better. If a company moves out of its areas of expertise, going to activities on which it has no experience, competitiveness can be affected, because it is operating from a position that is not its maximum ability. In the context of structural and strategic choices regarding marketing channels, if the company does not have the expertise to manage the related activities, it may be to its advantage to shift them to specialized subjects with the appropriate skills, technology and experience.

8.6. Conclusions

Marketing channels have changed dramatically in the last two decades due to the advent of the online channel and ongoing digitalization. As a consequence, many manufacturers and retailers' business models have been affected (Sorescu et al., 2011) as their marekting mix has changed and customers are behaving differently due to these developments. Multi-channel strategies have been adopted by both producers and retailers, and we are now moving to a new phase in multi-channelling. In recent years, a further digitalization in marketing and retailing with specific challenges occurred. (Leeflang et al. 2014). More specifically, with the starting of the mobile channel, tablets, social media, and the integration of these new channels in online and offline channels, the marketing channels landscape continues to change, moving from a multi-channel to an omni-channel retailing distribution (Rigby, 2011).

The different channels become blurred as the natural borders between channels begin to disappear. This development is affecting competitive strategies and is breaking down old barriers such as geography and consumer ignorance. Channels are interchangeably and seamlessly used during the search and purchase process and it is difficult or virtually impossible for companies to control this usage. Whereas in the multichannel phase research shopping gained some attention, in the omni-channel phase showrooming is becoming an important issue. Shoppers now frequently search for information in the store and simultaneously search on their mobile device to get more information about offers and may find more attractive prices. The opposite of showrooming also occurs, which is now referred to as webrooming, where shoppers seek information online and buy offline (Verhoef et al., 2015).

An important consequence is that interactive channels are becoming integrated with traditional mass advertising channels, and communication channels tend to correspond to sales channels. Thus, consumer switching across channels and devices such as desktop, laptop and mobile devices are all part of the shoppers' omni-channel experience and firms need to consider this to provide a seamless interaction.

In light of the above discussion, it is important to note that new models of marketing channels management are necessary, in which sales, communication and phisical distribution tasks and roles can be defined. In this issue, a key point refers to the leadership of the different channels, which in an omnichannel condition can vary channel by channel. Therefore companies, both at the production and distribution level, have to get used to dealing with situations where the channel leader changes from time to time, accepting the idea of being in some cases leader and in other cases side partners of the single channel.

References

Alderson W., *Marketing Behavior and Executive Action. A Functionalist Approach to Marketing Theory*, Irwin, Homewood, Ill., 1957.

Anderson Philip, Anderson Erin, *The New E-Commerce Intermediaries*, Sloan Management Review, 43(4), Summer, 53-62, 2002.

Artle R., Berglund S., *A Note on Manufacturers' Choiche of Distribution Channels*, Management Science, 5, July, 1959. https://doi.org/10.1287/mnsc.5.4.460.

Brondoni S.M., *Global Markets and Market-Space Competition*, Symphonya: Emerging Issues in Management, 1, 28-42, 2002. http://dx.doi.org/10.4468/2002.1.03brondoni.

Bucklin L.P., *A Theory of Distribution Channel Structure*, University of California, Institute of Business and Economic Research, Berkeley, 1966.

Cateora P.R., Graham J.L., *International Marketing*, Boston, McGraw-Hill Irwin, 2007.

Czinkota Michael R., Ronkainen Ilkka A., Tarrant John J., *The Global Marketing Imperative*, Lincolnwood, Illinois, NTC Business Books, 1995.

Dant M., Rajiv P., Schul. Patrick L., *Conflict Resolution Processes in Contractual Channels of Distribution*, Journal of Marketing, January, 38-54, 1992.

Davies R.L., *Retail and Commercial Planning*, Groom Helm, Beckenham, 1984.

Gulati R., Garino J., *Get the right mix of bricks & clicks*, Harvard Business Review, 78 (3), 107-114, 2000.

Hum S.H., Sim H.H., *Time-Based Competition: Literature Review and Implications for Modelling*, International Journal of Operations & Production Management, 16 (1), 75-90, 1996. http://doi/full/10.1108/01443579610106373.

Kalakota R., Whinston A.B., *Electronic Commerce*, Reading Massachusetts, Addison-Wesley, 1996.

Kaufman-Scarborough C., Forsythe S., *Current Issues in Retailing: Relationships and Emerging Opportunities*, Journal of Business Research, 62 (5), 517-520, 2009. https://doi.org/10.1016/j.jbusres.2008.06.010.

Leeflang P.S.H., Verhoef P.C., Dahlström P., Freundt T., *Challenges and Solutions for Marketing in a Digital Era*, European Management Journal, 32 (1), 1-12, 2014. https://doi.org/10.1016/j.emj.2013.12.001.

Mallen B., *Functional Spin-Off: A Key to Anticipating Change in Distribution Structure*, Journal of Marketing, July, 18-25, 1973.

McCammon B.C. Jr., *Perspective for Distribution Programming*, in Bucklin L.P. (ed.), Vertical Marketing Systems, Scott, Foresman & Co., Glenview, Ill., 1970.

Musso F., *Innovation in Marketing Channels: Relationships, Technology, Channel Structure*, Symphonya: Emerging Issues in Management, 1, 23-42, 2010. http://dx.doi.org/10.4468/2010.1.04musso.

Musso F., *Technology in Marketing Channels: Present and Future Drivers of Innovation*, International Journal of Applied Behavioural Economics, 1 (2), 41-51, 2012. http://dx.doi.org/10.4018/ijabe.2012040104.

Neslin S.A., Jerath K., Bodapati A., Bradlow E.T., Deighton J., Gensler S., Lee L., Montaguti E., Telang R., Venkatesan R., Peter C., Verhoef Z. , Zhang J., *The Interrelationships Between Brand and Channel Choice*, Marketing Letters, 25 (3), 319-330, 2014. https://doi.org/10.1007/s11002-014-9305-2.

Rigby D., *The Future of Shopping*, Harvard Business Review, 89 (12), 65-76, 2011.

Rosenbloom B., *Multi-Channel Strategy in Business-to-Business Markets: Prospects and Problems*, Industrial Marketing Management, 36, January, 4-9, 2007. https://doi.org/10.1016/j.indmarman.2006.06.010.

Rosenbloom B., *Six Classic Distribution Paradigms for Global Marketing Channel Strategy*, Symphonya: Emerging Issues in Management, 1, 7-17, 2010. http://dx.doi.org/10.4468/2010.1.02rosenbloom.

Rosenbloom B., Larsen, T., *Wholesalers as Global Marketers*, Journal of Marketing Channels, 15 (4), 235-252, 2008. https://doi.org/10.1080/10466690802063879.

Sorescu A., Frambach R.T., Singh J., Rangaswamy A., Bridges C., *Innovations in Retail Business Models*, Journal of Retailing, 87, S3-S16, 2011. https://doi.org/10.1016/j.jretai.2011.04.005.

Stigler G.J., *The Division of Labor is Limited by the Extent of the Market*, Journal of political economy, 59 (3), 185-193, 1951.

Tsay A.A., Agrawal N., *Modeling Conflict and Coordination in Multi-Channel Distribution Systems: A Review*, in Simchi-Levi D. et al. (eds.), Modeling in the E-Business Era, Kluwer, Boston, 557-606, 2004.

Verhoef P.C., Kannan P.K., Inman J.J., *From Multi-Channel Retailing to Omni-Channel Retailing: Introduction to the Special Issue on Multi-Channel Retailing.* Journal of retailing, 91 (2), 174-181, 2015. https://doi.org/10.1016/j.jretai.2015.02.005.

Wallace D.W., Giese J.L., Johnson J.L., *Customer Retailer Loyalty in the Context of Multiple Channel Strategies*, Journal of Retailing, 80(4), 249-263, 2004. https://doi.org/10.1016/j.jretai.2004.10.002.

Webb K.L., *Managing channels of Distribution in the Age of Electronic Commerce*, Industrial Marketing Management, 31 (2), 95-102 2002. https://doi.org/10.1016/S0019-8501(01)00181-X.

Yan R., *Managing Channel Coordination in a Multi-Channel Manufacturer-Retailer Supply Chain*. Industrial Marketing Management, 40 (4), 636-642, 2011. https://doi.org/10.1016/j.indmarman.2010.12.019.

Chapter 9
LARGE-SCALE RETAILERS, MARKETING CHANNELS AND COMPETITIVE CUSTOMER VALUE

Sabina Riboldazzi

ABSTRACT: *The growing complexity of today's business systems has led to the substantial modification of retailer policies. In particular, in recent years, large-scale retailers have found ways to become more competitive by devising new policies aimed at creating competitive customer value. The creation of such value translates into the entire marketing channel's ability to compete according to the principles of timeliness, effectiveness, efficiency, and optimization. Indeed, in over-supply markets, competition develops between the marketing channels where the processes are managed to quickly respond to market changes and satisfy unstable and changing demand.*

SUMMARY: 9.1. Large-scale retailers and global markets. – 9.2. Large-scale retailers, market-driven management and competitive customer value. – 9.3. Large-scale retailers, marketing channels and competitive customer value.

9.1. Large-scale retailers and global markets

In the past few years, the retail distribution sector has undergone profound structural changes where large corporations have increasingly acquired a leadership role in managerial activities, thereby contributing to the globalization process. These changes have occurred independently over different periods of time in various geographical areas, thus shaping current competitive markets.

The development of modern large-scale retailing first took place in the United States during the interwar period. In Europe, the gradual transition from traditional sales forms to modern distribution did not begin until after the Second World War. In particular, it is not until the 1980s that the Italian large-scale retail system began implementing a fast-paced modernization process, which led to a gradual but irreversible reduction in the number of traditional retail stores over a twenty-year period (Riboldazzi, 2005). This significant delay in the innovation process with respect to other devel-

oped countries has ultimately hampered the ability of large-scale Italian retailers to play a leadership role among top-ranking European and global
retailers. Indeed, those European retailers who first succeeded in implementing development strategies outside national boundaries have now become key players in an increasingly competitive global market as highlighted by the Deloitte survey of the top ranking global large-scale retailers by
revenue (Table 1).

As a result of modernization and globalization, large-scale retailing is
now characterized by the global presence of large multinational corporations. On the other hand, in Italy we can observe a much higher level of retail fragmentation due to the development of large-scale retailers, smaller in
size than their multinational counterparts (Table 2), which, with only few
exceptions, operate predominantly on the domestic market.

Table 1. The main large-scale retailers/wholesalers in the global market by revenues
2015.

Company	Country of origin	FY 2015 Retail revenue (US$M)	Dominant operational format	Countries of operation
Wal-Mart Stores, Inc	US	482,130	Hypermarket/Supercenter/ Superstore	30
Costco Wholesale Corporation	US	116,199	Cash & Carry/Warehouse Club	10
The Kroger Co.	US	109,830	Supermarket	1
Schwarz Unternehmenst reuhand KG	Germany	94,448	Discount Store	26
Carrefour S.A.	France	84,856	Hypermarket/Supercenter/ Superstore	35
Aldi Einkauf GmbH & Co. oHG	Germany	82,164	Discunt Stores	17
Tesco PLC	UK	81,019	Hypermarket/Supercenter/ Superstore	10

see next page

Target Corporation	US	73,785	Discount Department Store	1
Metro Ag	Germany	68,066	Cash & Carry/Warehouse Club	31
Aeon Co., Ltd.	Japan	63,635	Hypermarket/Supercenter/ Superstore	12
Auchan Holding SA (formerly Groupe Auchan SA)	France	59,050	Hypermarket/Supercenter/ Superstore	14
Albertsons Companies, Inc	US	58,734	Supermarket	1
Edeka Group	Germany	52,477	Supermarket	1
Casino Guichard-Perrachon S.A.	France	51,257	Hypermarket/Supercenter/ Superstore	31
Seven & i Holdings Co., Ltd.	Japan	47,795	Convenience/Forecourt Store	19

Source: Based on "Global Power of Retailing. The Art and Science of Customers", Deloitte, 2017.

Table 2. The main large-scale retailers in the Italian market. Market share in 2015.

Company	Market Share %
Coop Italia	14.5
Conad	11.9
Selex	9.7
Esselunga	8.9
Auchan	6.7
Carrefour	6.1

see next page

Eurospin	5.1
Vege	3.4
Pam	3.0
Finiper	2.8
Lidl	2.7
Agorà	2.5
Sun	2.5
Lillo	2.3
Aspiag	2.2
Crai	2.2
Sigma	2.2
Sisa	2.0
Others (< 2): 9.3	

Source: Conad Annual Report 2015

On the whole, the current large-scale retailing system is made up of large corporations that, in the context of high competition and market saturation, manage a large portfolio of spatially distributed points of sale, constantly reformulating their market offering to find new sources of value creation (Riboldazzi, 2005).

9.2. Large-scale retailers, market-driven management and competitive customer value

Hypercompetition, dynamism, and production which often exceed demand absorption capacity due to the development of economies of scale, along with consumption volatility, are all complex aspects of current global markets. These issues have forced large-scale retailers to pursue continuous innovation of products and solutions as well as improvement of business efficiency through market-driven management with the aim of creating competitive customer value.

A simplified customer value model is based on the difference between total perceived benefits and total perceived costs of a given product. However, in the presence of competitive alternatives, a high customer value is not any longer sufficient to ensure that the customer will purchase that product. Thus, retailers should always try to deliver a customer value that is higher than that of their competitors by predicting or identifying market changes that could translate into value determinants. It is therefore not enough for retailers to build customer value models only considering the value perceived by current customers with respect to their own market offerings. Instead, retailers should also take into account customer values offered by the competitors, relative to both current and potential customers, to gain a competitive advantage and become more suitable for larger markets (Riboldazzi, 2005).

The creation of competitive customer value therefore requires a market-driven management (Day, 1990, 1994, 1998, 1999; Narver and Slater 1990; Slater and Narver, 1994, 1998; Deshpandé and Farley, 1996; Fritz, 1996; Lambin, 1998; Jaworski, Kohli and Sahay, 2000; Best, 2009) able to quickly identify and fill the gaps in the market before their rivals, thereby meeting the ever-changing demand of customer aggregates.

In this context, thanks to the use of big data analytics, large-scale retailers have been increasingly cooperating with manufacturers in establishing multiple partnerships with other corporations (e.g. equity and non-equity such as R&S partnerships, joint ventures, cooperative marketing, franchising, etc.) to plan fast actions according to market changes and opportunities, thereby designing and launching new competitive market offerings before their competitors. Thus, competition is a process involving networks and/or marketing channels (Brondoni and Musso, 2010), where customer value is created mainly by manufacturers and large-scale retailers. Competitive customer value creation, therefore, requires collaboration and coordination between manufacturers and retailers to adequately deliver new offers that can efficiently meet customer dynamic demand, which ultimately represents a critical value assessment based on both the differential value of the product and the specific advantages afforded by the point of sale.

Overall, competitive customer value is the result of coordinated actions from all marketing channel subjects increasingly involving new partners in the context of a network characterized by dynamic relationships, spatial localization, and specific combinations of business activities.

9.3. Large-scale retailers, marketing channels and competitive customer value

A marketing channel can be defined as a network of business relations involving parties engaged in activities aimed at transferring goods from the manufacturer to the end user by activating multiple flows encompassing various degrees of cooperation, all within a certain setting.

In a global competitive market, marketing channels play a critical role in competitive customer value generation as effective and efficient flow management can lead to the to the creation of a superior customer value.

These principles are further analyzed below:

1. *Customer value is generated by the positive differential value of a market offering with respect to its alternatives.* – Briefly, customer value expresses the difference between customer benefits and "economic costs" associated with a given market offering; the benefit value relies on the customer's perception of the product-service provision and on the relationship with the supplier during the purchase; the costs or sacrifices that the customer has to bear relate to the price paid and to other monetary and non-monetary costs. Thus, competitive customer value is generally achieved when a company can generate superior customer benefits for the same cost or equal benefits for a lower cost compared to its competitors.

In this scenario, especially when dealing with fast-moving consumer goods, buyers tend to evaluate alternative offers, also known as consideration set, taking into account not only the value of the product being purchased, but also the specific advantages provided by the point of sale where the product is sold. Thus, competitive customer value is determined by the value of the product created by the manufacturer – this value depends on various attributes qualifying the product, such as its intended use and function, design, brand, quality, packaging, and so on – coupled with the advantages offered by the point of sale developed by the retailer. These latter benefits arise from each single components of the offer, such as assortment, during sales services (e.g. knowledge and professionalism of sales staff, store environment, available information on market offerings, user-friendly buying technologies, sales support services, billing transparency, payment diversification, etc.), access services (e.g. opening hours, parking lots, etc.), and pre- and after-sales services (e.g. reservations, guarantees, etc.). Consequently, it is of paramount importance for large-scale retailers to continuously innovate all the features of their market offerings (Brondoni, Corniani, Riboldazzi, 2013), as well as implement a dynamic management of their retail mix levers. In a broader context, retailers' policies that help maximize the positive differential value generated by a marketing channel to get a competitive advantage should take into account the following aspects: competitive pricing; dynamic aggregation of products forming the assortment and marketing offerings, which should be in line with the expectations of consumer associations; merchandising and exhibition space allocation required to maximize product exposure; and in-store and off-store communication.

2. Time is a strategic variable crucial for creating competitive customer value. – In today's new competitive markets, time plays a key role in delivering competitive customer value. In this regard, the ability to manage time has become a strategic variable strongly influencing the ability of a company to survive by gaining a competitive advantage.

All companies involved in each marketing channel must therefore devise time-based business strategies aimed at not only reducing the time needed to deliver the offer, but also choosing the optimal time to manage business operations. Consequently, the creation of competitive customer value requires a reduction/rationalization of time consumption across the entire marketing channel. In particular, time valorization should relate to the following business activities:

– identification, dissemination of data across the channel, and analysis and interpretation of critical information about possible value determinants;

– choice of intervention type and identification of critical phases during offer reformulation;

– choice of the optimal time for intervention and deliver of the reformulated offer.

3. Competitive customer value creation relies on effective and efficient management of channel flows. – A number of different flows, often involving external companies, can stem from each marketing channel. These flows can be divided into the following types (Rosenbloom, 2004):

– product flow: it relates to the physical movement of goods from the manufacturer to the end consumer, and it derives mainly from logistics and warehouse management activities;

– negotiation flow: it encompasses the series of sales and purchase negotiations associated with the transfer of the title of ownership of the product;

– ownership flow: it originates from the transfer of ownership of the goods between the various subjects of the marketing channel, and it also includes after-sales returned goods flows for unsold, defective, damaged or expired products;

– information flow: it concerns the diffusion within the channel of both internal and external information;

– promotion flow: it includes all types of communication flow implemented by the subjects of the marketing channel to outreach different market segments; it can also relate to the communication mix (i.e. advertising, sales force, sales promotion, publicity, and direct marketing);

– economic-financial flow: it relates to payment, financing, and pricing activities.

Creating a competitive customer value thus requires coordination, integration, speed, and efficient management of flows originating from each marketing channel. These complex processes can now be easily performed thanks to technological, organizational, and relational innovations. Listed below are some innovations that more than others have helped develop new channel flows by improving relationships across the manufacturer-retailer-consumer chain:

– Barcode and POS scanners together with fidelity cards have allowed large-scale retailers to better understand customer buying behaviors at the individual level, customize marketing activities, and collect data that could then be used to boost business activities. More recent innovations, such as self-checkout technology – similar to the traditional ones used by consumers to scan and pay for purchased products – and, in particular, self-scanning (i.e. portable scanners able to read product barcodes when the consumer picks up products displayed on shelves), along with personal shopping assistant technology (i.e. a technological crossover between a GPS device and a small computer that consumers can use while shopping) and fidelity cards, have allowed companies to gain an in-depth knowledge of consumer behaviors by recording not only the products that consumers choose, but also those that are initially entered and later on deleted from the shopping list.

– Reverse auctions, also known as procurement auctions, have played a key role in streamlining the supply of certain items to some large-scale retailers. These auctions are indeed based on a digital platform exchange process where suppliers underbid each other until the product is sold to the buyer according to rules established by the buyer itself (Riboldazzi, 2005). Typically, prices will decrease during this bidding process.

– Customer relationship management (CRM) is a collaborative effort to record and analyze data on customer behavior and market offering customization, which allows the development of long-lasting relationships with the consumer (i.e. customer fidelization), thereby generating superior customer value for both manufacturers and large-scale retailers.

– Near field communication (NFC) technology coupled with the ability to pay with smartphones has enabled consumers to spend their money more easily than in the past, thereby speeding up the overall buying process.

– Revolving cards allow consumers to choose deferred payment arrangements for the purchase of both durable and non-durable goods.

– Electronic shelf labels (ESLs) are digital labels placed on the shelves providing information about product prices and promotions. These labels allow retailers to automatically update prices displayed on the shelves according to channel requirements and demand variations.

– Radio-frequency identification (RFID) is a technology capable of tracking and reading out the information contained in smart labels (i.e. tags) attached to each product. Tag reading is performed thanks to a radio signal "captured" by a device that identifies the product's electronic code alongside any additional information. The tag allows tracking a certain product throughout all phases of the supply chain, including production, warehousing, in-store, and consumption, thereby improving the handling of the product itself and the overall information exchange.

– Continuous replenishment program (CRP) is a process that entrusts the manufacturer, once the information has been received from the retailer, with the responsibility of issuing order and managing stock levels at the distribution center. Collaborative planning, forecasting, and replenishment (CPRF) is a business practice that extends this collaboration between manufacturers and large-scale retailers also to the order forecasting and planning phases, shifting the focus towards medium/long-term objectives, thereby enhancing business efficiency.

– Cross-docking, multi-drop, multi-pick and multi-drop/multi-pick combination (Riboldazzi, 2015). Cross-docking is a distribution system characterized by the presence of a shared docking terminal where goods from multiple manufacturers are unloaded from inbound trucks and loaded directly into outbound trucks directed towards distribution centers or points of sale. In this regard, we can distinguish two types of cross-docking: 1) with the docking terminal inside the distribution center and the points of sale of a single retailer, or 2) point of delivery of multiple retailers. In contrast, the multi-drop system does not require the presence of a docking terminal as the manufacturer simply combines all orders made by multiple retailers and then deliver products to points of sale located in the same geographical area using the same means of transportation. Likewise, multi-pick transport does not require the presence of a docking terminal, thus avoiding its associated costs, as the goods are picked up from multiple manufacturers in neighboring areas and transported to a single point of delivery. A recent evolution of these transport practices is represented by the multi-drop/multi-pick combination, which organizes full truckloads of goods originating from multiple manufacturers to be delivered to different retailers. Thus, vehicle load saturation, synchronization of information between manufacturers and retailers, and virtually no storage time and warehouse needed for the goods have all allowed significant savings in product flow and transport logistics.

References

Basker E., Klimek S., Hoang Van P., *Supersize It: The Growth of Retail Chains and the Rise of the "Big-Box" Store*, Journal of Economics & Management Strategy, (21), 541–582, 2012. doi:10.1111/j.1530-9134.2012.00339.x.

Best R.J., *Market-Based Management*, Prentice Hall, New Jersey, 2009.

Boyle B., Dwyer F.R., Robicheaux R.A. and Simpson J.T., *Influence Strategies in Marketing Channels: Measures and Use in Different Relationship Structures*, Journal of Marketing Research, (29), 4, 462-473, 1992. http://wwwjstor.org/stable/3172712.

Brondoni S.M., *Market-Driven Management, Competitive Space and Global Network*, Symphonya. Emerging Issues in Management (www.unimib.it/symphonya), (1), 14-27, 2008. doi:http://dx.doi.org/10.4468/2008.1.02 brondoni.

Brondoni S.M., *Market-Driven Management, Competitive Customer Value and Global Network*, Symphonya. Emerging Issues in Management (www.unimib.it/symphonya), (1), 8-25, 2009. doi:http://dx.doi.org/10.4468/2009.1.02 brondoni.

Brondoni S.M., Musso F., *Ouverture de 'Marketing Channels and Global Markets'*, Symphonya. Emerging Issues in Management (symphonya.unimib.it), (1), 1-6, 2010. http://dx.doi.org/10.4468/2010.1.01ouverture.

Brondoni S.M., Corniani M., Riboldazzi S., *Global Retailers, Market-Driven Management and Innovation*, International Journal of Economic Behavior, (3), 27-40, 2013.

Bucklin L.P., *A Theory of Distribution Channel Structure*, University of California, Institute of Business and Economic Research, Berkeley, 1966.

Conad, *Annal Report*, 2015.

Day G.S., *Market-Driven Strategy: Processes for Creating Value*, Free Press, New York, 1990.

Day G.S., *The Capabilities of Market-Driven Organization*, Journal of Marketing, (58), 4, 37-52, 1994. http://www.jstor.org/stable/1251915.

Day G.S., *What Does It Mean to be Market-Driven?*, Business Strategy Review, (9), 1, 1-14, 1998. doi:10.1111/1467-8616.00051.

Day G.S., *Creating a Market-Driven Organization*, Sloan Management Review, (41), 1, 11-22, 1999.

Deloitte, *Global Power of Retailing. The Art and Science of Customers,* 2017.

Deshpandé R., Farley J.U., *Understanding Market Orientation: A prospectively Designed Meta Analysis of Three Market Scales*, Cambridge, MA: Marketing Science Institute, 96-125, 1996.

Fritz W., *Market Orientation and Corporate Success: Findings from Germany,* European Journal of Marketing, (30), 8, 59-74, 1996. https://doi.org/10.1108/03090569610130106.

Gundlach G.T., Bolumole Y.A., Eltantawy R.A. and Frankel R., *The Changing Landscape of Supply Chain Management, Marketing Channels of Distribution, Logistics and Purchasing*, Journal of Business & Industrial Marketing, (21), 7, 428-438, 2006. doi:10.1108/08858620610708911.

Gupta S., Loulou R., *Process Innovation, Product Differentiation, and Channel Structure: Strategic Incentives in a Duopoly*, Marketing Science, (17), 4, 301-316, 1998. http://dx.doi.org/10.1287/mksc.17.4.301.

Jaworsky B., Kohli A.K., Sahay A., *Market Driven Versus Driving Markets*, Journal of the Academy of Marketing Science, (28), 1, 45-54, 2000. doi:https://doi.org/10.1177/0092070300281005.

Lambin J.-J., *Capitalism and Sustainable Development*, Symphonya. Emerging Issues in Management (www.unimib.it/symphonya), (2), 3-9, 2009. doi:http://dx.doi.org/10.4468/2009.2.02lambin.

Lambin J.-J., *Le Marketing Strategique. Du Marketing à l'Orientation Marché*, Ediscience (Paris), 1998.

Lusch R.F, Brown J.R., *Interdependency, Contracting, and Relational Behavior in Marketing Channels*, Journal of Marketing, (60), 4, 19-38, 1996. http://www.jstor.org/stable/1251899.

Mohr J.J., *Communication Flows in Distribution Channels: Impact on Assessments of Communication Quality and Satisfaction*, Journal of Retailing, (71), 4, 393-415, 1995. https://doi.org/10.1016/0022-4359(95)90020-9.

Musso F., *Innovation in Marketing Channels*, Symphonya. Emerging Issues in Management (www.unimib.it/symphonya), (1), 23-42, 2010. doi:http://dx.doi.org/10.4468/2010.1.04musso

Narver J.C., Slater S.F., *The Effect of Marketing Orientation on Business Profitability*, Journal of Marketing, (54), 4, 20-35, 1990. http://www.jstor.org/stable/1251757.

Pellegrini L., Reddy S.K., *Retail and Marketing Channels. Economic nd Marketing Perspectives on Producer-Distributor Relationships*, Routledge Library Edition: Retailing and Distribution, 2013.

Riboldazzi S., *Global Retailers and Competitive Customer Value*, Symphonya. Emerging Issue in Management (symphonya.unimib.it), (2), 77-87, 2005. http://dx.doi.org/10.4468/2005.2.07riboldazzi.

Riboldazzi S., *Global Markets and Development Policies in Large-Scale Retailers*, Symphonya. Emerging Issues in Management (symphonya.unimib.it), (5), 8-28, 2015. http://dx.doi.org/10.4468/2015.5.02riboldazzi.

Rosenbloom B., *Marketing Channels: A Management View*, Thomson South Western, Mason, Ohio, 2004.

Rosenbloom B., *Six Classic Distribution Paradigms for Global Marketing Channel*

Strategy, Symphonya. Emerging Issues in Management (symphonya.unimib.it), (1), 2010, 7-17. http://dx.doi.org/10.4468/2010.1.02rosenbloom.

Slater S.F., Narver J.C., *Market Orientation, Customer Value, and Superior Performance*, Business Horizons, (37), 2, 22-28, 1994. https://doi.org/10.1016/0007-6813(94)90029-9.

Slater S.F., Narver J.C., *Customer-Led and Market-Oriented: Let's Not Confuse the Two*, Strategic Management Journal, (19), 10, 1001-1006, 1998.

Chapter 10

BUSINESS COALITIONS FOR SUSTAINABLE GLOBAL PROCUREMENT

Mario Risso

ABSTRACT: *The globalisation of markets has characterized the business landscape with an unprecedented, accelerating, and complex mix of risks and opportunities. Particularly in natural resource procurement markets, large global companies are called on to confront sustainable global goals and local problems, which require high investments in local areas and the involvement of local public regulators and civil society as a whole. A single large company, even if global, cannot easily achieve effective and efficient solutions with sustainable levels of risk. The aim of this chapter is to illustrate some initiatives where a collaborative approach among competitors (business coalitions) has facilitated long-term solutions that can generate shared value creation for all actors involved.*

SUMMARY: 10.1. Introduction. – 10.2. Sustainability and global procurement. – 10.3. Business-led coalitions for sustainable procurement. – 10.4. Two examples of successful business-led coalitions for sustainable global procurement. – 10.5. Concluding remarks.

10.1. Introduction

The globalisation of the economy is characterised by the progressive creation of internationalised and often fragmented production networks resulting from the process of productive delocalisation in emerging and developing countries. In fact, many international companies have outsourced their production to suppliers abroad. They have structured their supply networks in such a way to optimise costs and maintain their comparative advantage in order to maximise efficiency and corporate value creation (Emmelhainz, Adams, 1999; Manic, 2005). This process has been accompanied by the growing importance of logistical and distributive aspects, marketing and communication, and the outsourcing of low value-added upstream activities have become more prominent (Christopher, 2005).

However, the adverse human rights and environmental impacts often associated with the activities of suppliers directly or indirectly linked to large international companies have exposed the latter to greater reputational risks (Lemke, Petersen, 2013). The development of sustainable industries is therefore particularly important for large international companies that are held responsible for their environmental and social practices through their own activies, but also associated with any harmful activities of their suppliers (Handfield et al., 2005; Preuss, 2005; Bowen et al., 2006; Amaeshi et al., 2008; Andersen, Skjoett-Larsen, 2009).

In advanced markets the awareness of the social implications of relocation has increased. The pressure created by the behaviour of responsible consumers have the potential to strike the balance between the corporate benefits associated with production relocation and the externalities related to their fragmented activities (Pepe, 2007; 2013). In fact, responsible consumers are calling for sustainable practices throughout the supply chain. In response to this, large international companies have adopted new strategies aimed at developing new forms of competitive advantage, which is founded not only on economic efficiency, but also positive social environmental performance (Carter, Jennings, 2002; Logsdon, Wood, 2005; Musso, Risso, 2006; Brondoni, Pepe, 2007).

This paper aims to analyse new forms of industry-specific collaboration related to procurement practices in geographic areas at heightened risk of adverse social impact and environmental degradation.

The analysis starts by illustrating the different patterns of global supply chain governance in relation to the inclusion of sustainability principles in procurement practices, with specific regard to high risk areas where new collaborative models are gradually emerging (Brondoni, 2003; Porter, Kramer, 2011). The paper illustrates two examples of emerging business-led coalition initiatives for sustainable global procurement: the Electronic Industry Citizenship Coalition (EICC), which groups more than 80 of the world's leading electronics companies, and ITRI which is working to ensure the long-term sustainability of the tin industry globally.

The article concludes by illustrating the obstacles encountered by multinational companies and their suppliers in managing sustainable global procurement initiatives. The aim of the work is to illustrate innovative collaborative approaches among competitors and how they can facilitate the development and implementation of long-term solutions that can generate shared value for all actors involved and society at large (Prahalad, Ramaswamy, 2004; Porter, Kramer 2011).

10.2. Sustainability and global procurement

Today, enterprises are expected to contribute to the development of the countries and communities where they operate. In this respect, "stakeholders" are not only the shareholders and the customers of the companies that produce goods and services, but also local communities and the society at large. The pursuit of profit is undoubtedly a driver for efficient business processes. But, today achieving profit require companies to handle a variety of context variables that companies are no longer able to fully control.

The "multidimensional" potential adverrse impacts of corporate activies imply that every decision and every action should take into account not only the achievement of an economic result but also the impact that this result can have on:

• the company's ability to increase its value in terms of knowledge and professionalism;
• actors directly linked to the business activity, i.e. its customers;
• the whole socio-economic and environmental system.

The most innovative and forward-looking companies are therefore committed to incorporating sustainability into their values, by adopting a triple bottom line, which consists of taking on environmental and social responsibilities that go hand in hand with economic ones (Elkington, 1997). Sustainability can affect both the internal dimension, primarily the improvement of the working environment or the more effective management of the natural resources used in the business, as well as the external dimension, enabling greater integration of all the different stakeholders' interests (business partners, suppliers, customers, public authorities and nongovernmental organisations that represent the local community and the environment).

Global procurement is a matter of growing strategic importance as a result of the intensification of global competition, the spread of outsourcing practices involving emerging markets and the tight deadlines characterising supply chain activities (Andersen and Skjoett-Larsen, 2009). The ability to establish close and long-term relationships with suppliers and other strategic partners has become a crucial factor in determining the creation of a competitive advantage (Porter, van der Linde, 1995; Pedersen, Andersen, 2006). While recognising the diversity of approaches, recent studies converge to define sustainable supply chains as those characterised by the voluntary adoption of sustainable policies and tools for the selection of suppliers, the contractualisation of the relationship, the management, and the monitoring and evaluation of their performance (Roberts, 2003; Ansett,

2007; Worthington et al. 2008; Barkemeyer, 2009). Moreover, to implement sustainable solutions a new strategic approach to business management based on a relational and collaborative approach is needed (UN, 2015).

The coordinated management of the supply chain is an essential element for the implementation of sustainable strategies (Delbufalo, 2015). While every company is held responsible for its own activities within its business boundaries, the leading companies in the chain have the duty to use their co-ordinating power in a responsible manner. Where leverage exists, they are also expected to positively influence their suppliers, especially in emerging and developing countries, where the enterprise has the ability to effect change in the wrongful practices of the entities that may cause the harm (OECD, 2011). This can contribute to the progressive adoption and implementation of appropriate environmental and social standards and the spread of best practices across the entire supply chain (Carter, Jennings, 2002; Nidumolu et al., 2009; Vilanova et al., 2009; Isaksson et al. 2010; Esteves, Barclay, 2011; Iasevoli, Massi, 2012).

Responsible supply chain management can therefore be defined as the virtuous use of corporate purchasing power to influence a positive change in the production cycle, through the establishment of partnerships with suppliers, sharing responsibilities and promoting innovation for the simultaneous achievement of environmental, social and economic goals (Carter , Carter, 1998; Maloni, Brown, 2006; Vacho, Klassen, 2006; Locke, Romis, 2007; Lim Phillips, 2008; Müeller et a.l, 2009).

10.3. Business-led coalitions for sustainable procurement

The implementation of sustainability principles in supply chain management requires close consideration of the following issues:

• the development and adoption of codes of conduct (Jenkins et al, 2002; Lund-Thomsen, 2008, Preuss, 2009);

• the credible assessment of supplier sustainability practices (Xing, 2013);

• the design of tailored governance systems and data and communication management (Martin, 2016);

• co-ordination with business partners and joint strategic planning (Linnenluecke et al., 2017);

• appropriate prevention and corrective measures (Busse et al., 2017);

• monitoring and evaluation of performance (Motevali Haghighi et al., 2016).

Some companies have developed generic codes of conduct that include procurement sustainability criteria applicable throughout the whole supply chain consistent with applicable national laws and international guidelines from international organisations such as the ILO and the OECD.

However, individual attempts by international companies to cope with sustainable procurement challenges are not always an effective and efficient way to improve sustainable performance, especially when the production process is highly fragmented and suppliers may be exposed to conflicting requirements and audit procedures by different buyers. Although some initiatives already provide for shared standards for sustainable supply chains, they are not yet tailored to specific economic sectors, so they require adjustments with regard to specific contexts (Risso, 2012). Large international companies are also aware of the additional costs of individual approaches to promote sustainability in global procurement, in particular with respect to the identification and use of standards and monitoring and evaluation procedures that are not shared by all actors in the chain.

In response to this, collaborative horizontal approaches to managing sustainability challenges in global supply chains are gradually emerging. The objective of all of these initiatives is to reduce costs and risks, while improving sustainability performance in the relationships with suppliers, thus increasing the overall value created by products and services (Hutton, 2007; Teuscher, 2009). The participation in industry-wide collaborative efforts among enterprises that share common suppliers can help to coordinate supply chain policies and risk management strategies, including through information-sharing on good practices and independent monitoring and evaluation (Appolloni, Risso, Zhang, 2013). Enterprises may also engage with suppliers and other entities in the supply chain to improve their performance, in co-operation with other stakeholders, including through personnel training and other forms of capacity building.

Industry-specific collaborative initiatives, also referred to as business-led coalitions, provide a neutral and safe space where managers can freely interact to explore solutions to common sustainability challenges, in particular, with regard to management systems, incentives, key performance indicators, reporting, and experience sharing (Grayson, Nelson, 2013). This creates the conditions to develop new knowledge and financial, managerial, technical and logistical skills that otherwise would not be achievable.

The creation of a pre-competitive space to identify innovative solutions fosters dialogue among competitors and helps to build trust with other stakeholders, including governments and non-gouvernmental-organisations that may be involved in the process (Daboub, Calton, 2002).

Dialogue platforms linked to these forms of collaboration facilitate the mutual understanding of the challenges of operating in difficult contexts and the implementation of specific projects at local level as well as the provision of targeted services which go beyond the boundaries of individual organisations. This increases the positive impact of the activities of the entreprises and can also influence the policies of governments at national and regional level.

Industry-specific business-led coalitions are organised around business associations that are independent from their members. Their governing board usually includes top managers of member companies supported by technical staff composed of sustanibility experts. The governing board may also involve civil society rapresentatives. The inclusive nature of these organisations improves interactions with civil society and the mutual understanding of the issues at stake.

On the financial side, these organisations are supported by the contributions of their members that generally pay membership fees on annual basis. Alternative financial models include:

- revenues generate by counsultancies and services provided to members that benefit from the activities of the organisation;
- voluntary contributions given by philantropic organisations linked to the companies members of the coalition;
- public financial support and fundraising.

10.4. Two examples of successful business-led coalitions for sustainable global procurement

ITRI and its iTSCi Programme – ITRI is a not for profit membership based organisation representing the tin industry and is supported by the world's most important tin producers and smelters.

ITRI's main objective is to support and encourage the use of tin in existing and new applications by promoting a positive image of tin and the tin industry including through the creation of opportunities to differentiate between responsible producers and others and the promotion of sustainable tin procurement throughout the supply chain.

ITRI has established the iTSCi Programme designed to assist companies with traceability, due diligence and audit requirements on purchases of minerals from high risk areas in line with international standards set by the OECD Due Diligence Guidelines (2016) and UN recommendations. The Programme further aims to ensure compliance with the US Dodd Frank Law, section 1502 on conflict minerals.

Since its development in 2010, the Programme has rapidly evolved with the establishment of traceability in the upstream supply chain from mine to smelter, and downstream companies (product manufacturers etc) and it assists companies to carry out due diligence through independent audits and risk assessments (iTSCi, 2016).

The project is implemented in 1000 mine sites in Burundi, Rwanda and the DRC, shipping 100's of tonnes of minerals per month, and involving 80,000 miners. The programme counts 250 members spanning 35 countries.

By bringing together a wide range of different companies, from small cooperatives to large companies, iTSCi improves efficiency throughout the supply chain through avoidance of duplication, accurate management of extensive information and data, cost savings and helps to ensure that the procurement of minerals is managed and handled in line with international expectations.

iTSCi benefits from the collaboration with US based capacity building NGO Pact Inc. that acts as the Programme Operator for in-country traceability and the implementation of due diligence.

Regular independent audits, including preliminary audits, field governance assessments and company audits, are carried-out by third party auditing company, Synergy Global Consulting Ltd. Member companies can use this information to regularly check on suppliers and customers and manage risks.

iTSCi is also a useful tool for the small businesses and artisanal miners of central Africa to implement the complex international OECD Due Diligence Guidance. "*This rule based trading environment instils confidence and assures credibility thus allowing conflict-free African minerals to access international markets at fair prices. [...] iTSCi is a voluntary private sector initiative, understanding the importance of global markets, and trade opportunities, working hand in hand with Government services and international and local NGO's to deliver capacity building and improved governance*" (iTSCi, 2016).

iTSCi has demonstrated the power of market incentive to effect change in supply chain mangement to cope with complex challenges for responsible sourcing from high risk areas.

Electronic Industry Citizenship Coalition – The Electronic Industry Citizenship Coalition (EICC) is a nonprofit coalition of electronics, retail, auto and toy companies committed to setting and holding members accountable to core standards and providing training and assessment tools, with the objective of promoting co-operation for sustainable supply chain in the electronics industry.

Founded in 2004 by eight companies, today the EICC gathers more than 110 electronics companies with combined annual revenue of over $4.75 trillion, directly employing more than 6 million people. In addition to EICC members, thousands of companies that are Tier 1 suppliers to those members are required to implement the EICC Code of Conduct (http://www.eiccoalition.org).

Key to supply chain sustainability are strong management systems and institutional structures and practices that facilitate productive and sustainable manufacturing operations. These systems and structures are vital to prevent accidents and abuses that damage both businesses and communities. The EICC offers a range of educational tools to support members to make best use of these systems and structures that solve problems before they arise and reduce the need for costly auditing. The EICC further fosters dialogue and collaboration with governments and civil society, investors and academia to support and drive sustainable performance in global electronics supply chain (Liu et al., 2015).

With specific regard to the toolbox available, EICC members commit and are held accountable to a common Code of Conduct and utilise a range of EICC training and shared assessment tools to support continuous improvement in their supply chains.

The EICC has also established a Validated Asessment Process (VAP) for suppliers, which is used as a common standard for onsite compliance verification and effective, shareable assessments. The EICC has reported that since 2009, its members have completed more than 2,500 VAP onsite compliance assessments conducted in more than 20 countries by independent third-party audit firms that have been approved by the EICC to execute the VAP protocol (http://www.eiccoalition.org).

An important objective of the EICC programme is to provide support for risk assessment in raw materials supply chains. *"Assessing social and environmental risks in raw material extraction and processing, and industry's ability to appropriately manage such risks, remains a challenge for downstream companies due to the size and complexity of international supply chains. In addition to the difficulty of reaching suppliers beyond the first-tier supply chain levels, companies are confronted with a highly fragmented landscape of standards, initiatives and certifications related to responsible mining and minerals processing"* (EICC, 2016).

EICC members are required to complete self-assessments at the corporate level and at their own manufacturing facilities. Members are also strongly encouraged to use the self-assessment as a key part of their risk assessment of suppliers' facilities in their supply chain. The self-assessment checks for a range of supply chain risks that could constitute violations of the EICC Code of Conduct.

To facilitate this task, the EICC provides its members with a risk assessment template called the Self-Assessment Questionnaire (SAQ), as well as a high-level risk assessment tool. Members must use the SAQ on their own facilities and at the corporate level, and for supplier facilities they have the option of using the SAQ or a risk assessment tool.

The EICC also provides an on-line sustainability data management system (EICC-ON) designed to help its members to manage and share sustainability data, including from audits and self-assessment questionnaires, including online analysis by a company's customers (as authorized by the supplier). Audits are also carried out as a common tool used for corporate supply chain sustainability programs as they can establish a baseline and provide an important monitoring and evaluation check.

The EICC's conflict-free sourcing initiative provides an example of a targeted application of this toolbox which involves 350 companies from seven different industries, using a range of tools and resources including the Conflict-Free Smelter Program, the Conflict Minerals Reporting Template, Reasonable Country of Origin Inquiry data and a range of guidance documents on conflict minerals sourcing.

10.5. Concluding remarks

The growing importance of sustainable international supply chains is boosting new ways to cope with global procurement challenges through collaborative approaches between major buyers and local suppliers.

Emerging industry-specific business-led coalitions for sustainable global procurement show the usefulness of developing common codes of conduct and shared monitoring and evaluation systems to foster effective and efficient sustainable operations especially in high-risk areas.

Although large intrenational companies usually adopt codes of conduct to improve sustainable practices in their supply chains, the complexity of markets and the rapid expansion of highly internationalised networks have multiplied the issues at stake.

Individual approaches to deal with sustainibility in international supply chains have resulted in sub-optimal collective performance, given the proliferation of standards that are often not tailored to specific contexts and may impose conflicting requirements on suppliers, leading to additional costs of implementation (Risso, 2012).

Where control and the ability to influence suppliers clearly exist (hierarchical, captive and relational supply chains), the leading company may be able to support suppliers to adopt sustainable practices in a vertical collaborative rather than policing manner.

However, in highly fragmented supply chains vertical collaboration does not work. The complex network of actors and their interactions make vertical collaboration less effective. In these contexts, the resources invested by individual companies to promote sustainable procurement practices could be reallocated to support more collaborative industry-specific approaches (Risso, 2012).

In fact, innovative horizontal collaboration among competing companies sharing the same problems has proved more effective to ensure consistency and efficiency in the development and implementation of sustainable strategies throughout the supply chain (Appolloni et al., 2013; Delbufalo, 2015). Industry-specific collaboration can lead to collective solutions and the development of common tools that ensure harmonisation of standards throughout the supply chain, the reduction of implementation costs and mechanisms to support suppliers to comply with sustainibility principles through progressive improvement, training and capacity building.

The two pioneering examples described above show a significant shift in the organisational structures, procedures and processes of member companies providing for a pre-competitive space to identify innovative solutions to common issues. The collaborative approach adopted by business-led coalitions ultimately results in strengthened competitiveness of their individual members and fosters dialogue among competitors, helping to build confidence and trust with civil society by generating positive impacts. However, sustainable performance in global procurement largely depends on the degree of corporate and stakeholder participation and continuos involvement and commitment to such collaborative initiatives, which take time to develop due to the discussions and mediations needed to build consensus among all actors involved.

This embryonic analysis can prompt investigation of additional collaborative approaches to adopting sustainable global procurement solutions in international supply chains in order to conceptualise models and deepen the understanding of their performance.

References

Amaeshi K.M., Osuji O.K., Nnodim P., *Corporate Social Responsibility in Supply Chains of Global Brands: A Boundaryless Responsibility?*, Journal of Business Ethics, (81), 223-234, 2008. http://dx.doi.org/10.1007/s10551-007-9490-5.

Andersen M., Skjoett-Larsen T., *Corporate Social Responsibility in Global Supply Chains*, Supply Chain Management: An International Journal, (14), 75-86, 2009. https://doi.org/10.1108/13598540910941948.

Ansett S., *Mind the Gap: A Journey to Sustainable Supply Chains*, Employee

Responsibilities & Rights Journal, (19), 295-303, 2007. http://dx.doi.org/10.1007/s10672-007-9057-8.

Appolloni A., Risso M., Zhang T., *Collaborative Approach for Sustainable Auditing of Global Supply Chains*, Symphonya. Emerging Issues in Management, (2), 19-31, 2013. https://doi.org/10.4468/2013.2.02appolloni.risso.zhang.

Barkemeyer R., *Beyond compliance – Below expectations? CSR in the Context of International Development*, Business Ethics: A European Review, (18), 273-289, 2009. http://dx.doi.org/10.1111/j.1467-8608.2009.01563.x.

Beschorner T., Müller M., *Social Standards: Toward an Active Ethical Involvement of Business in Developing Countries*, Journal of Business Ethics, (73), 11-20, 2007. http://dx.doi.org/10.1007/s10551-006-9193-3.

Bowen F.E., Cousins P.D., Lamming R.C., Faruk A.C., *Horses for Courses: Explaining the Gap Between the Theory and Practice of Green Supply*, in Sarkis J., Greening the Supply Chain, Springer, London, 2006. http://dx.doi.org/10.1007/1-84628-299-3_9.

Brondoni S.M., *Network Culture, Performance & Corporate Responsibility*, Symphonya. Emerging Issues in Management, (1), 8-24, 2003. http://dx.doi.org/10.4468/2003.1.02brondoni.

Brondoni S.M., Pepe C., *Ouverture de 'Ethics in Global Supply Chains'*, Symphonya, Emerging issues in Management, (2), 1-4, 2007. http://dx.doi.org/10.4468/2007.2.01ouverture.

Busse C., Meinlschmidt J., Foerstl K. (2017), *Managing Information Processing Needs in Global Supply Chains: A Prerequisite to Sustainable Supply Chain Management*, Journal of Supply Chain Management, (53): 87-113, 2017. http://dx.doi.org/10.1111/jscm.12129.

Carter C.R., Carter J.R., *Interorganizational Determinants of Environmental Purchasing: Initial Evidence from the Consumer Products Industry*, Decision Sciences, (29), 659-684, 1998. http://dx.doi.org/10.1111/j.1540-5915.1998.tb01358.x.

Carter C.R., Jennings M., *Logistics Social Responsibility: An Integrative Framework*, Journal of Business Logistics, (23), 145-180, 2002. http://dx.doi.org/10.1002/j.2158-1592.2002.tb00020.x.

Christopher M., *Logistics and Supply Chain Management: Creating Value-adding Networks*, Prentice Hall, UK, 2005.

Daboub A., Calton J., *Stakeholder Learning Dialogues: How to Preserve Ethical Responsibility in Networks*, Journal of Business Ethics, (41), 85-98, 2002. https://doi.org/10.1023/A:102130220.

Delbufalo E., *Subjective Trust and Perceived Risk Influences on Exchange Performance in Supplier-Manufacturer Relationships*, Scandinavian Journal of Management, (31), 84-101, 2015. http://dx.doi.org/10.1016/j.scaman.2014.06.002.

Elkington J., *Cannibals with Forks*, Capstone Publishing Ltd, Oxford, 1997.

Emmelhainz M.A., Adams R.J., *The Apparel Industry Response to "Sweatshop" Concerns: A Review and Analysis of Codes of Conduct*, Journal of Supply Chain Management, Summer, 51–57, 1999. doi:10.1111/j.1745-493X.1999.tb00062.x.

Esteves A., Barclay M., *Enhancing the Benefits of Local Content: Integrating Social and Economic Impact Assessment into Procurement Strategies*, Impact Assessment & Project Appraisal, (29), 205-215, 2011. http://dx.doi.org/10.3152/146155111X12959673796128.

Grayson D., Nelson J., *Corporate Responsibility Coalitions: The Past, Present, and Future of Alliances for Sustainable Capitalism*, Greenleaf Publishing Limited, Sheffield, 2013.

Handfield R.B., Stroufe R., Walton S., *Integrating Environmental Management and Supply Chain Strategies*, Business Strategy and the Environment, (14), 1-19, 2005. http://dx.doi.org/10.1002/bse.422.

Hutton R., Cox D.B., Clouse M.L., Gaensbauer J., Banks B.D., *The Role of Sustainable Development in Risk Assessment and Management for Multinational Corporations*, Multinational Business Review (St. Louis University), (15), 89-111, 2007.

Iasevoli G., Massi M. (2012), *The Relationship Between Sustainable Business Management and Competitiveness: Research Trends and Challenge*, International Journal Of Technology Management, (58), 32-48, 2012. http://dx.doi.org/10.1504/IJTM.2012.045787.

Isaksson R., Johansson P., Fischer K., *Detecting Supply Chain Innovation Potential for Sustainable Development*, Journal of Business Ethics, (97), 425-442, 2010. http://dx.doi.org/10.1007/s10551-010-0516-z.

iTSCi, *iTSCi Joint Industry Traceability And Due Diligence Programme*, ITRI, www.itri.co.uk, 2016.

Jenkins R., Pearson R., Seyfang G. (eds.), *Corporate Responsibility and Labour Rights: Codes of Conduct in the Global Economy*, Earthscan, London, 2012.

Lemke F., Petersen H.L., *Teaching reputational risk management in the supply chain*, Supply Chain Management, (18), 413-429, 2013. http://dx.doi.org/10.1108/SCM-06-2012-0222.

Lim S.J., Phillips J., *Embedding CSR Values: The Global Footwear Industry's Evolving Governance Structure*, Journal of Business Ethics, (81), 143-156, 2008. http://dx.doi.org/10.1007/s10551-007-9485-2.

Linnenluecke M.K., Verreynne M., de Villiers Scheepers M.J., Venter C., *A Review of Collaborative Planning Approaches for Transformative Change Towards a Sustainable Future*, Journal of Cleaner Production, (142), 3212-3224, 2017. http://dx.doi.org/10.1016/j.jclepro.2016.10.148.

Liu C.C., Yu Y.H., Wernick I.K., Chang C.Y., *Using the Electronic Industry Code of Conduct to Evaluate Green Supply Chain Management: An Empirical Study of*

Taiwan's Computer Industry, Sustainability, (7), 2787-2803, 2015. http://dx. doi.org/10.3390/su7032787.

Locke R.M., Romis M., *Improving Work Conditions in a Global Supply Chain*, MIT Sloan Management Review, (48), 54-62, 2007.

Logsdon J.M., Wood D.J., *Global Business Citizenship and Voluntary Codes of Ethical Conduct*, Journal of Business Ethics, (59), 55-67, 2005. http://dx.doi. org/10.1007/s10551-005-3411-2.

Lund-Thomsen P., *The Global Sourcing and Codes of Conduct De-bate: Five Myths and Five Recommendations*, Development and Change, (39), 1005-1018, 2008. doi:10.1111/j.1467-7660.2008.00526.x.

Maloni M.J., Brown M.E., *Corporate Social Responsibility in the Supply Chain: An Application in the Food Industry*, Journal of Business Ethics, (68), n. 1, 35-52, 2006. http://dx.doi.org/10.1007/s10551-006-9038-0.

Mamic I., *Managing Global Supply Chain: The Sports Footwear, Apparel and retail Sectors*, Journal of Business Ethics, (59), 81-100, 2005. http://dx.doi.org/10. 1007/s10551-005-3415-y.

Martin G., Farndale E., Paauwe J., Stiles P.G., *Corporate Governance and Strategic Human Resource Management: Four Archetypes and Proposals for a New Approach to Corporate Sustainability*, European Management Journal, (34), 22-35, 2016. http://dx.doi.org/10.1016/j.emj.2016.01.002.

Min H., Galle W.P., *Green Purchasing Strategies: Trends and Implications*, International Journal of Purchasing and Materials Management, (33), 10-17, 1997. http://dx.doi.org/10.1111/j.1745-493X.1997.tb00026.x.

Motevali Haghighi S., Torabi S., Ghasemi R., *An Integrated Approach for Performance Evaluation in Sustainable Supply Chain Networks (with a case study)*, Journal of Cleaner Production, (137), 579-597, 2016. http://dx.doi.org/ 10.1016/j.jclepro.2016.07.119.

Müeller M., Gomes dos Santos V., Seuring S., *The Contribution of Environmental and Social Standards Towards Ensuring Legitimacy in Supply Chain Governance*, Journal of Business Ethics, (89), 509-523, 2009. http://dx.doi.org/10.1007/ s10551-008-0013-9.

Musso F., Risso M., *CSR within Large Retailers International Supply Chains*, Symphonya Emerging Issues in Management, (1), 79-92, 2006. http://dx.doi. org/10.4468/2006.1.06musso.risso.

Nidumolu R.C.K., Prahalad C.K., Rangaswami M.R., *Why Sustainability Is Now the Key Driver of Innovation*, Harvard Business Review, (87), 56-64, 2013. http://dx.doi.org/10.1109/EMR.2013.6601104.

OECD (2016), *OECD Due Diligence Guidance for Responsible Supply Chains of Minerals from Conflict-Affected and High-Risk Areas: Third Edition*, OECD Publishing, Paris.

OECD (2011), *OECD Guidelines for Multinational Enterprises*, OECD Publishing, Paris.

Pedersen E.R, Andersen M., *Safeguarding Corporate Social Responsibility (CSR) In Global Supply Chains: How Codes of Conduct Are Managed in Buyer-Supplier Relationships*, Journal of Public Affairs, (6), 228–240, 2006. http://dx.doi.org/10.1002/pa.232.

Pepe C., *Corporate Values in Global Supply Chains*, Symphonya, Emerging Issues in Management, (2), 5-11, 2007. http://dx.doi.org/10.4468/2007.2.02pepe.

Pepe C., *Values and Corporate Responsibility in Globalization Processes*, EMEE vol. 32, McGraw-Hill Education, Milan, Italy, 2013.

Pepe C., Musso F., Risso M., *The Social Responsibility of Retailers and Small/Medium Suppliers in International Supply Chains*, Finanza Marketing e Produzione, (28), 32-61, 2010.

Porter M.E., Kramer M.R., *The Big Idea. Creating Shared Value*, Harvard Business Review, Jan-Feb, (89), 62-77, 2011.

Porter M.E., van der Linde, *Toward a New Conception of the Environment-Competitiveness Relationship*, The Journal of Economic Perspectives, (9), 97-118, 1995. http://dx.doi.org/10.1257/jep.9.4.97.

Prahalad C.K., Ramaswamy V., *Co-Creating Experiences: The Next Practice in Value Creation*, Journal of Interactive Marketing, (18), 5-14, 2004.

Preuss L., *Ethical Sourcing Codes of Large UK-Based Corporations: Prevalence, Content, Limitations*, Journal of Business Ethics, (88), 735-747, 2009. http://dx.doi.org/10.1002/bse.435.

Preuss L., *Rhetoric and Reality of Corporate Greening: A View From The Supply Chain Management Function*, Business Strategy and the Environment, (14), 123-139, 2005.

Risso M., *A Horizontal Approach To Implementing Corporate Social Responsibility In International Supply Chains*, International Journal of Technology Management, (58), 64-82, 2012. http://dx.doi.org/10.1504/IJTM.2012.045789.

Roberts S., *Supply Chain Specific? Understanding the Patchy Success of Ethical Sourcing Initiatives*, Journal of Business Ethics, (44), 159-170, 2003.

Seuring S., Müller M., *From a Literature Review to a Conceptual Framework for Sustainable Supply Chain Management*, Journal of Cleaner Production, (16), 1699-1710, 2008. http://dx.doi.org/10.1016/j.jclepro.2008.04.020.

Teuscher P., Gruninger B., Ferdinand N., *Risk management in sustainable supply chain management (SSCM): lessons learnt from the case of GMO-free soybeans*, Corporate Social Responsibility and Environmental Management, (13) 1-10, 2006. http://dx.doi.org/10.1002/csr.81.

UN (2015), *Transforming Our World: The 2030 Agenda for Sustainable Development*, A/RES/70/1, United Nations.

Vacho S., Klassen R.D., *Extending Green Practices Across the Supply Chain*, International Journal of Operations & Production Management, (26), 795-821, 2006.

Vilanova M., Lozano J., Arenas D., *Exploring the Nature of the Relationship Between CSR and Competitiveness*, Journal of Business Ethics, (87), 57-69, 2009. http://dx.doi.org/10.1007/s10551-008-9812-2.

Walton S., Handfield R., Melnyk S., *The Green Supply Chain: Integrating Suppliers into Environmental Management Processes*, International Journal of Purchasing and Materials Management, (3), 2-11, 1998. http://dx.doi.org/10.1111/j.1745-493X.1998.tb00042.x.

Worthington I., Ram M, Boyal H, Shah M., *Researching the Drivers of Socially Responsible Purchasing: A Cross-National Study of Supplier Diversity Initiatives*, Journal Of Business Ethics, (79), 319-331, 2008. http://dx.doi.org/10.1007/s10551-007-9400-x.

Xing K., Wang H., Qian W., *A Sustainability-Oriented Multi-Dimensional Value Assessment Model for Product-Service Development*, International Journal of Production Research, (51), 5908-5933, 2013. http://dx.doi.org/10.1080/00207543.2013.810349.

Yakovleva N., Vazquez-Brust D., *Stakeholder Perspectives on CSR of Mining MNCs in Argentina*, Journal of Business Ethics, (106), 191-211, 2012. http://dx.doi.org/10.1007/s10551-011-0989-4.

Chapter 11
COMPETITIVE PRICING
AND ADVANCE SELLING

Giuseppe Cappiello

ABSTRACT: *The phenomenon of suppliers offering favourable conditions to customers who purchase in advance is increasingly recurrent in service management. This practice is known as "advance selling" and defines a scenario where customers purchase a service before they actually intend to use it. In exchange for the commitment of buying in advance, the buyer is offered a number of benefits, such as price discounts or the ability to choose before other customers. The aim of this chapter is to draw attention to this phenomenon (advance selling or advance pricing), which has become very popular with businesses, especially at the global level, but has still not been extensively analysed in economics and management literature, especially in relation to pricing and branding policies.*

SUMMARY: 11.1. Introduction. – 11.2. Competition and pricing policies. – 11.3. The advantages of advance selling. – 11.4. Strategies for advance selling. – 11.5. Conclusions.

11.1. Introduction

In today's world, as geographical borders expand and physical and technical barriers melt away, competitive perspectives have begun to shift from global production to global networks (Brondoni, 2014) and greater attention is being focused on pricing strategies to ensure that "no money is left on the table".

Thanks to new technology, companies can now take advantage of innovative, low cost solutions, such as electronic cards that can identify buyers and track purchase times and quantities, or geolocation marketing devices that target specific people in a specific place, at a specific time. And this is just the beginning, as with the development of IOT (Internet of Things), even more information will become available. This applies to customers as well, who now use novel technology to optimise their choices by consulting specialised websites that offer rapid comparisons of different prices and purchase conditions.

This degree of information means that systems and operations can now be designed more effectively than in the past and "dynamic prices" can be defined and applied to offer configurations that take into account a wide range of factors, including moment of consumption, purchasing channels and the behaviour of competitors (Fisher, Gallino, Li, 2017).

For all these reasons, a small number of scholars have suggested adopting a price strategy that offers a product or service at a special price if it is purchased a certain time before its actual consumption (*Advance Selling*). Such a decision seems to offer concrete advantages in terms of both production and profit optimisation (Shugan and Xie, 2000, 2004, 2005; Lee and Ng, 2001).

At first glance, this strategy may not seem particularly new, as there are numerous products and services that are purchased some time before their consumption. Think of concert or show ticket sales, holiday reservations, plane tickets or pre-launch product reservations. What qualifies Advance Selling is the emphasis that can be put on the uncertainty regarding the gap in time between the act of purchase and the act of consumption.

This chapter seeks to highlight this important price leverage - which businesses continue to underestimate - by illustrating the essential features of this interesting but often unmanaged phenomenon in existing literature and suggesting some possible focuses for future research.

11.2. Competition and pricing policies

"Pricing is the manager's biggest marketing headache" (Dolan, 1995) because it is difficult to find the right price for a product as the market has become global, less stable, less homogeneous, and each industry adopts different approaches to price fixing (Phillips, 2012). The ever-accelerating rhythm of innovation and the development of powerful tools for analysing large amounts of data, also continuously erode any advantages gained and creates competition in terms of both time and space (Brondoni, 2002).

In low competitive conditions prices can be fixed simply by adding an expected profit margin to the total cost or by differentiating the offer according to some specific demand request. This means that for some time price has bacome the "catalyst" (Cappiello, 2005) of new customer value-oriented business formulas (Woodruff, 1997). But now (D<O and over-supply) the actions of competitors often generate unpredictable reactions in the other actors in the system (Mc Kenzie, 2008).

Table 1. Market characteristics and pricing policies.

Market Characteristics	Pricing Orientation	Reference to	Differentiating elements
Stability (D>O)	Costs	Demand (quantity)	Product Features
Differentiation (D=O)	Demand	Demand (quality)	Value for the customer
Volatility (D<O)	Competition	Demand (structure)	Emotions/time space/channels

In today's markets, products either seem to be "priceless" (Poundstone, 2010) or to have a wide range of prices (Raju and Zhang, 2010), as the same products are offered at very different prices on different channels and at different times. Customers themselves may also dictate prices with "pay what you want" formulas (Weisstein et al., 2016). Sports teams and other organizations have also followed the example of airlines, hotels and restaurants, by adopting revenue management practices in the sphere of event ticket sales (Smith et al., 1992, Enz et al., 2012, Bouchet, 2016).

To complicate matters further, the Sharing Economy has turned ownership into a commodity by means of a business model based on an international network that creates relationships between customers and businesses. For example, Airbnb is one of the world's leading tourism players without owning a single room and Uber is a highly successful transport service without owning a single vehicle. Netflix has definitively changed the way we use television services, as happened some years ago with the distribution of music products and books. The prices of the services offered on these platforms do not follow traditional rules, and therefore continue to create headaches for anyone attempting to analyse them.

In the public service sector, too, authorities now have less control over prices, as strategies drawn from the private sector are increasingly adopted and service providers now seek to offer service packages with a greater focus on customer value and competition.

In the contexts outlined above, the strategy of fixing a different price for those who buy in advance (*Advance Selling*) is becoming more and more common. When a customer decides to make a product or service purchase, it is not certain what their status will be at the time of use, as health problems or an unavoidable commitment may arise. If you wish to go on a skiing holiday you cannot be sure there will be enough snow, or if you want to visit a Middle Eastern country a security issue may arise that will encourage you to stay away. Then there is the problem of travel companions who may need more time than others to come to a decision.

To look at another example, when a pop star announces a concert for a certain date, many fans buy their ticket immediately without worrying about whether they have to pay a booking fee or if they will be able to attend. Conversely, when reserving a vacation, customers may select a last minute option, even if this restricts their choice of destination. In the event of a new service, they may also wait for "pioneers" to test quality standards first.

To anticipate or simply facilitate these choices, sometimes companies offer solutions like, no penalties in case of cancellation, a free trial period, or even a refund in case of customer dissatisfaction. Lastly, by purchasing in advance, the customer chooses whether to consume the product in parts or change their decision over time at a small surcharge. "Carnet 10 Travels" offered by Trenitalia, for example, is a ten-ticket package for a single route purchased in advance and has to be used within 180 days. The offer includes a 20% or 30% discount on the total travel price, but has some limitations, like the price returning to the normal rate if the reservation is changed.

These examples indicate that demand and supply require a range of options that take it account the uncertainty of the future and can therefore be modified as the moment of consumption draws nearer. This may involve specifying an approximate time of consumption and attempting to manage any uncertainty as to what might happen between the moment of purchase and consumption. This is what has made Advance Selling increasingly popular in recent years.

Advance sales should not be considered to be a special case of the Yield Management Systems (McGill, Van Ryzin, 1999; Kimes, 2003; Dana, 2008) widely adopted by large-scale companies. This is because, to be effective, these systems require limited capacity, a predominantly fixed and very low variable cost configuration, and also a significant difference in price sensitivity between the various customers. These conditions are so binding that Yield management can only be used in a limited number of industries.

At the same time Advance Selling is not a traditional form of price discrimination because it does not target predetermined customer categories (third-degree discrimination) and does not necessarily induce self-selection in relation to certain service classes (second degree discrimination).

11.3. The advantages of advance selling

Advance Selling is a price strategy, or part of a more complex commercial strategy, which involves the application of a different, usually lower, price for customers who purchase well before the actual time of consumption.

Services are a favourable context for pricing policies based on time of purchase as services are perishable, i.e. they cannot be used after production (Shostack, 1977). When a plane takes off, for example, any unsold seats cannot be used on the next flight, and a hotel reservation has no value after the night it has been booked for. There are, however, two ways of overcoming the constraints of perishability. Firstly, by adapting production capacity to demand, and secondly, by influencing demand to shift quotas from more "high season" to "low season" periods. The first hypothesis has a rather contained margin for manoeuvre on account of the rigidity of its production structure, while the second hypothesis offers considerably better results.

In the planning phase, production plants are designed to meet peak demand but excess capacity entails higher costs and sometimes damages perceived quality. In the same way, a large restaurant with few customers may communicate poor quality or numerous unrented parked cars at a car hire firm may cause logistics as well as financial problems.

Ng, Wirtz and Lee have investigated how service companies face the problem of unused capacity management by identifying seven strategies that leverage supply and demand and customer relations. Other authors suggest rationing the service range to influence buying strategies (Liu, Van Ryzyn, 2008).

Advance Selling allows businesses to address the issue of profitability and capacity management by influencing market demand through price leveraging.

In addition to a greater use of production plants, other benefits that can be enjoyed by Advance Selling, include:

– diluting contact with customers, which reduces queues and expectations and leaves time for personalising services to meet customers' requirements more efficiently;
– allowing the company to create a temporary monopoly by securing a portion of sales before its offer is compared to those of its competitors;
– generating valuable revenues, which may be lower than market values but still create a cash flow that allows a large part of the fixed costs needed to set up the service to be paid off;
– widening the company's service range and extending its potential market thanks to a differentiated offer that includes early booking and re-

duced prices even if there may be some limitations, such as penalties in the case of cancellation or a return to full price payments for variations in dates;

– allowing more time for demand to be monitored, which is useful for making plant planning decisions (Boyaci and Ozer, 2010) and anticipating new product sales.

Forecasting the time and quantity of demand is one of the most difficult problems that faces marketers. Comparing anticipated to later sales can help create useful predictive models (Moe and Fader, 2002) that can be used to adapt supply conditions rapidly or provide more efficient services. For example, how much fresh fish should a restaurant buy for the following day, or how many extra staff should a business hire, etc.

Generally speaking, the company's goal is to increase profits; Shugan and Xie are the authors who have contributed most to the study of early sales. To demonstrate the affordability of early pricing, they give this simple, but significant example (Shugan and Xie, 2004). Imagine a Chinese restaurant that offers its customers a buffet service on Saturday nights. The customer's willingness to pay for this special offer depends on the value they attach to it and on how much Chinese food they would actually eat. Of course, only the customer knows this value, but one thing is certain: the further away the date is, the more difficult it is to make a decision. On Monday you are not sure whether you will be hungry and feel like eating Chinese food on Saturday. To simulate a situation, let's assume that 100 consumers come to the buffet every Saturday evening, who are equally divided between those who are in a "favorable state" of consumption with regard to appetite and type of cuisine and those who are not. Let's suppose, finally, that they are willing to pay $ 10 for the dinner when they are in a favorable state and only $ 4 when they are in an unfavorable state and that the average cost to serve a customer is $ 2.

The restaurateur must determine the price and choose whether to charge $ 10 or $ 4 per person, i.e. which of the two types of customer value are most likely to apply to a Chinese dinner on a Saturday evening. In the first case, only half of the 100 potential consumers will come, but they will be in a favourable state of consumption and willing to pay the higher price (half, i.e. 100/2 = 50), equivalent to a profit of (10 − 2) * 50 = $ 400. In the second case, the dinner will be sold to all 100 potential customers, but at a low price, which will make a profit of (4 − 2) * 100 = 200 $.

The restaurateur, therefore, decides to introduce a constraint stating that reservations have to be made before the previous Monday. In this case, favorable and unfavorable conditions are equally likely, as on Monday customers have no idea of their appetite and desire for Chinese food on Saturday and are therefore willing to spend $(10 * 0.5) + (4 * 0 , 5) = 7$ $ for the dinner. At this price, the restaurant maximizes profits by earning $ 500 $(7 - 2) * 100 = 500$.

A similar example is that of a car rental company near an airport that offers two types of contract: with the first, the customer purchases a full tank of fuel in advance at a fixed and advantageous price, while the second option allows the customer to return the car with a full tank. By subscribing to the second type of contract the customer decides to run the risk of not finding a petrol station near the airport to fill the tank at a more favourable rate than the car rental or not having the time to refuel and therefore having to pay for the missing fuel at the spot price and not the price booked in advance.

It should be noted that without the advance sale, no price would reach a certain level of profit, not because this kind of sale is more likely to extract the so-called consumer surplus, but because it involves more buyers in the buying process.

No "spot" sale (i.e. a sale made at the moment of consumption) could have allowed these levels of profit, unless the seller, in the case of the Chinese restaurant, is able to distinguish, immediately and without cost, which customers are willing to pay $ 10 and which only $ 4 . This is the case for first-rate price discrimination that creates profits for a total of $(4 - 2) * 50 + (10 - 2) * 50 = 100 + 400 = 500$ $, which is exactly the same as the advance sales calculated previously.

11.4. Strategies for advance selling

The benefits shown and these two simple examples inevitably raise some questions, such as, when is it worth anticipating service bookings and under what conditions?

Unfortunately, not many studies address this issue with concrete examples.

Lee and NG (2001) propose a model that suggests creating a service with an excess capacity, so part of it can be sold in advance. The amount reserved for early sale can be varied according to price sensitivity at the time of consumption. The greater the price sensitivity at the time of consumption, the higher the amount sold in advance, and conversely, if there is little price sensitivity, only a few discounted seats will be sold in advance.

Xie and Shugan (2001) have instead identified five different price strategies that they consider to be optimal in relation to two variables: the level of production capacity and marginal cost.

[S1] – High spot price and no advance sales: with this strategy the service is not offered in advance and the purchase price is high. This is the best strategy when capacity is very limited or marginal costs are high.

[S2] – Discounted and limited advance sales: with this strategy the service can be booked in advance at a discounted price compared to the spot price but the number of seats is limited so as to leave a significant quantity of full price sales. Here again, this works with a limited capacity and marginal costs must be low to justify the discounted prices for those buying in advance.

[S3] – Discounted and unlimited advance sales. This is the best strategy in two cases: when costs are neither too high, nor too low and capacity is very large or even unlimited.

[S4] – If the ability to provide the service is wide but insufficient to meet all requirements, then it is also advisable to arrange limitless pre-sales at an increased price. This assumes that buyers are willing to pay a premium price to make sure they can use the service.

[S5] – Lastly, if capacity is unlimited and marginal costs are medium or low level, then the best strategy is to anticipate sales to keep them at a low price compared to spot sales, so they can then be sold at a higher price at the last minute.

The question of long-term dynamic price strategies can also be addressed in relation to the competitive context in which the service is offered, i.e. the competitive intensity of the reference market. In a low demand situation (demand>offer), prices can be higher even if they are distanced from the moment of consumption, because the buyer is willing to pay a higher price to make the reservation and ensure they enjoy the product. Any eventual leftover products can then be sold at the marginal cost of production (last minute prices).

In the case of over-supply (demand<offer), the customer is aked to accept a risk (due to the uncertainty of the future) and therefore the advance price will be lower than the spot price.

11.5. Conclusions

Global competition requires careful attention to be paid when fixing prices for products and services. The price of a product or service identifies the offer made to the market, communicates the value provided and directly influences the revenue stream. Managers are constantly judged on the results achieved in these areas.

In this chapter, a pricing strategy based on the moment of purchase has been presented that proposes a different (usually lower) price for advance sales. In the service industry, on account of its specific production and consumption characteristics, creating a time distance between the moment of purchase and the moment of consumption can be extremely advantageous.

New technologies reduce the risk of arbitrage, i.e. the possibility of something purchased at a lower price being resold at higher price. So, for example, the tickets required to enter a stadium have the name of the holder printed on them so they cannot be given to someone who has no ticket and is willing to pay more to attend the event. In the same way, e-commerce shortens the distribution chain by directly linking supply and demand services and eliminating expensive distribution channels.

More and more companies from a wide variety of sectors, have adopted this strategy, but there are still very few studies that analyse actual results, both in terms of its effectiveness and customers' reactions to it. Existing literature is mainly concerned with the construction of theoretical models and many aspects of the phenomenon have not been explored.

Conversely, there are a number of consolidated theories that could use Advance Selling practices as an interesting testing ground. For example, it is known that buyers attribute value to what they buy in relation to what they are going to use it for (state dependent utility). For example, in the case of a laundered dress, the perception of price varies depending on whether you are going to use the dress immediately or put it in the closet for next season. According to Construal Level Theory (Liberman and Trope, 1998) people or events are perceived differently in terms of spatial or temporal distance; so it would be interesting to apply this to the period between the purchase and actual consumption and the benefits reaped over time.

Likewise, existing literature has analysed the kind of emotion that arises after a purchase when the buyer thinks they should have done something different (regret). This may also apply to Advance Selling as even if the product has been bought at a reasonable price, the limitations laid down by the seller may lead to second thoughts or regrets near the time of consumption, especially if other information has become available.

Another aspect of interest is that of refunds for those who decide or need to change the reservation they have made.

Lastly, there is the question of credibility. Here, it would be interesting to analyse the relationship between the customer's moment of choice and the company's reputation to see if certain companies receive higher value ratings when an advance sale is made. Dynamic pricing and Advance Selling could also raise a fairness issue (Maxwell, 2008), as considering the challenges of today's market, pricing strategies must be perceived as sustainable and fair, as well as competitive.

References

Bouchet A., Troilo M., Walkup B., *Dynamic Pricing Usage in Sports for Revenue Management*, Managerial Finance, (42), 913-921, 2016. https://doi.org/10.1108/MF-01-2016-0017.

Boyaci T., Ozer O., *Information Acquisition for Capacity Planning via Pricing and Advance Selling: When to Stop and Act?*, Operation Research, (50), 1328-1349, 2010. https://doi.org/10.1287/opre.1100.0798.

Brondoni S.M., *Global Markets and Market-Space Competition*, Symphonya. Emerging Issues in Management (symphonya.unimib.it), (1), 28-42, 2002. http://dx.doi.org/10.4468/2002.1.03brondoni.

Brondoni S.M., *Global Capitalism and Sustainable Growth. From Global Products to Network Globalisation*, Symphonya. Emerging Issues in Management (symphonya.unimib.it), (1), 10-31, 2014. http://dx.doi.org/10.4468/2014.1.02brondoni.

Cappiello G., Price Policies, *Over-Supply and Demand Bubbles*, Symphonya. Emerging Issues in Management, (symphonya.unimib.it), (2), 2005. http://dx.doi.org/10.4468/2005.2.06cappiello.

Dana J., New Direction *Revenue Management Research*, Production and Operation Management, (17), 399-401, 2008. doi 10.3401/poms.1080.0040.

Dolan R., *How do you know when the Price is Right*, Harvard Business Review, (73), 174-180, 1995.

Enz C.A., Canina L., Noone B., *Strategic Revenue Management and the Role of Competitive Price Shifting,* Cornell Hospitality Report, (12), 6-11, 2012.

Fisher M., Gallino S., Li J., *Competition-based Dynamic Pricing in Online Retailing: A Methodology Validated with Field Experiments*, Management Science, Published Online: June 27, 2017. https://doi.org/10.1287/mnsc.2017.2753.

Kimes S., *Revenue Management: A Retrospective*, Cornell Hotel and Restaurant Administration Quarterly, (44), 131-138, 2003. http://scholarship.sha.cornell.edu/articles/472/.

Kumar V., Reinartz W., *Creating Enduring Customer Value*, Journal of Marketing, (80), 33-68, 2016. https://doi.org/10.1509/jm.15.0414.

Lee K.S., Ng I.C.L., *Advanced Sale of Service Capacities: a Theoretical Analysis of the Impact of Price Sensitivity on Pricing and Capacity Allocations*, Journal of Business Research, (54), 219-225, 2001. https://doi.org/10.1016/S0148-2963(00)00119-3.

Liberman N., Trope Y., *The Role of Feasibility and Desirability Considerations in Near and Distant Future Decisions: A Test of Temporal Construal Theory*, Journal of Personality and Social Psychology, (75), 5-18, 1998. http://dx.doi.org/10.1037/0022-3514.75.1.5

Liu Q., Van Ryzyn G., *Strategic Capacity Rationing to Induce Early Purchases*, Management Science, (54), 1115-1131, 2008. https://doi.org/10.1287/mnsc.1070.0832.

Maxwell S., *The Price is Wrong*, John Wiley, 2008.
McGill J., Van Ryzin G., *Revenue Management: Research Overview and Prospect*, Transportation Science, (33), 233-256, 1999. https://doi.org/10.1287/trsc.33.2.233.
McKenzie R.D., *Why Popcorn Costs So Much at the Movies*, Springer New York, 2008.
Moe W., Fader P., *Using Advance Purchase Orders to Forecast New Product Sales*, Marketing Science, (21), 347-364, 2002. https://doi.org/10.1287/mksc.21.3.347.138.

Nasiry J., Popescu I., *Advance Selling when Consumer Regret*, Management Science, (58), 1160-1177, 2012. https://doi.org/10.1287/mnsc.1110.1473.
Ng I.C.L. , Wirtz J., Lee K.S., *The Strategic Role of Unused Service Capacity*, International Journal of Service Industry Management, (10), 211-244, 1999. https://doi.org/10.1108/09564239910264352.

Phillips R., *Why are Prices Set the Way They Are?*, in Ozer O., Phillips R., The Oxford Handbook of pricing management, Oxford University Press, 2012.
Poundstone W., *Priceless: The Myth of Fair Value (and How to Take Advantage of it)*, Hill and Wang, New York, 2010.

Raju J., Zhang Z.J., *Smart Pricing*, Wharton School Publishing, 2010.

Sasser W.E., *Match Supply and Demand in Service Industries*, Harvard Business Review, (54), 133-140, 1976.
Shostack G., *Breaking Free from Product Marketing*, Journal of Marketing, (43), 73-80, 1977. https://DOI: 10.2307/1250637.
Shugan S.M., Radas S., *Services and Seasonal Demand*, in Swartz T., Iacobucci D. (eds.), *Handbook of Services Marketing and Management*, Sage Publications, 147-170, 1999.
Shugan S.M., Xie J. *Advance Pricing of Services and Other Implication of Separating Purchase and Consumption*, Journal of Service Research, (2), 227-239, 2000. https://doi.org/10.1177/109467050023001.
Shugan S.M., Xie J., *Advance Selling for Services*, California Management Review, (46), 37-54, 2004. https://doi.org/10.2307/41166220.
Shugan S.M., Xie J., *Advance-selling as a Competitive Marketing Tool*, International Journal of Research in Marketing, (22), 351-373, 2005. https://doi:10.1016/j.ijresmar.2004.11.004.
Smith, B., Leimkuhler J., Darrow R.M., *Yield Management at American Airlines*, Interfaces, (22), 8-31, 1992. https://doi.org/10.1287/inte.22.1.8.

Weisstein F., Monika Kukar-Kinney L., Monroe K.B. (2016), *Determinants of Consumers' Response to Pay-what-you-want Pricing Strategy on the Internet*, Journal of Business Research (69), 4313-4320, 2016. https://doi.org/10.1016/j.jbusres.2016.04.005.

Woodruff R. (1997), *Customer Value: The Next Source for Competitive Advantage*, Journal of the Academy of Marketing Science, (25), 139-153, 1997. http://dx.doi.org/10.1007/BF02894350

Xie J., Shugan S.M, *Electronic Tickets, Smart Cards and Online Prepayments: When and How to Advance Sell*, Marketing Science, vol. 20, n. 3, Summer. 219-243, 2001. https://doi.org/10.1287/mksc.20.3.219.9765.

Zeithaml V., Birtner M. (2000), *Service Marketing: integrating Customer Focus Across the Firm*, Mc-Graw-Hill.

Chapter 12

BRAND STRATEGIES
AND MARKET-DRIVEN MANAGEMENT

Flavio Gnecchi

ABSTRACT: *An enterprise inspired by a market-based business approach is better able to understand and relate to the market through defining and anticipating the consumption trends and competitive horizons. With market-driven management, companies focus their efforts on identifying what their customers value, thereby capitalising on the system of intangible resources. In particular, brand management in a market-driven approach becomes a critical factor in affirming the company's offer in global markets with intense competition. In excess supply conditions, the brand encapsulates the evolution of products or services, both in relation to the development of demand and its benefits, emotions, and experience.*

SUMMARY: 12.1. Corporate communications and market-driven management. – 12.2. The brand in a competitive market orientation. – 12.3. Market relations and customer value.

12.1. Corporate communications and market-driven management

In recent years, manufacturing and service companies in most traditionally considered economic sectors have struggled to confront the crisis whose origin, beyond political or financial reasons, can decidedly be attributed to the irrefutable and entrenched excess supply conditions; overabundant (and steadily increasing) production due to a number of factors including globalisation, logistics modernization, supranational agreements, business transaction simplification, and improved technologies, colliding with demand that struggles to grow.

Since the early 80s, the economy has seen a reversal in trends with respect to the past: demand is no longer able to absorb the supply of manufacturers or service providers. This enduring condition of quantitative demand saturation particularly affects mature markets, even if also impacting innovative product or service offerings (Brondoni, Lambin, 2001).

In the modern economy, companies are confronted with global markets, continuous improvements, decreasing costs, and market volumes far above the absorptive capacity of demand. Globalisation has therefore led to increasing production overcapacity and thus unprecedented excess supply. Excess supply is consequently a structural development factor that forces businesses to deal with purchasing and consumption patterns characterized by irregular growth rates, unstable demand and, above all, potentially different repurchasing intentions.

Under these conditions, which have long concerned most of the manufacturing as well as all types of service sectors, companies that are more attentive to the needs and prerogatives of the markets no longer exclusively build their offer on a product or service, but also on critical intangible factors. These companies define their own supply strategy by widening the analysis to a multiplicity of factors and aspects, not constrained to a partial vision, and thus favouring a market orientated competitive approach (Market-Driven Strategy). Brondoni (2014) notes that in such a changing scenario, *"with the globalisation of markets, numerous borders and barriers disappear, the intangible becomes more important than the tangible, time becomes a critical aspect of competition, and mobility (of capital, people, goods, knowledge and ideas) emerges as a vital condition of the organisation's existence. The extension of the competitive space generates complex relations that the global firm is obliged to build up and manage"*.

Hence, in markets under excess supply conditions, companies that have opted for market-driven management systems have proven able to affirm successful proposals, achieve profitable economic flows, generate financial resources, and are recognized for their ability to listen to the market and consequently ensure that supply meets demand. As Lambin and Chumpitaz (2007) observe, *"in a market economy, the role of market-driven management is to design and promote, at a profit for the firm, added value solutions to people and/or organizations problems"*.

Webster (2002) notes that market-driven management is more pervasive than a customer-driven orientation and requires greater commitment. In fact, while the latter remains a fundamental element of marketing, a market-driven strategy implies the firm's attention to their competitors' offerings and capabilities or how they are perceived by customers. It also means understanding how the firm's capabilities meet customer needs and how the company's offerings are measured against those of competitors. These three variables contribute to the definition of value that customers assign to the offer. The adoption of a market-driven strategy therefore requires that every decision taken be consistent with the information on customers and competitors, and based on a coherent value proposition.

Market-driven organizations are thus characterised by a complex combination of several factors, amongst which Day (2007) indicates the simultaneous presence of:

- A corporate culture oriented to the outside;
- Distinctive capabilities in perceiving the market;
- An appropriate structural configuration.
- With regard to the last element, in a market-based enterprise, the vocation towards a competitive market orientation is fully validated when all functions that contribute to the structural configuration itself lead to:
- Knowing, understanding, and evaluating the behaviour of competitors;
- Sensitivity to the tangible needs of demand (and thus characterized by distinctive expertise in understanding customer needs), but also the willingness to transfer value to customers;
- The pursuit of management solutions to overcome the entrenched organizational boundaries of each corporate function and the traditional physical spaces of competition.

In addition, these companies are recognized for their strong and shared culture, the pursuit of sources of competitive advantage, and oriented precisely towards the outside.

Indeed, Brondoni (2009) notes that *"Market-driven management strategies (dominated by customer value and by direct, constant benchmarking with competitors) have developed in line with globalisation since the 1980s, particularly as an effect of the many innovations introduced by Toyota and other leading Japanese companies (lean production, just in time, total quality, mass customization, demand bubble management). In global markets populated by increasingly voluble and non-loyal consumers, market-driven management is very attractive because it favours: 1. activities focused on the profitability of competition, rather than on simple customer satisfaction; 2. market policies based on innovation and competitive pricing, to stimulate uncertain and unstable customers to purchase; 3. and finally, performance metrics even with very short timeframes"*.

The market-driven enterprise is aware of the need to transfer higher value to customers, which includes understanding them, but above all, grasping the competitive differential. The enterprise consequently places the recipient in a position to appreciate what has been received, evaluating it in relation to the ex-ante perceived need and ex-post satisfaction with regard to the economic-monetary sacrifice, the price they must pay, together with the figurative costs that the same customer bears, against the benefits of the service received, to the satisfaction of the expected need.

Gnecchi (2009) notes, *"Globalisation has accentuated the collapse of spatial boundaries, assisted by the development of telecommunications and transport (and therefore by the evolution in logistics); this has fostered a gradual consolidation of the intangible factors of supply, and not only corporate, which the best prepared businesses have been able to achieve"*.

As a result, market-driven organizations have the goal of transmitting greater benefits to those who turned to them to meet their needs; the transferable benefits are of a dual nature, thereby contributing to both an economic and emotional value proposition.

The propensity to condense a series of concrete benefits that could be called 'collateral' for the benefit of customers becomes, together with the capacity to make their offer more appropriate and advantageous compared to competitors, one of the key factors of market-driven management, able to determine the success of corporate initiatives.

In a market-driven vision, one of the strategic concepts with the greatest impact is expressed precisely by the value proposition, understood as the explanation of how the company intends to convey the superior value of its offer to customers and differentiating it from competitors.

In this regard, Best (2005) states that companies must develop and adapt (to customer needs) a value proposition appropriate to each positioning strategy that conveys value to the target customers. Each value proposition includes all the key elements of the context and the benefits that the target customer seeks in the purchasing decision.

The positioning is consequently the development of the value proposition. Webster (2002) states in this regard that in essence the positioning statement coincides with the value proposition.

Thus, recalling the original Ries and Trout (2001) observation, *"positioning is not what you to a product. Positioning is what you to the mind of a prospect. That is: you position the product in the mind of the prospect"*.

Of primary importance and contributing to the definition and affirmation of the offer are the corporate communications.

Among the most important elements of communications is the key role assigned to the brand, namely, the specific and capacitive relationship, observed at a precise moment in time, between the company's offer and its target market.

Corporate communications can be defined as the set of activities and actions aimed at disseminating information flows and consequently establishing a relationship with the recipients of those flows to pursue specific objectives in terms of responding. This is the set of actions taken to disseminate messages characterized by content (descriptive or quantitative, rational or emotional) aimed at affecting the behaviour of the recipients or their observations and needs. This is therefore an activity aimed at the construction, development, and maintenance of relationships with others.

With regard to the environmental dynamics (both internal and external), corporate communications lend themselves to changes that take into account the concrete experiences, technological elements, and regulatory factors. In view of the above, a fundamental criticality lies in the need to constantly adapt corporate communications to changing contextual situations, not only from a conceptual point of view, but also in terms of their application.

Previously, we introduced the concepts underlying a competitive market orientation strategy. Building a lasting relationship, not only with customers, but with all the players in the entire market, requires a related and consistent corporate communications policy, in line with the prerogatives and determinants of a market-driven strategy.

In excess supply conditions, companies have become aware of the importance of communications, dedicating resources to affirm their presence and disseminate their offer, defining tools (and ways of using them) increasingly adapted to the times and to technology developments (Brondoni, 2002).

A common view is that corporate communication are critical for the company's long-term presence in the market, where the 'market' is not just the competitive arena but the wider context (social, economic, cultural, etc.) that permeates its existence.

A further indispensable reflection on the importance of culture that characterizes every business reality is that this factor also determines the precise communications culture that distinguishes each firm.

Recent years have seen a cultural evolution, in some ways imposed (not only by regulatory obligations, but importantly by the changed behaviours of all stakeholders and the development of new tools) and in other cases, expressly pursued by individual companies.

However, as mentioned, corporate communications cannot but be primarily influenced by the entrepreneurial culture that characterizes every organization, as well as the development of new technologies, new tools, and new "territories".

In light of the difficulties seen in markets, it is therefore natural to expect that business economics and management will determine further developments in corporate communications.

Regardless of this expectation, all service providers, considering the influencing factors (size, type and range of services offered, user bases, legal form, etc.), cannot avoid setting coherent communication objectives that are able to effectively translate their aims.

Before proceeding further, to note is that such a market-driven vision by its very nature does not allow defining a hierarchy of communication objectives, since all are an expression of the 'market' components the company has to consider not only in the formulation of its offer, but also in the enterprise's superordinate management.

Consequently, all communication objectives are relevant, consistent with the needs of a competitive market orientation. Indeed, both the "institutional" and "organizational", and consequently not just the "persuasive" nature of the relationships are critical to achieving such goals.

With reference to the aforementioned, a company qualifies as a market-driven organization when manifesting:

• A specific *culture oriented to the outside,* reflected in the prerogatives of institutional communications;

• *Distinctive capabilities* to grasp the needs of its trading partners, which affect the content of persuasive communications;

• A *structural configuration* based on sharing objectives and commitments correlated to the organisational communication activities.

12.2. The brand in a competitive market orientation

As previously recalled, amongst the business communication objectives, the brand holds a leading position that gains strength over time.

Brondoni (2004) notes that, albeit relevant, a brand's function cannot be limited to labelling, since the changed economic conditions call for wider considerations. Indeed, in contexts where market capacity is able to absorb the entire supply (in scarce economies and even dynamic equilibrium economies), the labelling function ensures some potential counterfeiting protection (favoured by the attractiveness of a receptive market able to attract other operators). In conditions where supply is structurally greater than demand, the brand has other purposes. Indeed, *"in a highly competitive environment, the brand synthesizes the notoriety and image that an offer has been able to assert to a particular public of reference and therefore, in a business-to-business sense, can be defined as a specific relationship established with a given market for the affirmation of a particular offer".*

This specific relationship is expressed by the functional and symbolic values that the demand, precisely through the brand, associates with a clearly identifiable offer and therefore distinguishable from that of competitors.

In practice, the brand summarizes the evolution of products or services, both in relation to the development of supply and the benefits, emotions, and experience gained by demand. The brand thus becomes the bearer of a promise and at the same time "*succinctly sums up the resources the company dedicates resources to competition processes and in particular investments to developing knowledge and relationships with the market*".

Consequently, in the context of corporate communications, the brand, as the promise underpinning the formation of concrete expectations, is associated with a system of responsibilities towards a specific public of reference.

As noted, from the early 80s, excess supply was determined and progressively accentuated up to the point of substantiating in the crisis that in the second half of 2008 gripped the entire planet. Consider that in excess supply conditions, companies are unable to increase their sales even through price reductions. Also to take into account are complex aspects that become apparent in the purchasing and consumption processes, whereby the "*contexts affirm where the intangible component of supply predominate that tend to direct the competition of entire business sectors towards new competition trends that are unstable and based on intangible factors*" (Gnecchi, Corniani, 2003), amongst which the brand plays a prominent role, which companies that have developed market-driven management policies are conscious of.

Which factor determines the specific requirements of end buyers that can affect the choices of intermediate demand by favouring some offers over others? The product/service itself, certainly; the price, of course; the offer combination, as well; quality, undoubtedly, but a significant impetus of the purchasing decision is the brand, seen as the most immediate relationship the company has with the market.

In fact, the brand among the intangible supply factors (brand, design, pre/post sales services, etc.) decidedly draws the most attention and is highly critical in the long-term phase of the excess supply of modern markets characterized by intense competition.

Brand management, considering the importance that the brand plays, requires a major commitment, but there is no certainty on the outcome of the efforts undertaken. In this regard, Haig (2008) observes, "*consumers don't truly believe there's a huge difference between products, which means brands have to establish 'emotional ties' with their customers. ... Once a brand has created that necessary bond, it has to handle it with care. One step out of line and the customer may not be willing to forgive. This is ultimately why brands fail. Something happens to break the bond between the customer and the brand. This is not always the fault of the company, as some things beyond are really their immediate control (global recession, technological advances, international disasters, etc.). However, more often than not, when brands struggle or fail it is usually down to a distorted perception of either the brand, the competition or the market".*

However, under these particular conditions, demand is still unable to absorb the entire volume of supply and the brand essentially contributes to the construction of a lasting relationship with demand.

12.3. Market relations and customer value

Previously, we recalled the potential opportunities that market-driven companies can seize in times of marked economic difficulties, characterized by the distinctive ability to grasp the relevance of some of the key factors to define a competitive market orientation strategy. These include:

1. Culture;
2. Relations with the market;
3. Creating value for the customer;
4. The value of customers for the enterprise.

This strategy, in addition to a solid, shared and widely communicated enterprise culture, requires constant attention to the signals that the market explicitly or not transmits to the market itself, and is therefore one of the founding elements in defining market-driven management (Davis and Dunn, 2002).

The enterprise is thus called on to make a substantially commitment to rationalize two distinct activities that require specific competencies (Day, 1999): *the perception of the market (market sense)* and the *relations with the market (market relations).*

These competencies are closely interrelated: in fact, the former is a fundamental requirement to activate the second, as in the absence of the capacity to grasp and measure the market dynamics or all those forces that constitute it, each relational action is limited, detached from a real interpretation.

In relation to the above, the market perception cannot be immune from the culture that distinguishes every business. However, this does not mean that perceiving the market is a mere complement of culture, and as such, an action that is entirely natural. On the contrary, an articulated process must be defined that develops an appropriate system targeted at market relations.

This process, developed through the firm's market-driven management, is characterized by constant learning, without continuity solutions, placing the market in the foreground and elevating it to the primary cognitive objective for the organizational configuration.

The approaches can be numerous, given that reference does not only have to be made to the recurring behaviour of the forces that constitute the market, but also the occurrence of unplanned (nor programmable) events, or the introduction of innovations that necessarily entail a reconsideration of the messages that the market itself transmits.

Clearly therefore, a cultural factor, such as perception (a combination of sensitivity, evaluation skills, predispositions, etc.) is coupled with a technical factor, such as the information system the company has been able to define and develop.

The effort targeted at market sensing must be related to a series of actions aimed at:

- Fostering a spirit of inquiry and investigation characterized by the propensity to listen and open up towards what the market projects;
- Analysing with adequate attention the actions of direct and indirect competitors, or the opportunities/rigidity expressed by the external environment;
- Listening to those professional figures who before others capture market opportunities and fluctuations;
- Investigating areas of unmet or latent needs not explicitly expressed by customers for different reasons;
- Encouraging proactive, constant and continuous experimentation, identifying sensitive and open customers or groups of solicitous customers when necessary, thereby demonstrating a marked propensity to innovation;
- Considering the whole market, and thus also the most remote areas that are more distant or peripheral, yet providing the impetus to adjust and improve the offer.

This subsequently entails, prior to utilizing the findings, rationalizing the information collected, classifying and categorizing it into coherent aggregates.

This sense-making phase is necessary to develop models shared within the company that move in a common direction to avoid individual or partial dystonic behaviours with respect to the market orientation.

As noted, an important role is assumed by the information system and thus the instruments used and the deliberated procedures, without neglecting the necessary time and cost evaluations. In particular, the economic aspects, characterized by substantial cost invariance (or preponderance of fixed costs), cannot take second place or in any case represent an underestimated limit pending the criticality of market relations for the success of the strategy outlined.

Hence, this set of activities cannot be regarded as residual or complementary, but call for adequately planning the allocated resources (and related organizational levels and responsibilities), market sensing and market making programs, as well as the underlying actions.

With regard to market relations instead, the brand (in both B2C and B2B contexts) is the most immediate expression but also has the greatest potential. Earlier we recalled that the concept of the brand itself must be extended and enriched as a result of the changing economic conditions in which enterprises operate. As Brondoni (2004) observes, *"from the manufacturer's point of view, the brand imposes a multiplicity of obligations defining the nature and intensity of the relationship established with a given demand. In other words, it tends to express the set of resources (typically credibility, legitimacy, and affect) that in reality substantiate the supply-demand relationship and requires behaviours aimed at meeting the specific obligations of coherence, continuity, and socio-cultural; obligations that manifest on the one hand in the technical characteristics of the product and the ways in which it performs (a tangible component of a given offer) and, on the other, in the business communication activities (intangible component of supply and of primary importance in excess supply conditions)".*

In a market-driven vision, this relation is further enriched and corroborated by the potential influence that can be exercised on the customer/consumer by the four categories of key actors who contribute to the functioning of the market (customers, distributors, competitors, and prescribers).

Therefore, above all in the B2B context, the role of consultants/prescribers is paramount, capable of radically influencing final demand, determining specific requirements from intermediate demand to be transmitted to the offer. This consideration is all the more relevant when related to durable consumer goods.

The brand thus clearly assumes a critical connotation in affirming the company's offer. If, as many observe, the brand in B2C contexts is able to substitute the autonomous customer/consumer choice (creating "convictions" and representing "support"), thereby becoming a formidable lever in the hands of manufacturing companies, in the B2B context, the brand becomes a powerful relational driver, focused on the awareness and willingness to form an essential problem solving reference.

Brand management, inscribed in the perception of what the market represents and requires is thus externalised in a fundamental relational effort, and must hence represent a weighted option exercised by enterprises that are cognisant of the potential opportunities they can develop and the resulting extractable benefits.

As noted, an enterprise inspired by a market-based business approach demonstrates superior expertise in understanding the market, relating to it, and defining and anticipating consumption trends. As Best (2005) states, *"our evaluation of product often needs to go beyond economic and price-performance measures of customer value. Customer perceptions of service quality, brand reputation, and costs other than price also affect customer value"*.

Enterprises must focus their efforts on identifying what their customers consider as value, and managing the competitive space contributes to this objective. The ability to capture these aspects determines the success of companies, placing them in a position to affirm their offer before and better than competitors (direct or indirect).

Value is not a dimension that, in relation to customer satisfaction, only consists in the act that is substantiated in the service provision. Instead, the relationship established with the customer must also be viewed in terms of the value created for the enterprise (Gnecchi, 2009).

Such value legitimises and supports the presence of the company in the market, and has an economic/financial but also a cognitive and relational dimension.

In particular, the appropriate knowledge of customers, their personal characteristics (or company characteristics, if a business customer), their purchasing and consumption behaviours, contribute to creating value for the company in the same way as the economic-financial value deriving from the exchange.

This requires going beyond some evaluation measures, such as determining market share, or at least must be accompanied by an in-depth study of the value that the customer represents for the enterprise.

A strategy based on the quality of the offer is clearly different, which on the one hand can legitimize high prices and the correlated levels of profitability, and on the other hand, can lead to growth in demand that increases market share and volumes, reducing unit production costs and thus improving revenues.

In the case of market share, worth noting is that companies need to ask whether it is actually the market share held that determines their profitability. Consider the GE example that Webster (2002) presents. Back in 1969, General Electric defined a different approach, called PIMS ("Profit Impact of Market Strategy"), under which it is not the market share that determines profit, but the opposite, namely, the increase in market penetration is favoured by the profitability of the activities, the achievement of which contributes considerably to the qualitative aspects of the offer. This approach is based on a regressive analysis and on the timely - and repeated - feedback of some indicators.

According to GE, the fundamental driver on which to build this strategy is precisely the quality of the offer, which must be communicated and perceived, on which the value transfer process is anchored. In essence, setting aside the traditional (low) price approach that leads to higher market share, or rather, a greater volume of activities that in turn reduces unit production costs and consequently increases revenue.

Market-driven management is based on the pursuit of a quality offer that meets user needs, in line with the market opportunities and prerogatives, and anticipating the offers of competitors, which allows increasing the rate of use of the services provided and improving the production and provision cost structure.

References

Aaker D.A., *Strategic Market Management*, John Wiley & Son, Hoboken, 2004.
Aaker D.A., Joachimsthaler Eric, *Brand Leadership,* The Free Press, New York, 2002.
Anderson J.C.-Narus J.A.-van Rossum W., *Customer Value Proposition in Business Markets*, Harvard Business Review, March, 2006.
Arrigo E., *Alliances, Open Innovation and Outside-in Management*, Symphonya. Emerging Issues in Management (symphonya.unimib.it), (2), 53-65, 2012. http://dx.doi.org/10.4468/2012.2.05 arrigo.

Best R.J., *Market-Based Management*, Prentice Hall, Upper Saddle River, 2005.
Brondoni S.M, *Global Markets and Market-Space Competition,* Symphonya. Emerging Issues in Management (symphonya.unimib.it), (1), 28-42, 2002. http://dx.doi.org/10.4468/2002.1.03brondoni.
Brondoni S.M., *Market-Driven Management, Competitive Customer Value and Global Networks*, Symphonya. Emerging Issues in Management (symphonya. unimib.it), (1), 8-25, 2009. http://dx.doi.org/10.4468/2009.1.02brondoni.
Brondoni S.M., *Global Capitalism and Sustainable Growth. From Global Products to Network Globalisation*, Symphonya. Emerging Issues in Management (symphonya.unimib.it), (1), 10-31, 2014. http://dx.doi.org/10.4468/2014.1.02 brondoni.
Brondoni S.M., Lambin J.-J., *Ouverture de "Market-Driven Management"*, Symphonya. Emerging Issues in Management (symphonya.unimib.it), (2), 1-11, 2001. http://dx.doi.org/10.4468/ 2001.2.01ouverture.

Davis S.M., Dunn M., *Brand-Driven Business*, Jossey Bass, San Francisco, 2002.
Day G.S., *The Market Driven Organization*, The Free Press, New York, 1999.
Day G.S., *Market-Driven Winners*, Symphonya. Emerging Issues in Management (symphonya.unimib.it), (2), 12-22, 2001. http://dx.doi.org/10.4468/2001.2.02day.

Gerzema J., Lebar E., *The Brand Bubble*, Jossey Bass, New York, 2008.

Gnecchi F., *Brand Portfolio and Over Supply*, Symphonya. Emerging Issues in Management (symphonya.unimib.it), (1), 56-65, 2005. http://dx.doi.org/10.4468/2005.1.05gnecchi.

Gnecchi F., *Market-Driven Management, Market Space and Value Proposition*, Symphonya. Emerging Issues in Management (symphonya.unimib.it), (2), 33-45, 2009. http://dx.doi.org/10.4468/2009.2.04gnecchi.

Gnecchi F., *Retailing, Private Label and Global Competition,* Symphonya. Emerging Issues in Management (symphonya.unimib.it), (2), 79-87, 2013. http://dx.doi.org/10.4468/2013.2.06gnecchi.

Haig M., *Brand Failures*, Kogan Page, London, 2008.

Hitt M.A., Ireland R.D., Hoshisson R.E., *Strategic Management: Competitiveness and Globalization*, South Western College, Stamford, 2013.

Hooley G., Piercy N.F., Nicoulaud B., *Marketing Strategy & Competitive Positioning*, Pearson, Harlow, 2012.

Keegan W.J., Green M., *Global Marketing*, Pearson, Harlow, 2016.

Kotler P., Jain D.C., Maesincee S., *Marketing Moves*, Harvard Business School Press, Boston, 2002.

Lambin J.-J., *Changing Market Relationships in the Internet Age*, UCL Presses, Louvain-la-Neuve, 2008.

Lambin J.-J., *Market-Driven Management Strategic and Operational Marketing*, Palgrave Macmillan, Basingstoke, 2012.

Lambin J.-J., Brondoni S.M., *Ouverture*, Symphonya. Emerging Issues in Management (symphonya.unimib.it), (1), 1-4, 2001. http://dx.doi.org/10.4468/2001.1.01ouverture.

Lambin J.-J., Chumpitaz R., Schuiling I., *Market-Driven Management*, Palgrave Macmillan, Basingstoke, 2007.

McDonald M., Christopher M., Knox S., Payne A., *Creating a Company for Customers. How to Build and Lead a Market Driven Organization*, Prentice Hall, Englewood Cliffs, 2001.

Riboldazzi Sabina, *Global Markets and Development Policies in Large-Scale Retailers*, Symphonya. Emerging Issues in Management (symphonya.unimib.it), (3), 8-28, 2015. http://dx.doi.org/10.4468/2015.5.02riboldazzi.

Ries A., Trout J., *Positioning: The Battle for Your Mind*, Harper Business, New York, 2001.

Vorhies D.W., Harker M., *The Capabilities and Performance Advantages of Market-Driven Firms: an Empirical Investigation*, Australian Journal of Management, Vol. 25, (2), 145-171, September, 2000. https://doi.org/10.1177/031289620002500203.

Webster Jr. F.E., *Market-Driven Management*, John Wiley & Sons, Hoboken, 2002.

Chapter 13

GLOBAL FIRMS AND NEW STANDARDS OF CORPORATE SOCIAL RESPONSIBILITY

Luca Bisio

ABSTRACT: *In global firms, corporate responsibility is aimed at pursuing partial and overall business results characterized by high levels of profitability and efficiency with a focus on sustainable development. For this reason, CSR represents an action that a firm chooses to take and potentially affecting the social welfare of stakeholders. Promoting the effectiveness of a CSR-oriented strategy requires enterprises to govern their costs and benefits, and develop dynamic relationships with stakeholders. This chapter highlights the new standards of sustainability and the cost drivers of CSR strategies that favour the correct balance between content knowledge requirements and stakeholder engagement.*

SUMMARY: 13.1. Corporate social responsibility as a competitive lever. – 13.2. Costs and benefits of Corporate Social Responsibility. – 13.3. New standards of Corporate Social Responsibility. – 13.3.1. The Global Reporting Initiative (GRI). – 13.3.2. Accountability 1000 (AA1000).

13.1. Corporate social responsibility as a competitive lever

"Several socio-economic mutations and technological breakthrough innovations are currently modifying the competitive environment and the functioning of today's economies" [1].

"The debate over corporate conduct in a context of sustainable development has taken on new importance in recent times. It is an area that generates great interest among public opinion; a public increasingly well-informed and attentive to the ethical aspects of the company and prepared to recognise the lead played by those companies with responsible and socially oriented behaviour" [2].

---

[1] J.-J. Lambin, *Rethinking the Market Economy*, in Symphonya. Emerging Issues in Management (symphonya.unimib.it), n. 2, 2014.

[2] S.M. Brondoni, *Network Culture, Performance and Corporate Responsibility*, in Symphonya. Emerging Issues in Management (www.unimib.it/symphonya), n. 1, 2003.

While this is deemed valid in the different competitive conditions prevailing in the world economy (Table 1), it is particularly important in the presence of excess supply. In this case, corporate responsibility must ensure the enduring pursuit of the company's mission in an open and unstable competitive system.

"The firm is exposed to large-scale socio-environmental tensions, which with modern Corporate Social Responsibility (CSR) made explicit through global corporate responsibility, can lead to sustainable growth"[3].

"Corporate responsibility in global markets therefore aims to pursue business results (partial and total) that feature high levels of profitability and efficiency, but also a priority concern for sustainable development. Corporate responsibility in a global context is consequently in practical terms finalized by corporate social responsibility"[4].

Table 1. Corporate Responsibility, CSR and competitive conditions.

Competitive Conditions	Responsibility business	Social Responsibility (CSR)
Scarce economies (Demand > Supply)	Predominantly focused on profitability.	The company's welfare conditions reflect the company's CSR, directly associating the company's growth (increased turnover and workers employed) with the development of relationships with the environment and sociability.
Controlled competition economies (Demand ≈ Supply)	Maintaining solid monolithicity, as the parent-company sets the rules of conduct for subsidiaries. The objective is to balance the growth of the central organization with the subsidiary's basic economic outcomes, while respecting the host country's social and/or environmental expectations. Recognizes the existence of the diversity of individual operational contexts.	Tends to assume autonomous and relevant configurations, with distinct local characterizations, albeit always within an enhanced central-peripheral monodirection. Aimed at interfacing the social and environmental phenomena of different markets, which must be respected and managed to ensure local business development.

---

see next page

[3] K. Annan, *The Global compact. Corporate Leadership in the World Economy*, in Symphonya. Emerging Issues in Management (www.unimib.it/symphonya), n. 2, 2002.

[4] S.M. Brondoni, *Network Culture, Performance and Corporate Responsibility*, in Symphonya. Emerging Issues in Management (www.unimib.it/symphonya), n. 1, 2003.

Excess supply economies (Demand < Supply)	Ensuring the long-term pursuit of the company's mission within an open and unstable competitive system.	Understood as a critical corporate intangible for success in a global economy.
	Dominated by the externalities of social and environmental relations, and therefore reconciling the business profitability goals with those of sustainable growth within a dynamic equilibrium system.	Aimed at managing stakeholder relations.
	Tailored to corporate social responsibility.	

Source: Own construction.

With this in mind, it is therefore important to assume a very pragmatic interpretation of corporate social responsibility – typical of the US approach and focused on the problem of social responsibility measurement as a corporate intangible that is critical for success in a global economy – defined as an "Action by a firm, which is a firm choice to take, that significantly affects an identifiable social stakeholder's welfare"[5].

"Relationships between companies and societies are therefore critically important determinants of:

– On the one hand, managing the diversity of the social and environmental systems in which they operate;

– On the other hand, the competitive tensions linked to the stakeholder system with the aim of identifying in advance and resolving the social and environmental problems generated by the competitive activity"[6].

More specifically, "In a global economic perspective, corporate responsibility is required to deal positively with specific social and environmental conditions pertaining to each operating context. This context, consequently, does not qualify as being referred to as 'local phenomena of divergence' but rather as 'elements of competitive market characterization', namely or-

[5] J. Frooman, *Socially Irresponsible and Illegal Behavior and Shareholder Wealth*, in Business & Society, n. 3, 1997, 221-249; R.E. Freeman, *A Stakeholder Theory of the Corporation*, in T.L. Beauchamp-N.E. Bowie (eds.), *Ethical Theory and Business*, 6th ed., Prentice-Hall, Englewood Cliffs, NJ, 2001, 56-65.

[6] L. Bisio, *Global Company and Global Regulation*, in Symphonya. Emerging Issues in Management (www.unimib.it/symphonya), n. 1, 2005.

ganisational components of which it is essential to know the evolving trends in order to ensure the company's or companies' local and global growth"[7].

This requires focusing on specific issues, such as profitability, maintaining financial equilibrium, compliance with ethical codes of conduct, attention to the environment, and social profiles in general.

"Acting in this way guarantees the vitality of the enterprise, minimizing its risk profile. The role of stakeholder relations is therefore re-evaluated as the essential condition for business durability"[8].

"Resource procurements, their optimal use in implementing activities aimed at obtaining a well-qualified supply in line with customer expectations, the ability to create wealth and its balanced target, are all elements that contribute to defining the ways of interacting between the enterprise and the environment according to business excellence. These measures first determine, in compliance with fairness, competition, and behavioural transparency, the requirements that should permeate an effective and correct corporate governance approach"[9].

The above clarifies that CSR needs to be increasingly subject to careful assessments, bearing in mind that the ongoing economic and financial crisis since 2008 requires modern capitalism to be based on the pursuit of more sustainable development[10]. In fact, companies need to learn to deal with global-scale socio-environmental tensions that lead to identifying in CSR a corporate intangible asset critical to their succes.

With these premises, it is clear that CSR should be analysed with reference to at least three essential elements:

– the company's competence in directly addressing the "social and environmental concerns" referred to in the Green Paper of the European Commission on Corporate Social Responsibility[11];
– the measurability of its effectiveness as an intangible at the corporate

[7] S.M. Brondoni, *Network Culture, Performance and Corporate Responsibility*, Symphonya, Emerging Issues in Management (www.unimib.it/symphonya), n. 1, 2003.

[8] D.M. Salvioni, *Corporate Governance and Global Responsibility*, Symphonya, Emerging Issues in Management (www.unimib.it/symphonya), n. 1, 2003.

[9] D.M. Salvioni, *Corporate Governance and Global Responsibility*, Symphonya, Emerging Issues in Management (www.unimib.it/symphonya), n. 1, 2003.

[10] S.M. Brondoni, *Ouverture de 'Global Networks and Sustainable Development-1'*, Symphonya. Emerging Issues in Management (symphonya.unimib.it), n. 1, 2014.

[11] Commission of the European Communities, *Green Paper: Promoting a European framework for Corporate Social Responsibility*, Bruxelles, 2001.

level that generates certain costs and returns of complex verifiability, both in terms of quantification and causality;

– the most suitable means of communicating social responsibility.

13.2. Costs and benefits of Corporate Social Responsibility

A first important reflection concerns the interpretation of the enterprise's role within the global market. Indeed, a question that arises is whether companies are expected to deal with the socio-environmental issues, common to other institutions (of all public administrations), penalizing shareholders in terms of net profits.

Even before the 2008 crisis, The Economist [12] – espousing Milton Freeman's vision and summing up the contributions of a major part of literature – reiterated that, "There is one and only one social responsibility of business – to use its resources and engage in activities designed to increase its profits so long as it stays within the rules of the game" [13].

However, just three years later, The Economist [14], while maintaining a critical attitude towards CSR, admitted the significant spread of the phenomenon within global businesses, also following the increasing pressure exerted by a number of stakeholder categories [15].

In particular, CSR actions can be interpreted according to three conceptual approaches:

– CSR as business philanthropy, which is the most traditional and less strategic form of such a business function;
– CSR as a component of risk management;
– CSR as a competitive advantage that contributes to creating value for the enterprise.

The last conception is inspired by Porter and Kramer's (2007) contribution identifying corporate social responsibility as a source of opportunity, innovation, and competitive advantage, albeit aware of the costs and the not-always measurable benefits that this practice entails.

However, the same authors are critical of many of the commonly used

---

[12] C. Crook, *The Good Company*, The Economist, January 2005.

[13] M. Friedman, *Capitalism and Freedom*, Chicago University Press, Chicago, 1962.

[14] D. Franklin, *Just Good Business*, The Economist, January 2008.

[15] To be noted, however, is that the increasing attention that businesses dedicate to CSR is not always an entirely voluntary choice. Many have only taken note after having been surprised by public opinion on issues they never previously considered part of their responsibilities.

sustainability practices. Social and environmental reports rarely provide a coherent framework of CSR activities, especially from a strategic point of view. They often describe only non-coordinated initiatives, with the aim of demonstrating the firm's social sensitivity. The information that is omitted from these publications is as revealing as that which is included. For example, it may occur that the reduction of pollutants is documented for certain divisions or specific areas, but not for the company as a whole. Philanthropic initiatives are usually described in terms of money spent or volunteer hours, almost never in terms of impact. Even rarer is businesses committing themselves to achieving declared performance targets in the future.

The four main arguments put forward by CSR advocates at the base of their theories are also not entirely convincing. Moral obligation, sustainability, license to operate, and reputation have the same weakness: they place emphasis on the tension between business and society, rather than on their interdependence.

The absent pursuit of interdependence often generates uncoordinated CSR actions, separated from the business strategy, which do not have a significant impact on society or enhance the company's competitiveness. Internally, CSR activities and initiatives remain isolated from operating units, and even separate from philanthropic ones. Externally, the company's social impact is dispersed in non-synergistic initiatives, each responding to the pressures of a different stakeholder group or a different lobby.

Advancing CSR requires a widespread awareness of the relationship between the enterprise and society, and at the same time rooted in the strategies and activities of individual companies.

Frequently, the economic and social objectives are opposed. In fact, this is often a false dichotomy because businesses do not work in isolation of the context of belonging, but are an integral part of it. For example, improving the level of education of the population could be considered a purely social problem, but training the workforce is linked to potential competitiveness. In this sense, in the medium term, the social and economic goals are mutually reconciled.

The mutual dependence of enterprises and societies implies that business decisions and social policies must therefore follow the principle of shared value. That is, the choices made must bring benefits to both parties. In particular, according to Porter, analysing the four constituent elements of the competitive environment, the enterprise can identify within each of the overlapping areas economic value and social value, and thus improve its economic-social performance in the medium term.

More precisely, CSR actions can have a positive impact on:

– The presence of an experienced workforce, qualified scientific institutions, and adequate infrastructure (impact on inputs);

– The volume and qualitative dimension of demand (impact on demand);

– The transparency and degree of cooperation of competitive contexts of reference (impact on the strategic and competitive environment);

– The degree of development of interbusiness agreements and the solidity of support agreements (impact on related and support sectors).

All this leads to understanding that good strategic CSR management can also be of value in excess supply markets and periods of economic instability, as any other action that is conducive to creating a competitive advantage.

In addition to the purely strategic aspect, CSR initiatives and the main functional tools for their communication must refer to the correct representation methods and techniques. Useful to this end is providing an overview of the new sustainability standards, which are tools to prepare a proper definition of the structure and content of reports produced, and the engagement methods used to generate virtuous relationships with their stakeholders.

13.3. New standards of Corporate Social Responsibility

Literature and business practice offer a wide range of tools to support the identification of CSR profiles and manage these efficiently and effectively. Here, however, we do not intend to provide a complete taxonomy of such tools, but to highlight two different types with substantial synergies in their use:

– Sustainability reporting;
– Stakeholder relationship management.

Traditionally, sustainability reporting is much more cautious than the definition of the communication plan and, above all, the stakeholder relationship management systems. This is also due to the development of some significant national and international standards such as GBS[16], SA8000[17], and above all, GRI[18].

---

[16] GBS, *Study Group for the Social Report* (www.gruppobilanciosociale.org).

[17] SA8000, *Social Accountability* (www.sa8000.info).

[18] GRI, *Global Reporting Initiative* (www.globalreporting.org).

To be noted, however, is that stakeholder relationship management practices are also finding a strong point of reference in the affirmation, improvement, and dissemination of the AA1000 standard, especially in recent years.

13.3.1. The Global Reporting Initiative (GRI)

GRI is an independent international organization that helps businesses, governments, and other organizations understand and communicate the impact of business on critical sustainability issues, such as climate change, human rights, corruption, and many others.

GRI, founded in 1997, is promoted by the non-governmental organization CERES (Coalition for Environmentally Responsible Economies) in collaboration with the United Nations Environment Program (UNEP), associations, certification institutes, and business coalitions.

The assumption behind the GRI is that a sustainable global economy should combine long-term viability with ethical behaviour, social justice, and respect for the environment. This means that GRI-friendly organizations should consider the economic, environmental, social, and governance impacts of their operations. In fact, the GRI Sustainability Reporting Framework can be defined as a reporting system that allows all businesses and other organizations to measure, understand, and communicate such information responsibly and transparently.

The basic aim of this standard is to:

– Encourage the drafting of reports incorporating the economic, environmental, and social dimensions of the business (Triple Bottom Line);
– Bring social and environmental sustainability information to the same level as economic-financial information;
– Promote and disseminate reporting practices by creating an adaptable standard for any sector;
– Represent a permanent institution that works efficiently and effectively to support and protect this project.

In the revised version of October 2016, the GRI standards are divided into:

– Universal standards;
– Topic-specific standards, differentiated by economic, environmental, and social profiles.

The universal standards (Table 2) have as their starting reference the GRI 101 (Foundation), which structurally outline the use of reporting parameters, introducing their fundamental principles, and clarifying the techniques for drafting a sustainability report accordingly.

In parallel to GRI 101, two other universal standards should also be applied:

– GRI 102 (General Disclosures) is used to report contextual information about an organization and its sustainability reporting practices. This includes information about an organization's profile, strategy, ethics and integrity, governance, stakeholder engagement practices, and reporting process;

– GRI 103 (Management Approach) is used to report information about how an organization manages a material topic. It is designed to be used for each material topic in a sustainability report, including those covered by the topic-specific GRI Standards (series 200, 300, and 400) and other material topics. Applying GRI 103 with each material topic allows the organization to provide a narrative explanation of why the topic is material, where the impacts occur (the topic Boundary), and how the organization manages the impacts [19].

Table 2. GRI Universal Standards.

Standard		Scope
GRI	101	GRI 101: Foundation applies to any organization that wants to use the GRI Standards to report about its economic, environmental, and/or social impacts. Therefore, this Standard is applicable to: – An organization that intends to prepare a sustainability report in accordance with the GRI Standards; or – An organization that intends to use selected GRI Standards, or parts of their content, to report on impacts related to specific economic, social, and/or environmental topics (e.g., to report on emissions only). GRI 101 can be used by an organization of any size, type, sector, or geographic location.
GRI	102	GRI 102 sets out reporting requirements on contextual information about an organization and its sustainability reporting practices. This Standard can be used by an organization of any size, type, sector or geographic location.
GRI	103	GRI 103 sets out reporting requirements about the approach an organization uses to manage a material topic. This Standard can be used by an organization of any size, type, sector or geographic location.

Source: GRI – Consolidated set of GRI sustainability reporting standards 2016.

---

[19] GRI – Consolidated set of GRI sustainability reporting standards 2016 (p. 7).

The topic-specific standards are used to report information on an organization's impacts related to economic (Table 3), environmental (Table 4), and social topics (Table 5).

To prepare a sustainability report in accordance with the GRI Standards, an organization applies the Reporting Principles to define the report content from GRI 101 to identify its material economic, environmental, and/or social topics. These material topics determine which topic-specific standards the organization uses to prepare its sustainability report. Selected topic-specific standards, or parts of their content, can also be used to report specific information, without preparing a sustainability report.

Table 3. Topic-Specific Standards – GRI 200 Economic.

Standard		Scope
GRI	201	GRI 201: Economic Performance sets out reporting requirements on the topic of economic performance. This Standard can be used by an organization of any size, type, sector or geographic location that wants to report on its impacts related to this topic.
GRI	202	GRI 202: Market Presence sets out reporting requirements on the topic of market presence. This Standard can be used by an organization of any size, type, sector or geographic location that wants to report on its impacts related to this topic.
GRI	203	GRI 203: Indirect Economic Impacts sets out reporting requirements on the topic of indirect economic impacts. This Standard can be used by an organization of any size, type, sector or geographic location that wants to report on its impacts related to this topic.
GRI	204	GRI 204: Procurement Practices sets out reporting requirements on the topic of procurement practices. This Standard can be used by an organization of any size, type, sector or geographic location that wants to report on its impacts related to this topic.
GRI	205	GRI 205: Anti-corruption sets out reporting requirements on the topic of procurement anti-corruption. This Standard can be used by an organization of any size, type, sector or geographic location that wants to report on its impacts related to this topic.
GRI	206	GRI 206: Anti-competitive Behaviour sets out reporting requirements on the topic of anti-competitive behaviour. This Standard can be used by an organization of any size, type, sector or geographic location that wants to report on its impacts related to this topic.

Source: GRI – Consolidated set of GRI sustainability reporting standards 2016.

Table 4. Topic-Specific Standards - GRI 300 Environmental.

Standard		Scope
GRI	301	GRI 301: Materials sets out reporting requirements on the topic of materials. This Standard can be used by an organization of any size, type, sector or geographic location that wants to report on its impacts related to this topic.
GRI	302	GRI 302: Energy sets out reporting requirements on the topic of energy. This Standard can be used by an organization of any size, type, sector or geographic location that wants to report on its impacts related to this topic.
GRI	303	GRI 303: Water sets out reporting requirements on the topic of water. This Standard can be used by an organization of any size, type, sector or geographic location that wants to report on its impacts related to this topic.
GRI	304	GRI 304: Biodiversity sets out reporting requirements on the topic of biodiversity. This Standard can be used by an organization of any size, type, sector or geographic location that wants to report on its impacts related to this topic.
GRI	305	GRI 305: Emissions sets out reporting requirements on the topic of emissions. This Standard can be used by an organization of any size, type, sector or geographic location that wants to report on its impacts related to this topic.
GRI	306	GRI 306: Effluents and Waste sets out reporting requirements on the topic of effluents and waste. This Standard can be used by an organization of any size, type, sector or geographic location that wants to report on its impacts related to this topic.
GRI	307	GRI 307: Environmental Compliance sets out reporting requirements on the topic of environmental compliance. This Standard can be used by an organization of any size, type, sector or geographic location that wants to report on its impacts related to this topic.
GRI	308	GRI 308: Supplier Environmental Assessment sets out reporting requirements on the topic of supplier environmental assessment. This Standard can be used by an organization of any size, type, sector or geographic location that wants to report on its impacts related to this topic.

Source: GRI – Consolidated set of GRI sustainability reporting standards 2016.

Table 5. Topic-Specific Standards – GRI 400 Social.

Standard		Scope
GRI	401	GRI 401: Employment sets out reporting requirements on the topic of employment. This Standard can be used by an organization of any size, type, sector or geographic location that wants to report on its impacts related to this topic.
GRI	402	GRI 402: Labor/Management Relations sets out reporting requirements on the topic of labor/management relations. This Standard can be used by an organization of any size, type, sector or geographic location that wants to report on its impacts related to this topic.
GRI	403	GRI 403: Occupational Health and Safety sets out reporting requirements on the topic of occupational health and safety. This Standard can be used by an organization of any size, type, sector or geographic location that wants to report on its impacts related to this topic.
GRI	404	GRI 404: Training and education sets out reporting requirements on the topic of training and education. This Standard can be used by an organization of any size, type, sector or geographic location that wants to report on its impacts related to this topic.
GRI	405	GRI 405: Diversity and Equal Opportunity sets out reporting requirements on the topic of diversity and equal opportunity. This Standard can be used by an organization of any size, type, sector or geographic location that wants to report on its impacts related to this topic.
GRI	406	GRI 406: Non-discrimination sets out reporting requirements on the topic of non-discrimination. This Standard can be used by an organization of any size, type, sector or geographic location that wants to report on its impacts related to this topic.
GRI	407	GRI 407: Freedom of Association and Collective Bargaining sets out reporting requirements on the topic of freedom of association and collective bargaining. This Standard can be used by an organization of any size, type, sector or geographic location that wants to report on its impacts related to this topic.
GRI	408	GRI 408: Child Labor sets out reporting requirements on the topic of child labor. This Standard can be used by an organization of any size, type, sector or geographic location that wants to report on its impacts related to this topic.
GRI	409	GRI 409: Forced or Compulsory Labor sets out reporting requirements on the topic of forced or compulsory labor. This Standard can be used by an organization of any size, type, sector or geographic location that wants to report on its impacts related to this topic.

see next page

GRI	410	GRI 410: Security Practices sets out reporting requirements on the topic of security practices. This Standard can be used by an organization of any size, type, sector or geographic location that wants to report on its impacts related to this topic.
GRI	411	GRI 411: Rights of Indigenous Peoples sets out reporting requirements on the topic of rights of indigenous peoples. This Standard can be used by an organization of any size, type, sector or geographic location that wants to report on its impacts related to this topic.
GRI	412	GRI 412: Human Rights Assessment sets out reporting requirements on the topic of human rights assessment. This Standard can be used by an organization of any size, type, sector or geographic location that wants to report on its impacts related to this topic.
GRI	413	GRI 413: Local Communities sets out reporting requirements on the topic of local communities. This Standard can be used by an organization of any size, type, sector or geographic location that wants to report on its impacts related to this topic.
GRI	414	GRI 414: Supplier Social Assessment sets out reporting requirements on the topic of supplier social assessment. This Standard can be used by an organization of any size, type, sector or geographic location that wants to report on its impacts related to this topic.
GRI	415	GRI 415: Public Policy sets out reporting requirements on the topic of public policy. This Standard can be used by an organization of any size, type, sector or geographic location that wants to report on its impacts related to this topic.
GRI	416	GRI 416: Customer Health and Safety sets out reporting requirements on the topic of customer health and safety. This Standard can be used by an organization of any size, type, sector or geographic location that wants to report on its impacts related to this topic.
GRI	417	GRI 417: Marketing and Labeling sets out reporting requirements on the topic of marketing and labeling. This Standard can be used by an organization of any size, type, sector or geographic location that wants to report on its impacts related to this topic.
GRI	418	GRI 418: Customer Privacy sets out reporting requirements on the topic of customer privacy. This Standard can be used by an organization of any size, type, sector or geographic location that wants to report on its impacts related to this topic.
GRI	419	GRI 419: Socioeconomic Compliance sets out reporting requirements on the topic of socioeconomic compliance. This Standard can be used by an organization of any size, type, sector or geographic location that wants to report on its impacts related to this topic.

Source: GRI – Consolidated set of GRI sustainability reporting standards 2016.

These two types of standards form an integrated and modular system of guidelines for sustainability reporting. Such integration and modularity enables upgrading the existing standards and adding new ones without interfering with the overall system.

13.3.2. Accountability 1000 (AA1000)

Important to highlight after clarifying the essential elements of the most important "product" standard (aimed at encouraging the proper drafting of the sustainability document) is that this standard should also be accompanied by both the communication and "process" methods, such as for example, the AA1000 standard[20] (aimed at facilitating the relationship and active engagement with stakeholders).

Emerging from the analysis of best business practices is the joint use of the AA1000 standard and product standards, such as SA8000 (Social Accountability), ISO14001 (International Standard Organization), and GRI (Sustainability Reporting Guidelines).

AccountAbility 1000 (AA1000) is a process standard developed in 1999 and subsequently updated by ISEA (Institute of Social and Ethical Accountability) according to a stakeholder-based approach. This is one of the first accountability standards framework created to meet the need to standardize approaches to social reporting, and thus render information from different entities comparable.

Although AA1000 was born as – and continuous to be – a unitary standard, it is appropriate to specify that its evolution led to the creation of the so-called AA1000 Series (AA1000S), articulating the standard in three modules. In particular:

– AA1000APS (AccountAbility Principles), approved in 2008, provides a framework for organizations to respond to the sustainability question and represents the basis on which the subsequent AA1000AS and AA1000SES modules were built;
– AA1000AS (Assurance Standard), also approved in 2008, essentially provides the tools to assess the adherence of social reporting and the information provided under the AA1000 principles;
– AA1000SES (Stakeholder Engagement Standard) of 2015, which represents a framework to improve the quality of design, implementation, validation, communication, and stakeholder engagement.

A particular feature of A1000, as in the case of other process standards, is that it focuses mainly on the construction of social reports outlining the prin-

---

[20] AA1000, *Accountability 1000* (www.accountability.org).

ciples that should underlie its drafting, but focusing mainly on the stakehold-er engagement path to follow, contrary to the so-called content standards, which mainly deal with the structure of reports and the information that needs to be provided to the bearers of interest. This is because to recover trust and positive expectations from their stakeholders, it is not enough to produce information, but essentially requires disseminating and sharing it through a programmed and structured relationship with them.

To this end, three key accountability principles defined by the AA1000 Accountability Principles Standard (AA1000 APS 2008) become important in stakeholder relationship management:

– Transparency, understood as the ability to "account" for their activi-ties;

– Correspondence, understood as the ability to respond to the expecta-tions of the bearers of interest;

– Compliance with law, standards, codes, principles, policies, and other voluntary regulations.

This standard is generally applicable to a framework of companies open to experimentation to improve the quality of their design, implementation, and validation of stakeholder relationship management practices, and is functional to different types of internal and external stakeholder involve-ment, such as for example, customer care actions, focus on specific issues of a social or environmental nature, internal reporting and re-orientation man-agement paths.

It is not designed to technically manage the legal and/or formal commit-ments between the organization and its stakeholders, but rather to facilitate the achievement of such agreements and to support the parties involved.

Faced with the proliferation of investigations, inquiries, information and misinformation campaigns, all widely disseminated by the press, companies see the constant management of stakeholder dialogue (also guided by the above-mentioned standards) as a form of "civil diplomacy" that allows them to take part in social debate through a practice that could be defined as:

– Restoring the role of social as well as economic actors[21];

– Enhancing the concept of sustainability performance[22], which includes policies, decisions, and actions that result in social, environmental, and eco-nomic-financial outcomes.

---

[21] J.M. De Leersnyder, *Corporate culture and Geopolitics*, in Symphonya. Emerging Issues in Management (www.unimib.it/symphonya), n. 2, 2002.

[22] Accountability AA 1000, *Stakeholder Engagement Standard. Exposure Draft*, in www.accountability21.net.

References

AA1000, *Accountability 1000* (www.accountability.org).
Accountability AA 1000, *Stakeholder Engagement Standard. Exposure Draft*, in www.accountability21.net.
Annan K., *The Global compact. Corporate Leadership in the World Economy*, Symphonya. Emerging Issues in Management (www.unimib.it/symphonya), n. 2, 2002. http://dx.doi.org/10.4468/2002.2.02annan.

Bisio L., *Global Company and Global Regulation*, Symphonya. Emerging Issues in Management (www.unimib.it/symphonya), n. 1, 2005. http://dx.doi.org/10.4468/2005.1.07bisio.
Brondoni S.M., *Network Culture, Performance and Corporate Responsibility*, Symphonya, Emerging Issues in Management (www.unimib.it/symphonya), n. 1, 2003. http://dx.doi.org/10.4468/2003.1.02brondoni.
Brondoni S.M., *Ouverture de 'Global Networks and Sustainable Development-1'*, Symphonya. Emerging Issues in Management (symphonya.unimib.it), n. 1, 2014. http://dx.doi.org/10.4468/2014.1.01ouverture.

Commission of the European Communities, *Green Paper: Promoting a European framework for Corporate Social Responsibility*, Bruxelles, 2001.
Crook C., *The Good Company*, The Economist, January 2005.

De Leersnyder J.M., *Corporate culture and Geopolitics*, Symphonya. Emerging Issues in Management (www.unimib.it/symphonya), n. 2, 2002. http://dx.doi.org/10.4468/2002.2.06deleersnyder

Franklin D., *Just Good Business*, in The Economist, January 2008.
Freeman R.E., *A Stakeholder Theory of the Corporation*, Beauchamp T.L., Bowie N.E. (eds.), *Ethical Theory and Business*, 6th ed., Prentice-Hall, Englewood Cliffs, NJ, 2001.
Friedman M., *Capitalism and Freedom*, Chicago University Press, Chicago, 1962.
Frooman J., *Socially Irresponsible and Illegal Behavior and Shareholder Wealth*, in Business & Society, n. 3, 1997.

GBS, *Study Group for the Social Report* (www.gruppobilanciosociale.org).
GRI, *Global Reporting Initiative* (www.globalreporting.org).
GRI – *Consolidated Set of GRI Sustainability Reporting Standards*, 2016.

Lambin J.-J., *Rethinking the Market Economy*, Symphonya. Emerging Issues in Management (symphonya.unimib.it), n. 2, 2014. http://dx.doi.org/10.4468/2014.2.02lambin.

SA8000, *Social Accountability* (www.sa8000.info).
Salvioni D.M., *Corporate Governance and Global Responsibility*, Symphonya, Emerging Issues in Management (www.unimib.it/symphonya), n. 1, 2003. http://dx.doi.org/10.4468/2003.1.05salvioni.

AUTHORS

Silvio Mario Brondoni is Full Professor of Management at the University of Milano-Bicocca, Department of Economics, Management and Statistics, Milan (Italy). He also served in the Management and Marketing Programs at Bocconi University, Bologna University, and the University of Calabria. His interests lie in global business management, global competition, and market-driven management. He teaches advanced competitive management and price management at the University of Milano-Bicocca. He is Editor in Chief of "Symphonya. Emerging Issues in Management" (http://symphonya.unimib.it/) and Coordinator of ISTEI - Business Management Section – Dept. Economics, Management and Statistics, The University of Milano-Bicocca.

Jean-Jacques Lambin is Professor Emeritus from the Université Catholique de Louvain (Belgium) and Professore Emerito from the University of Milano-Bicocca (Italy). A Doctor in Applied Economics from Louvain University, Lambin is interested in Strategic Marketing, in Market-driven Management and in the impact of globalization in the market economy system. A past Editor in chief of European Bunsiness Forum (EBF) Lambin is the author of several text books. His main text – Strategic Marketing – has been translated in eight languages.

Daniela M. Salvioni is Full Professor of Business Administration in the Department of Economics and Management (DEM) at Brescia University (Italy). She has also taught at Milan University, Bologna University, and Bocconi University. She has coordinated international and national research projects on corporate communications, web reporting, corporate and school governance, and is a member of many Italian and international scientific institutions. Professor Salvioni's research articles have been published in various international peer-reviewed governance and management journals. She has also edited several books on corporate governance, corporate social responsibility, internal control, financial communication, cost accounting, and financial control. She teaches "Corporate Governance and Control Systems" and "Sustainability Report" at the University of Brescia. Due to her internationally recognized scientific reputation and competence, she is a referee of scientific publications and research projects in many universities.

Nicola Bellini is Professor of Management at the Scuola Superiore Sant'Anna in Pisa (on leave) and Director of the Tourism Management Institute at the La Rochelle Business School. He has been visiting and affiliate professor at the Stanford University Center in Florence, University of Sassari, University of Pisa, GSSI L'Aquila, and Grenoble Ecole de Management. From 2009 to 2011 he was Director of the Regional Institute for Economic Planning of Tuscany – IR-PET. From 2007 to 2014 he was Director of the Galileo Galilei Italian Institute in Chongqing and Co-Director of the Confucius Institute in Pisa. He has also served as an expert for the EU Commission on regional strategies for smart specialisation. He is the author and editor of books and articles on industrial policy, local and regional development, business support services, place branding, and urban tourism.

Elisa Arrigo, is Associate Professor of Management at the University of Milano-Bicocca, Department of Economics, Management and Statistics, Milan (Italy). She holds a Ph.D. in Marketing and Business Management from the University of Milano-Bicocca. During her Ph.D. studies, she was a visiting scholar at the Stockholm School of Business (Sweden) and London Business School (UK). She teaches marketing and global communication at the University of Milano-Bicocca. Her research interests lie primarily in global business management with particular reference to luxury and fashion.

Paolo Rizzi is Director of Local Economy Laboratory and Associate Professor in Political Economy at the Università Cattolica del Sacro Cuore in Piacenza (Italy), Department of Economic and Social Science (Dises). He teaches Political Economy and Place Marketing at Università Cattolica of Piacenza and Tourism Economics at University of Milan-Bicocca. His main research topics are: Local Economic Systems Analysis and Local Development Policies; Territorial Planning; Place Marketing; Social Capital Theory; Policy Evaluation. He is Country Representative of Rsa-Regional Studies Association, Editor of Eyesreg-online Journal of Italian Association of Regional Science and Editorial Team Member of Symphonya. Emerging Issues in Management

Federica Codignola is an Assistant Professor of Management at the University of Milan-Bicocca, Department of Economics, Management and Statistics, Milano (Italy). Her main expertise is in the field of: art market dynamics; arts and cultural management; cultural economics & globalization; cross-cultural management; consumer behavior. Since 2009, she is a tenured Assistant Professor in Management. In that capacity, and previously as a PhD student, in the past few years she was able to study and teach in a number of international environments, such as Italy, France, Switzerland, England, Canada, the Netherlands.

Fabio Musso is Full Professor of Business Management at the Carlo Bo University of Urbino, Department of Economics, Society and Politics, Urbino (Italy). He is interested in internationalization of companies, marketing channels, retailing, logistics. He teaches Advanced International Marketing and International Business Management at the Carlo Bo University of Urbino. He is Chairman of the M.S. in Marketing and Communication at the Carlo Bo University of Urbino and Vice-Rector for Knowledge Transfer in the same University. He is Editor in Chief of the "International Journal of Economic Behavior") (http://ijeb.faa.ro/) and Associate Editor of the "International Journal of Applied Behavioral Economics" (http://www.igi-global.com/journal/international-journal-applied-behavioral economics/49170).

Sabina Riboldazzi, is Assistant Professor of Management at the University of Milano-Bicocca, Department of Economics, Management and Statistics, Milan (Italy). She graduated from the University of Piemonte Orientale, Novara, and gained her Ph.D. in Marketing and Business Management from the University of Milano-Bicocca. During her Ph.D. studies, she was a visiting scholar at the London Business School. She teaches market-driven management and global marketing management at Milano-Bicocca University. She is Director of the Master Program "Executive Security Management" at the University of Milano-Bicocca. Her interests lie in global business management with particular reference to competitive customer value, marketing channels, and large-scale retailers.

Mario Risso is Full Professor of Management and he is Dean of School of Economics at the Niccolò Cusano University-Rome (Italy). He holds a PhD in Banking and Finance from University of Rome Tor Vergata, a Master in Asset Management and a Master in Retail Management. He holds University Degree in Business Administration, from University of Rome "Tor Vergata".
His research interests include retailing, global supply chain management, corporate social responsibility, international business. He teaches Business Management and Marketing at the Niccolò Cusano University and Retail Management at the University of Rome Tor Vergata. He is member of Editorial Team of "Symphonya. Emerging Issues in Management" (http://symphonya.unimib.it/) and member of the Scientific Advisory Board of the International Journal of Economic Behavior.

Giuseppe Cappiello is Assistant Professor at the Department of Business Science at the University of Bologna where he teaches "Business Economics and Management" and "Marketing". He earned the PhD in "Strategy, Management and Quantitative Business Methods" at the University of Milan-Bicocca and was a Visiting Scholar at the Kellogg Graduate School of Management in Evanston, Illinois. The main research interests are Pricing Policy and Public Management. The last publication is related to the value creation in public services.

Flavio Gnecchi is Full Professor of Management at the University of Milan-Bicocca, Department of Economics, Management and Statistics, Milano (Italy). He is graduated at Parma University. He is interested in global business management, B2B Marketing, Market-Driven Management. He teaches Marketing and Global Corporate Finance Communication at University of Milan-Bicocca. He's the current Coordinator of two degree courses, "Marketing, Corporate Communication and Global Markets" (1st level) and "Marketing and Global Markets" (2nd level).

Luca Bisio is Assistant Professor of Management at the University of Milano-Bicocca, Department of Economics, Management and Statistics, Milan (Italy). He graduated from Bocconi University, Milan. His research interests include market-driven management, global communication, and corporate social responsibility. He teaches corporate global communication and marketing communication at the University of Milano-Bicocca.

For Product Safety Concerns and Information please contact our EU
representative GPSR@taylorandfrancis.com
Taylor & Francis Verlag GmbH, Kaufingerstraße 24, 80331 München, Germany

www.ingramcontent.com/pod-product-compliance
Ingram Content Group UK Ltd.
Pitfield, Milton Keynes, MK11 3LW, UK
UKHW020957180425
457613UK00019B/726